SOCIAL POLICY FOR S
WELFARE PROFESSIO

Tools for understanding, analysis and engagement

Graeme Simpson and Stuart Connor

First published in Great Britain in 2011 by

The Policy Press
University of Bristol
Fourth Floor
Beacon House
Queen's Road
Bristol BS8 1QU
UK

Tel +44 (0)117 331 4054
Fax +44 (0)117 331 4093
e-mail tpp-info@bristol.ac.uk
www.policypress.co.uk

North American office:
The Policy Press
c/o International Specialized Books Services (ISBS)
920 NE 58th Avenue, Suite 300
Portland, OR 97213-3786, USA
Tel +1 503 287 3093
Fax +1 503 280 8832
e-mail info@isbs.com

British Library Cataloguing in Publication Data
A catalogue record for this book is available from the British Library.

Library of Congress Cataloging-in-Publication Data
A catalog record for this book has been requested.

ISBN 978 1 84742 265 1 paperback
ISBN 978 1 84742 913 1 hardcover

Cover design by The Policy Press
Front cover: image kindly supplied by Paul Green
Printed and bound in Great Britain by Hobbs, Southampton
The Policy Press uses environmentally responsible print partners

Contents

Acknowledgements

This book was first discussed over poached eggs on toast, bacon sandwiches, teas and coffees in Jay's Café, a source of sustenance (if not inspiration) to several generations of Wolverhampton University's staff. It developed further at a rainswept Swansea, and was begun in earnest when Wolves were missing out on promotion and Derby County were recording the lowest ever Premiership points total. The work stalled following the theft of a computer that contained several chapters, but a fresh impetus was gained following the shocking, if unsurprising, events of 2008 – thanks Lehman Brothers et al. The book's eventual completion is due to the continuing support, help and encouragement – not to mention the discussions and disagreements – we have had with many people over the last four years (and more). There are too many to name them all, but there are some who deserve a special mention. Paul Grant and Vicky Price have been there since the beginning. Richard Huggins, Danny Mulvihill, Dee Cook, Karen Rowlingson and Akwugo Emejulu have not only shared their knowledge and expertise but have demonstrated what can be done. An extra-special mention goes to Ani Murr, who not only read the drafts and commented extensively upon them, but did so often at short notice when either football or Doctor Who was a viable alternative. Our students, too, also played their part in helping us develop these ideas.

We would also like to thank all of those at The Policy Press who made this possible and who persevered with us (even though they may, at times, have wondered if we would ever finish it). The comments of the anonymous reviewers have also helped shaped the final version, but as always this is solely the authors' responsibility.

Many of the ideas which shaped the thinking behind this book were formed in the Black Country and south Derbyshire, and in turn influenced by 'moms', 'mams' and 'dads' – thank you for the vital lessons that you have shared. Of course, there are those who have been there no matter what and have shown us what being valued really means – Hils, "yo am bostin"; Vicky, thank you for your love and patience.

Finally, we couldn't forget Eve (who reminds us that there is no party without dancing), Oliver (just starting out at university) Becky and Sarah (beginning their own careers) and Michael, who is, like so many others, paying the price of the bankers' excesses and mismanagement. The world they are entering is not the world we would necessarily wish for them. The opportunities that were made available to us are being attacked like never before. We hope this book will be a resource for those who will continue to engage, organise and ensure that the principles of equality and social justice are not only defended, but realised. The book has drawn inspiration from all those writers and activists, who not only believe that another world is possible, but continue to work to help bring it closer. This book is dedicated to them.

Graeme Simpson & Stuart Connor,
February 2011

INTRODUCTION

The ideas behind the book

Discussions of social policy, particularly when aimed at those who work in and receive welfare services, are frequently presented in terms of scene-setting. That is, it is argued that an awareness of social policy is required in order to better understand the context in which those engaged in social welfare are expected to operate. In this respect, social policy can be likened to the use of 'bluescreens' in film and television, where they are used to provide a projected backdrop for actors. There is no physical connection between the actor and digital scenery, but the actor is required to respond to and operate as if the scene is in place. For example, as part of the 'new age of austerity' announced by the Conservative and Liberal Democrat coalition government in October 2010, the Chancellor of the Exchequer, the Rt Hon George Osborne MP, argued that a far-reaching programme of public service reform was necessary. This reform was to include: substantial cuts across government departmental spending; delivering changes in public services so that they were 'fit for the modern age'; leaving 'no stone unturned' in the search for waste; and, arguably most notably, changing the 'aspirations and expectations' of public services in the minds of today's population. Like actors in front of a bluescreen, those individuals and groups who provide and receive welfare services are just expected to accept this new backdrop to their lives and seek ways to adapt and rise to the challenge of this new context.

We start from a different position; one that recognises that those engaged in social welfare are not just (policy) actors on a stage, but also can, do and should seek to play a greater part in setting the scene and directing the action. It is for this reason that we argue that social welfare professionals need to engage with social policy. To this end, we aim to outline a particular way of engaging social welfare professionals with the business of social policy, and specifically welfare policy. We use the term 'welfare professionals' as an inclusive concept, similar to the continental European concept of 'social professionals', which covers all the groups of people who work in the direct provision of welfare services – it would include social workers, social care workers, community workers, health care professionals, teachers and other educationalists, to identify but a few.

Social welfare workers are frequently motivated by a desire to 'work with people', to 'bring about change' or to 'make a difference', yet often find themselves compromised by aspects of policy. Our approach is to focus upon the development of 'skills for analysis' or 'tools for understanding', which we believe are of paramount importance, enabling social welfare professionals to make the links between policy and practice over the course of their careers. So, while we include policy examples and some history of policy development, the approach is less about explaining what the current policy is, although we have incorporated historical analyses of specific welfare policies as case studies to help explore how these tools for understanding can be used. There is a strong tendency within today's managerialist culture for welfare professionals to develop a narrow task-focused approach, which ever increasingly concentrates upon the 'task' without making the connections to the external factors that shape the task. Policy is something that surrounds the daily routines of welfare professionals.

Policy literacy: tools for understanding and analysis

Our approach begins with the view that policies play an important part in shaping people's lives, but that people should also play an important part in shaping policies. Intentionally and unintentionally, social policies impact on the experiences, opportunities and outcomes of all our lives. In an attempt to better understand and exert influence over the choices that shape policies, we suggest that a form of 'policy literacy' needs to be developed by all citizens and by practitioners of social welfare in particular.

Like traditional literacy, policy literacy includes the ability to both read (comprehend), write (create, design, produce) and perform policies. It does not just include a knowledge of particular pieces of legislation, but includes an understanding and analysis of the institutions and relationships that operate in the name of social welfare. Policy literacy aims to make recipients and practitioners of social welfare more critical and discriminating readers, performers and producers of policies.

There are three phases to this. The first is to understand and become aware of the extent of the impact of policy on people's lives. In addition, these should be seen as not simply a set of instructions to be followed, but particular prescriptions from a range of available options. In other words, despite efforts of countless politicians to persuade people otherwise, there is an alternative.

The second phase is learning to analyse and question how policies have been constructed and what may have been left out. We argue that all policies embody 'points of view' about the world and form a particular policy narrative, which draws on and represents a number of assumptions about the way the world works. These viewpoints result in the variety of choices made by the people and groups who make policies. So, throughout the book, we explore questions such as:

- Who has created and advocated for the policies?
- What story is being told? More specifically, what social issues have been identified, what justifications are provided for examining these social issues and what solutions are recommended?
- How are individuals and groups represented within these policies and what relationships exist within and across these individuals and groups?
- What is our role as 'recipients' of the policies in identifying with, or questioning, what we see and hear?
- How have policies been developed, administered and implemented?

The third phase is to explore deeper issues of who produces the policies that shape our experiences – and for what purpose? In other words: who profits, who loses and who decides? This stage of social, political and economic analysis looks at how each of us (and all of us together in society) plays a part in the policy process and society as a whole. At this stage we consider:

- Why do particular policies exist (or not exist)?
- Who is doing the speaking and from whose perspective is a policy story being told?
- What resources/signs are being used in the telling of a policy story and in efforts to persuade the reader that the message and actions prescribed in the policy are legitimate?
- Whose viewpoint is not heard and what alternatives are or are not available?

The book is an attempt to encourage and enable social welfare professionals to engage with these questions, and as such we address that audience specifically, drawing upon the arenas in which they operate to provide examples to illustrate responses to the questions. Throughout the book we will draw upon a current work in progress, in which we are exploring the views of welfare professionals in relation to their work in a series of interviews. While this work is as yet incomplete, we have decided to include some of the comments in this text to illuminate some of the concepts through the everyday concerns of those who work in social care and social work, health and education. All these comments are suitably anonymised and where these appear they will be referenced to the role of the person making the comment.

At the end of each chapter the key concepts and skills are summarised in a conclusion, which is followed by a number of what have been called 'reflective exercises'. These can be used to trigger a wider debate and discussion about the ideas contained within the chapter either within teaching groups or as prompts for the individual reader. The aim is to develop a deeper engagement with the ideas and foster the skill of critical analysis and engagement.

The structure of the book

The book is notionally divided into four sections: working with people; working in society; setting people and society in context; and the final section is a response to the question frequently asked by social welfare professionals, 'Why study social policy?', as we conclude with chapters aimed at creating a more engaged policy practice. Throughout the chapters we will introduce ideas and explore these in the context of welfare debates and how they impact upon the lives of service users and welfare professionals. We will use case studies, often drawn from history, which have the added advantage of establishing the historical context and a striking circularity in how welfare has always been seen as 'problematic'.

The reader will be challenged to consider and understand the theoretical underpinnings of a range of academic disciplines, which combine to form the subject of social policy. Despite this, we attempt to make social policy accessible and, by the use of examples, relevant to welfare professionals. In the context of the economic and social trajectory set by the UK government in 2010, it is important to be able to access not just ideas, but also the conceptual language behind these, as we anticipate welfare, and those who deliver it, will be the subject of ever increasing political assaults.

We begin, in Chapters 1–3, with a focus upon aspects of working with people set within a historical account of developments leading to early 21st-century practice. This is the point at which most social welfare workers begin their engagement with policy. By exploring the history of welfare, we examine how the balances of power have seemingly shifted over time from one where the professional had considerable authority and legitimacy, to the contemporary position of partnerships and 'users by experience'. We conclude with an examination of how policies at both a local and national level reinforce the idea that service users have been transformed into 'citizen consumers' and the impact this has upon social welfare professionals. We then move on to examine debates about welfare in general and the role of welfare workers in this, notably Victorian philanthropy and the debates between the Charity Organisation Society (COS) and the Fabians around the turn of the 20th century. Many of these debates have a very contemporary resonance, with their significance not merely being historical, and we examine what contemporary welfare professionals could usefully develop from this analysis. The final chapter in the section examines more recent policy developments, specifically the policy shift towards deinstitutionalisation. This is often couched in terms of 'service user choice' set against 'monolithic, one-size-fits-all' provision. We examine the nature of choice in greater depth and question the extent to which new forms of 'monolithic provision' are being promoted, premised upon the language of individualism and the illusion of choice.

Having followed the advice of Mayer and Timms (1970), who, in one of the first books to explore the views of service users (then termed 'clients'), argued that it was important to 'start where the client is', we move into a less familiar arena of the policy forces that shape welfare policy. This takes the form of a policy examination of current trends in society, which provides the context for the delivery of social welfare. Chapter 4 focuses upon the mixed economy of welfare and its constituent elements: the state (central and local government); the private sector (independent agencies providing welfare for profit); and civil society (this includes the family; individuals as volunteers – the 'informal' sector; and the not-for-profit independent sector). We then move into a discussion of social inequalities, and we explore the question of whether or not poverty, and its consequences, are located within individuals or structures. We explore economic dimensions and argue that social class needs to be reinstated upon the agenda of welfare professionals, since it is largely neglected in many more recent accounts, which often privilege 'choice'. In the final part of the section we explore the actual work context of the welfare professional in relation to managerialism and the attendant decline of the trades union movement.

The third section moves into the important arena of the economy. Welfare and services cost money and these chapters aim to develop knowledge and skills in understanding this key area. Chapter 7 offers a guide to make sense of the economy and includes explanations of many terms that are frequently heard but rarely understood. We then move on to discuss the relationship between work and welfare, again something that is likely to become of increasing significance. Chapter 8 extends this analysis to that of global capital and how this impacts upon the economic conditions for welfare. This chapter also explores questions of the movement of people and how that impacts upon the work of welfare professionals, including the movement of welfare professionals themselves in relation to recruitment of nurses and social workers from overseas. The final chapter in the section explores how the creation and sustainment of wealth for a minority has been a constant feature of UK policies and how this makes 'welfare' problematic. We advance the view that this is a result of very specific political choices that have been made.

Our final chapters begin with a theoretical exposition of how a policy-oriented practice could be developed, through exploring questions of 'agency' (i.e. individual and collective actions) and 'structure' (i.e. social structures that provide the context for actions). This draws upon some earlier chapters, where we show how 'agency' in relation to service-user movements, for example, has impacted upon the development of social welfare. Chapter 11 deals quite explicitly with policy stereotyping. This is where targets for policy are 'demonised', thereby presenting as reasonable sets of policies that target particular groups, and how these stereotypes are created and sustained in media representations. We highlight the poor, specifically those who have been on long-term benefits, often referred to as the underclass, as well as asylum seekers. We argue that a first step for welfare professionals is to engage in countering these negative stereotypes as a practical first step towards a more engaged practice. The final chapter argues that welfare professionals need to engage with policy to reclaim the radical agenda, attempts to answer the question 'Why study social policy?', and offers some suggestions as to how social welfare professionals could develop a more active and engaged practice.

Part One
Working with people

CHAPTER 1

From the care of the poor to service users: experts by experience

We begin at the point that engages most social professionals – contact with people. By exploring the history of welfare from this perspective, we can examine how the balances of power have changed over time: from one where the professional had considerable authority and legitimacy, to the contemporary position of partnerships, individualisation and 'users by experience'.

The key skill here is being able to understand the nature of the 'professional' relationship and how this is shaped by the twin effects of 'agency' and 'policy'. We have touched on the idea of agency in the introduction and it will be a recurring theme throughout the text. What we want to do at this stage is offer a definition which argues that all people who are part of the policy process have 'agency', which for us means that their actions have an impact upon those with whom they have an immediate interaction, and that, crucially, they can have an impact upon how policy is developed, sustained and changed.

The comfort of strangers – the philanthropic impulse

While there has been a long-standing tradition of welfare provision, from charity dispensed by religious orders to the first Poor Law (1553), our focus for developing an understanding of social policy begins in the 19th century. There are two connected reasons for this: first, the century saw the beginning of industrial capitalism and a particular social and economic order that, we argue, still prevails (Thompson, 1963); and, second, it also saw the origins of much contemporary welfare work (Payne, 2005; Price and Simpson, 2007). This was across the whole spectrum of what is now included as 'social policy': education; health care; housing; social care and social work; as well as campaigns for better employment rights, social insurance and pensions (Wilson, 1977; Thane, 1984). It is important to acknowledge that this was not merely a British phenomenon, but one that emerged throughout much of the industrialised world at the time (Reidegeld, 2006).

We are concerned with the way in which the welfare subject (Jones and Novak, 1993) was, and is, constructed by those who delivered welfare, in the age in which they acted. This becomes an important tool for analysis, since it develops a focus upon those who receive a 'service' rather than those who deliver it. Naturally, to suggest that the two are easily separated is highly problematic, but it allows an analysis by which the contemporary social professional can explore current, as well as historical, policies. Central to this is the argument that most people who enter welfare work do so because of a wider concern, as can be seen by the simple juxtaposition of two statements, over 100 years apart, expressing similar views as to the motivation for entering into a form of 'welfare work':

> I wanted to do a job where I felt I was doing something positive for other people. I wanted to work with people, to care for them and to show some sort of compassion. (Nurse, thinking about why she started out in the profession in the 1980s)

> I should give them any help I could, such as I might offer without insult to other friends – sympathy in their distresses; advice, help and counsel in their difficulties. (Octavia Hill, 1888, in Whelan, 1998: 69)

So, if people are motivated by a concern for the 'welfare subject', there is a need to explore how they are actually perceived, since, while the motivational factors may be similar, the context in which welfare is delivered has most certainly changed.

The 19th century saw 'welfare' being provided largely to the poor by the middle classes, for a variety of reasons, but frequently it was generated by their religious and social beliefs. Octavia Hill was a Christian belonging to the Anglican Church, who, while accepting much of the legitimacy of the existing social order, sought to improve the lives and conditions of the poor, arguably in a highly individualistic and moralistic fashion (Spicker, 1987). 'Rational Dissenters' were one group who rejected the Anglican Church's hierarchical systems. They believed that while preparation for the 'hereafter' had a place, it was imperative that life on earth should be characterised by 'justice, rationality and happiness for all' (Hilton and Hirsch, 2000: 4). Indeed, as the following two brief case studies illustrate, much of the philanthropic impulse came from Christians of all denominations.

Case study: Catherine McAuley

In the early to mid-19th century, discrimination against Roman Catholics in Ireland was eased, but there was a concern that their religious belief was being subtly repressed through education. Catherine McAuley was one of several Roman Catholic women who were concerned with promoting education among young women, especially those who were poor and unlikely to receive any education. She inherited a considerable amount of money in 1822 and founded the 'House of Mercy' and organised women helpers in this task. She later founded schools for the poor in Dublin and after her death her followers founded schools across Ireland and England, including one in Derby, between 1840 and 1860 as a result of the migration of Irish labourers. (Adapted from Minns, 2000: 52–6)

The 'welfare subject' was, more often than not, seen as less than equal to the 'welfare provider' and 'equality' was rarely an aim. Minns (2000: 52ff) analyses the impact of the legacy of Catherine McAuley who established a system of education for poor Irish girls that continued well into the 19th century. Her aim was to:

> visit and take care of the sick in hospital and their own homes, to educate poor Catholic girls, and to provide accommodation and domestic training for vulnerable young women. (Minns, 2000: 53)

However, as Minns acknowledges, there was no attempt to enable those 'poor Catholic girls' to 'rise above their allotted station in life' (2000: 53). Thus, while education and opportunity were to be provided, this was primarily to attain a degree of respectability, with the more successful of the girls going on to become teachers themselves, as the records of the McAuley school in Derby in the mid-19th century show (2000: 53).

Case study: Octavia Hill

Octavia Hill was a key Victorian figure who used her inherited wealth to develop a number of projects, the most well-known of which was her commitment to social housing. She believed that the conditions in which poor people were housed led to poor habits of industry and cleanliness among the poor and accordingly developed systems for providing better-quality housing alongside 'training' for those who lived in them. She became an influential figure in the COS and argued against welfare as a 'right' without any 'responsibilities'.

Octavia Hill saw the poor as very much in need of personal improvement and her housing schemes aimed to promote this. She described one of her schemes, where she collected rent, as 'truly lawless' (quoted in Whelan, 1998: 68), and wrote of how these 'evils' were compounded when people lived in blocks, as opposed to small houses, since it was 'almost impossible to train them. The temptations are greater [and] relapse far greater' (Whelan, 1998: 107).

In his review of interventions with the poor, Pearson (1975) notes that, throughout much of the 19th century, deprivation and depravation were almost synonymous. The welfare subject was, therefore, seen as someone in need of reform, betterment and improvement. The welfare provider, by contrast, already has the means of a 'better life', as was a feature of much of the writings of Barnett and Barnett (1972) and other prominent Victorian philanthropists. Indeed, at the extreme was the characterisation of the East End of London as 'Outcast London' and this imagery helped to create a generation of 'missionaries' who went into what Booth described as 'darkest London' (Stedman-Jones, 1981).

Thus, a clear pattern emerges that establishes the welfare subject as someone on the receiving end of a series of interventions, which confirms the position of *both* in a social hierarchy. Even though the philanthropist would engage in actions to bring about reforms, though crucially not 'revolution', Clark's argument is that this type of intervention and provision of 'welfare' maintains the existing order. This theme will be developed in subsequent chapters, but in the fields of education, health care, social housing and other aspects of social welfare there are numerous examples of moving from philanthropic 'charity' to arguing for a more sustainable form of welfare intervention. In the 19th century all of these fields and such forms of action were often seen as 'social work'.

Nonetheless, it was not always the case that the relationship was so 'one-way'. In some instances, those who were intent on providing some welfare intervention often engaged in some form of collaboration, either out of desire, as in the case of the settlements movement (Barnett, 1880, in Moore, 1988), or necessity, as recorded by an unknown preacher in 1875, commenting that 'a committee, consisting entirely of working men (*for we had no others*) gladly gave up their time to minister to the [cholera] sufferers' (Barnett, 1880, in Moore, 1988: 282, emphasis added).

Moreover, in some instances contact with the so-called welfare subject had a life-changing effect. Heaseman describes the impact of working with prostitutes upon some middle-class women, citing an excerpt from a pamphlet in 1882, which speaks of one moral welfare worker's experience:

> when she made for herself the discovery that these nameless ones were her sisters, made of her own flesh and blood, only poor, only weak, only ground into a foul serfdom by the tender mercies of Christian civilisation, it revolutionised her life. She had been taught that it was wrong to know of their existence. When the scales fell from her eyes she saw that in that teaching lay the root of half their wrong. (1962: 167)

This not only shows the capacity for people's views about the poor to be changed, but it also identifies an aspect that will be discussed elsewhere in this book, namely the power of society to define certain behaviour as 'problematic' and to sustain this through negative stereotyping.

The philanthropic impulse was criticised by many people at the time as they saw it as weakening both the economic and social nature of Victorian society (Smiles, 1997 [1851]). With the advent of 'social Darwinism' – a belief that the principle of natural selection, developed by Darwin in relation to the *natural world* (often referred to as the survival of the fittest), could be applied to *social structures* – such charitable interventions were seen as weakening the species (Arnold, in Stedman-Jones, 1981). In this sense both the welfare provider and the welfare subject were seen as problematic.

The philanthropic impulse has been the subject of much discussion and debate (Heaseman, 1962; Clarke, 1993b; Whelan, 1998). There is also a clear strand of contemporary analysis that is critical of philanthropy, and to a degree legitimately so (see Chapter 9). Clarke's (1993a) description of 19th-century welfare work as providing a 'comfort to strangers' is important here. He argues that the focus adopted was upon the individual, and accordingly individual, not collective, remedies were sought. This is a theme that will be examined in subsequent chapters and there is clear evidence that, in political terms, Clarke's analysis holds. For those who are involved in the provision of welfare, Clarke's analysis ignores a desire to engage in the immediate; the plight of the poor stranger may well have been best addressed in the long term by socialism, as Clarke argues, but in the short term they would have remained a poor, comfortless stranger (a theme expanded on in Chapter 6). This dilemma lies at the heart of all welfare work, and it is one of its 'enduring tensions' (Price and Simpson, 2007: 23–31).

Summarising this brief overview of the nature of the welfare subject in the Victorian period, we can see that the motivations of those who provided some form of 'service' were not dissimilar to those of people entering social welfare professions some 100–150 years later. Yet, the way the recipient was constructed was largely one that pathologised the poor, rendering them responsible for their own poverty. Crucially this was contested, not just through a historical analysis, but also by those involved *at the time*. Finally, the goal of welfare provision, imbued as it was with 'Christian charity', was contingent upon beliefs about the social order – a theme to which we will return throughout the book.

State welfarism – professionals know best

From the end of the 19th century and into the 20th, the state gradually began to assume greater responsibility for 'welfare'. The development of 'new sciences' gave a legitimacy to intervention into personal lives (Sapsford, 1993), as did elements of social Darwinism (Stedman-Jones, 1984), and, in some notable areas, so did organised labour. Essentially though, state welfarism developed as a price paid by capital for its security (Saville, 1957), though the 'price' had to be 'won' – a theme that will be explored in more detail in Chapter 6. Part of the welfare response was to begin to organise key aspects of previously philanthropic concern into areas of welfare provision: health, education and social work. Accordingly the welfare professional was created as part of the emerging welfare state.

The professional derived their power and legitimacy from knowledge, while the welfare subject was the recipient of a service, because the professional 'knew best'. Thus, nurses knew what was best for those in their care; teachers taught; and social workers provided services through the medium of casework, which cemented the professional–client relationship. Whether or not the position of the welfare subject changed in a significant way is contested. There is unquestionably the development of a view that 'welfare' was a right, articulated most clearly in the two pillars of state welfare that have expanded during the 20th century – health and education – though both have always retained significant 'private' provision (Klein, 2001). Nevertheless, it is now firmly established that both education and health should be provided as a 'right' and that this transcends class boundaries. It is relatively easy to see that the nurse has specialist skills and knowledge, particularly as the profession has developed in the late 20th century. Likewise the teacher – and both these professions (or semi-professions; see Etzioni, 1971) deal with 'service users' in a largely non-stigmatising service. The power of these groups, though, to define the 'pupil' or 'patient' has long been recognised. Foucault (1977, 1980) developed the view that the 'professional's' power to define is a form of regulation and control of the potential 'deviant' subject. This comes to the fore in the influential work *Discipline and Punish*, which argues that the range of state control not only punishes deviant behaviour, but also determines what behaviour is to be termed 'deviant'. While this may appear obvious for those who have committed a crime, it is no less relevant to definitions of the 'good' pupil or student and the 'good' patient.

For those engaged in social work the position is more complex. While there was a discernible 'struggle' for health and education, Wilson (1977) argued that this was not the case with the provision of 'social work'. Thus, the state professional's power to define problematic behaviour assumes greater significance and this is manifest in the so-called 'casework relationship', which we would argue can be seen as a general metaphor for overarching state welfarism. Within social work, casework became the dominant expression of the client–worker relationship. Casework emerged from the practices of the COS in the late 19th century. The system was one that saw each volunteer having a number of cases, which they worked and, importantly, recorded their actions (Whelan, 2001). The nature of the type of work undertaken and the ethical rationale behind the COS will be explored in the next chapter, but it should be noted that some of the criticisms made of the COS (for example, Clarke, 1993a) often overlooked some of the creative work they did in attempting to meet perceived 'need', as noted by Professor Muirhead in his year-end report of the Birmingham COS, who cites the case of a man who had 'signed the pledge', that is, committed himself to not drinking alcohol, where the local committee 'had thought it only right to supply him at home with a gramophone to counteract the siren strains of a neighbouring public house' (1911: 59). Younghusband, in her history of social work, argued that the COS attempted to integrate casework, group-work and community work, but that 'the three disastrously fell apart and only case work was conceptualized ... a failure for which we paid and continue to pay dearly' (1981: 13).

Despite these criticisms, casework is highly significant in the shaping of contemporary social work. Biestek (1961), a Jesuit priest, developed a set of ethical guidelines to establish a clear framework for this type of work: acceptance, being non-judgemental, individualisation of the client, purposeful expression and controlled emotional involvement, confidentiality, and self-determination. Thus, the key was a genuine 'helping' relationship, governed by confidentiality and premised upon the client having 'agency' and the power of self-determination. Harris Perlman (1970), a major supporter of the casework approach, argued that it 'stubbornly asserts the importance of individual man (sic) and of the individual small frail clusters of persons called families' (quoted in Fitzgerald et al, 1977: 97).

The significance of this for policy analysis in the UK is that the late 1960s saw the development of social work into a state-sponsored activity (Jones, 2001), leading to the establishment of a national qualification in 1970 (Payne, 2005), with casework as its bedrock. The formulation of the welfare state in 1948 was based upon the Beveridge report (1942), which identified 'five pillars' that were to militate against the worst excesses of capitalism: full employment; universal education; universal health care, free at the point of need; good-quality housing, initially 'council'-owned, but later encompassing 'social housing'; and a systematic system of insurance benefits. These were intended to eradicate poverty, yet in the late 1960s, generic social work was established through the Seebohm report (Seebohm, 1968) with the aim of ensuring that those who were unable (or unwilling) to benefit from the post-war welfare state could receive the individual help and support to do so. It was not, however, without criticism, and two elements of the critique will be explored here, since they offer a clear tool for a policy analysis of the 'helping relationship'.

The first aspect is that of *power* and the question of '*who defines* the need' or even the grounds of legitimate discussion. Parkinson (1970) provides a brief, yet telling, ethnographical account of the casework relationship. He begins with a comment found on file from a fellow probation officer, who recounts that a 'client' had visited the day before and began with a request for money, but soon revealed that his marriage had broken down and that there were potential difficulties in this for him. When the man subsequently visited Parkinson, he said that he had talked about the marriage breakdown because it was obvious that that was what interested the other probation officer. Parkinson gave him 10 shillings (a significant sum of money in 1970) and told him to keep in touch. Parkinson argues that essentially casework is 'associated with insight', whereas he stated that:

> I give most of my clients money. I give it because it is the one thing they accept joyfully; it makes them feel valuable.... It shows my concern in the only way they understand. I give money with all the difficulties and dangers of dependence it can produce because I feel I have precious little choice within the context of the situations my clients offer me. (1970: 220)

As noted earlier, in their seminal book, *The Client Speaks*, Mayer and Timms (1970) focused upon the power struggles between the professional and their clients over who controlled the agenda of the interaction. It is a fuller analysis of the situation that Parkinson described, but one that shows that the casework relationship, in which the professional defined what the 'problem' was, dominated social work and other 'helping professions' at that time. In psycho-analytical terms, the key was to discover the underlying (unconscious) problem (which the 'client' lacks the insight to spot). The presenting problem (perhaps a request for money) needed to be worked through to discover the 'real' problem. Textbooks of the time set out this approach in detail and there was no doubt that the client was perceived as lacking the necessary insight, which needed to be developed, and arguably in this was a denial of 'agency'. Indeed, Parkinson suggests later in his article that the only 'agency' open to the client was often conning the probation officer out of money – interestingly a continuation of what Parkinson describes as 'delinquent' activity, the opposite in fact of what the probation officer's role was.

A second critique was focused upon what the function or outcome of casework interventions were, and again this relates to power, but rather than this being a struggle in the personal domain, it was a struggle in the social or political domain. Casework is little more than a way in which structural deficiencies are reduced to and refocused as individual weaknesses (Pearson, 1975; Corrigan and Leonard, 1978; Ferguson, 2008). This argument has a long-standing tradition among radically minded welfare professionals. Heaseman cites a 19th-century radical churchman who argued that the Church (and by extension its philanthropic and 'charitable' actions) should not be 'an ambulance to gather up the casualties of our industrial system' (1962: 66). He, and many others, argued that the role of those who were engaged in philanthropic activities, or 'social work' (and it needs to be remembered that this included a range of provisions that contemporary society would locate within health, education and social care services), needed to address the causes of the difficulties those groups had. In their study of social work and health services, Homfeldt and Sting (2006: 17, our translation) argue that those involved in health provision in 19th-century Europe saw much of their work as 'social' rather than narrowly 'medical', and that doctors were the 'advocates for the poor'. In his critique of the origins of social work, Clarke (1993a) argued that a defining feature was that philanthropy sought individualised (casework) solutions, rather than collective (political) solutions, and that this shaped welfare policy throughout the 20th century.

Perhaps the zenith of the critiques of casework from *within* the profession can be found in the 1970s, ironically within years of establishing social work as a major welfare profession. These critiques focus upon the consequences of casework as a professional tool in maintaining existing social and economic relationships through the reconstruction of public ills as private problems (Pearson, 1973). Thus, the second element of analysis here is the 'outcome' of interventions that seek to regulate and control, what Loney (1983) and others frequently termed the 'iron fist in the velvet glove', whose origins lie in the nature of discourse and power to 'construct' the acceptable 'problem'. This power and control lies with the welfare professional (de Montigny, 1995) who sees it as a discourse that controls not only the service user, but also the work of the welfare professional.

New social movements and user control – experts by experience?

There have, however, been a number of challenges to professional power from those who use services, that is, from *outside* the discourse of welfare professionals. This development augmented the internal professional critiques and formed the basis of a different radicalism, built around those experiences (Dominelli, 1988; Braye and Preston-Shoot, 1995; Dalrymple and Burke, 1995), given an added impetus by the implementation of the 1990 NHS and Community Care Act.

A particular example of this movement, which has affected different groups of welfare professionals, is that of the disability rights movement.

While there are several strands to the movement (Finkelstein, 1980; Brechin and Swain, 1983; Ryan with Thomas, 1987; Morris, 1991), Oliver (1990) is one of its leading voices. He argued that disabled people had a right to services, and that they should not be dependent upon the 'expertise' of professionals. Moreover, one of the key arguments is that previous forms of welfare services had served to create and maintain a particular image of disability and disabled people as being dependent and inferior to the able-bodied person, which was identified as a 'medical' model, and a critique of these services emerged. Disabled people were 'medicalised', that is, they were subjected to a range of 'expert' diagnoses that saw the disability as something in need of treatment or intervention under the control of various 'experts'. The writers draw upon the history of interventions that frequently kept people with disabilities segregated, often in hospitals. Their conditions were 'diagnosed' in medical terms as either 'treatable' or 'untreatable': the former 'diagnosis' would lead to attempts to 'normalise', for example, prosthetic limbs; while the latter diagnosis led to a system of 'warehousing'.

Within the arena of learning disability, Nirje (1969) and Wolfensberger (1992) had earlier developed their concept of 'normalisation' as a response to the institutionalisation and infantilisation of learning-disabled people. This model has been subject to criticism, notably from those who are strongly attached to the 'social model', which is premised upon the belief that it is the nature and structure of society that 'disables' people: people may have an impairment, for example, reduced mobility, and therefore need to use a wheelchair, but it is how society is built, for example, the lack of dropped kerbs, ramps or lifts, which renders the wheelchair-user disabled. This was later developed into a 'materialist social theory' by Oliver (1999), where he argues in this critique of normalisation that:

> Normalization theory offers disabled people the opportunity to be given valued social roles in an unequal society which values some roles more than others. Materialist social theory offers disabled people the opportunity to transform their own lives and in so doing to transform the society in which they live into one in which all roles are valued. (1999: 172)

He concludes with his personal and rhetorical comment that 'As a disabled person I know which of those choices I prefer and I also know which most of the disabled people I meet prefer.' In his rejoinder, Wolfensberger (1999: 175–9) argues that in an unequal society there will always be those who have a valued role and those who do not: crucially, Wolfensberger sees society as being inevitably 'unequal' whereas Oliver argues strongly for equality premised upon Marx's dictum that inequality is a 'material and not a mental act' (Marx, and Engels, 2004 [1845/1923]: 30). Thus, for Oliver 'agency' is concerned with the transformation of society as a whole – whereas Wolfensberger seeks a transformation of the way in which learning-disabled people are viewed and treated. An important point that emerges here is that learning-disabled people themselves – contrary to Oliver's implied argument – have been active agents in attempting to transform their own circumstances and much of this has been recorded from the 1960s onwards (Hreinsdóttir et al, 2006). Thus, those who traditionally are perceived as being 'powerless' can, through group and self-advocacy, begin to challenge professional power and discourse and assume levels of control over their own lives (Brandon et al, 1995). Finally, Race et al (2005) argue that both models have high levels of relevance for all disabled people. They note that for many severely learning-disabled people, Oliver's position that 'individuals must transform themselves through collective action, not be transformed by others who know what's best for them or what's best for society' (Oliver, 1999: 170) is simply not attainable, and that without 'the support of other people to "act on them" or on their behalf, they may be "unable" to transform their own lives or the society in which they live' (Race et al, 2005: 516). They conclude by arguing that both models 'would agree that most of the oppressive and discriminatory treatment experienced by people with learning difficulties is socially ascribed, and both would strive to fight oppression and achieve equality' (Race et al, 2005: 520), thereby highlighting their commonalities.

Another highly influential group of service users who campaigned for control over their own lives and experiences were people who had experienced mental ill health. They argued for services that were driven by them, rather than those premised upon medicalised interventions, and placed a strong emphasis upon self-advocacy and 'survivor' accounts (see Sweeney et al, 2009). People with disabilities, both learning and physical, and people who have experienced mental ill health, alongside other service user groups, have developed alliances to promote the view that service users be seen as 'experts by experience' and that their accounts of their situations should be given equal weight (Branelly and Davis, 2006). More recently a range of service user groups has been increasingly involved in social work education as directed by the General Social Care Council, the body responsible for the social work curriculum and the registration of social care workers, and have established 'centres' or 'hubs' to organise such involvement. A group in West Sussex – *Experts by Experience* – typically promote their services thus:

> What we have in common is the desire to use our expertise to give professional health and care staff an insight into our world. We also work with groups that wish to raise their understanding and awareness of disability. As well as promoting disability awareness, we take our experience of accessing health and social care services and use it to instruct and inform care workers, social workers and health workers in training and education settings. (Available at: http://www.expertsbyexperience.org.uk/)

The service user movement has arguably become 'mainstreamed' and while this brings clear benefits, there are also 'dangers' in that the authentic voice, even the campaigning voice, becomes part of the established practices that they seek to change. Nevertheless in a short period of time, service users have ceased to be 'passive recipients', and have increasingly become 'active partners' in the provision of services. A central tenet here is that of 'agency', which is one of this book's core themes. The point we make is that these changes did not come about by accident, but were developed in response to action and demand. We would also note in passing at this stage, that the timing of these developments, and particularly the way in which they have been seized upon by government, suggests that it is not entirely a result of 'agency', but that other factors are at work. A critical question to ask is 'Why this and why now?', as did Scull (1983), who argued that while the 'decarceration' of people with mental ill health was long overdue and had been campaigned for long and hard for many years, it should be asked why it did occur at that certain point in history. His response was that policies were developed to reflect 'the structural pressures to curtail sharply the costly system of segregated control' (1979: 152). This point has been developed further in response to some contemporary policy shifts in relation to learning-disabled people by Simpson and Price (2010), who argue that the combination of a socially liberal ideology with the demands of economic liberalism results in a series of policies where social liberals have their views appropriated by economic demands.

Finally, Annetts et al (2009: 44ff) locate social welfare movements in a broader and long-standing context of resistance, linking them together in a 'moral economy of protest'. They draw upon the historical work of both E.P. Thompson (1963) and Eric Hobsbawm (1987) and extend their analysis to the field of 'welfare' as a whole, incorporating housing, poverty and unemployment. While much of their analysis is beyond the scope of this text, their conclusion remains apposite for our analysis of agency within 'social welfare' and the social professions. Whether it is, as it once was, that social professionals or volunteers engage in action on behalf of groups of people, or whether those groups of people activate their own 'agency' to take control for themselves, or whether it is in coalitions (Beresford and Croft 2004; Ferguson, 2008), 'social welfare movements are always related to concrete struggles over immediate demands for resources in one form or another' (Annetts et al, 2009: 257).

Conclusion

This chapter has sketched out a shift from a philanthropic impulse in the provision of welfare 'services' through to the dominance of state professionalism, where the 'superior' expertise of the 'professional' dominated, to more recent developments, which have seen the rise of the service user or 'expert by experience'.

The aim has been to provide a background to policy developments as well as contemporary policies by focusing not upon 'policy development' per se, but upon specific positions adopted by those who were engaged in this activity either as service providers or service users. The key to understanding these developments, we would suggest, and the key 'skill' to reflect upon at the chapter's close is the use of 'agency' and how this is reflected in policy development. We, therefore, close the chapter with an exercise for the reader.

REFLECTIVE EXERCISES

- ➔ Consider the particular field in which you are interested or (if you are already qualified) work. How much has it been influenced by the actions of service users and also those who are engaged as service providers? How do you think this has benefited people who use services and those who deliver them?
- ➔ If you are qualified, or are coming to professional training after a period of working in an 'unqualified' role, think about how it has changed in your career span (of course, this will be a rich source of material for some, and less so for others).
- ➔ As we develop our ideas and promote different areas of skills that can be developed to understand policy, you can return to this throughout, adding new insights, we hope, along the way.

CHAPTER 2

From caseworkers to networks: partnership and collaboration

This chapter continues by arguing that it is not just a shift in the personal construction of the relationship that has defined contemporary welfare work, but also the relationships between welfare professionals and how their work is organised or, in other words, the extent to which 'welfare work' has become an integral part of state activity. Beginning with Victorian philanthropy and the debates between the COS and the Webbs about the fundamental nature of welfare, we explore how welfare work gained its legitimacy as part of a welfare state. The shifts outlined in Chapter 1 have been mirrored by policy changes to inter-professional relationships aimed at increasing partnerships and collaboration.

The previous chapter explored welfare through the lens of the service user and developed the concept that understanding the position of the service user is an important critical tool for the welfare professional in understanding social policy. In this chapter we will examine how the nature of the 'welfare professional's' own role has changed in the same period, since they work within a specific social and political framework that shapes their working environment and determines the nature of their role. Thus while the position of service users should not be forgotten, it is not the focus of this chapter, the purpose of which is to underline what is an important aspect of policy, namely that analyses have to incorporate different perspectives, all of which act to shape it.

We also aim to link some of these ideas with debates about the nature of welfare, so, even though some of the material here is 'historical' in its nature, we are going to draw out themes that still shape the way people think about welfare and the role of the professional and the provision of welfare.

'Doing good': the methodology of casework and its Fabian critics

The previous chapter introduced the COS as one of the key groups in the provision of early 'welfare' interventions. It is regarded as having a lasting legacy for both the 20th and early 21st century, namely the development of 'casework', which is even acknowledged by those who are largely antagonistic to its overarching aims (for example, Marshall, 1967; Pinker, 1972; Clarke, 1993b). Stedman-Jones (1984) argues that the casework methodology of the COS needs to be seen in the context of its wider theoretical position. This leads into our focus upon the question of the wider ideological context of welfare, rather than the specifics of how it is delivered.

The ideological position that underscored much of the COS's philanthropic impulse was that of 'idealism' developed largely by C.S. Loch and Bernard Bosanquet (Vincent, 1984; Whelan, 2001; Moffat and Irving, 2002). Their philosophy has been termed a crucial element in the 'British Enlightenment', following on from Hegel, arguing that there was a need to collect and examine all social facts, because they are all only a partial reality – hence the need for a casework approach that allows for a constant examining and re-examining of these 'facts'. Moffat and Irving suggest that the Hegelian position here was 'how to reconcile the pervasive tension between the ideals of individuality ... [and the] need to find meaning and significance in a wider collective community' (2002: 416). Thus, the logic of the philosophical underpinning of the COS (and hence early social work) was to investigate the whole and not just part of the 'problem'. We need, however, to move further into idealist thought to clarify what the 'whole' was actually concerned with.

Idealism was not merely concerned with the nature of 'ideas' (following Hegel), but how to build a democratic society based upon the general good, and casework, with its individualised approach, was designed to enable people to contribute towards this common good. As C.S. Loch wrote in his article entitled *On Charity*, the question was 'not whether or not the person was "deserving" or "undeserving", but whether, given the facts, distress can be stayed and self-support attained' (quoted in Whelan, 2001: 22). Whelan continues to draw attention to the point that the central question was not whether or not people were 'bad', or had been 'bad', but whether or not they wanted to be 'good', citing a COS pamphlet which argued that 'sometimes those who deserve least sympathy sometimes need it the most' (quoted in Whelan, 2001: 22). Octavia Hill, in one of her letters to fellow housing workers, summed up the emphasis upon betterment for the common good thus:

> get all this well into your heads and hearts, and in very deed believe that your subtlest work is by no means ameliorating the outward condition of your people, but making them better, and that you will do this by helping their weak wills to do what they know to be right. (Quoted in Whelan, 1998: 37)

While Octavia Hill provided good-quality housing for poor people, the unambiguous aim was to promote 'goodness': first, in the individual who provided the support (taken as read by Hill, since her fellow workers were demonstrating their 'goodness' by volunteering); second, in the recipients of the support; and, finally, this (hopefully) would be translated into general 'goodness' in bringing about the good society. Welfare, therefore, is provided to encourage and bring about the common good.

On the other side of the late Victorian debate, however, stood those who placed far greater emphasis upon environmental, as opposed to individual, factors. The group that promoted this view were the Fabians, epitomised by Sydney and Beatrice Webb. The Fabian approach was essentially located in an understanding of the 'environment', as opposed to individual character traits. The Fabians believed in the transformation of society through the organised working class, and this was the founding principle of so-called 'Fabian-socialism' (see www.fabians.org.uk). The state had the *moral* duty and responsibility to intervene to prevent chronic poverty, and attempts to locate the causes of this in individual 'character' were misguided. Harris (2009) argues that their seminal publication was the 1909 Poor Law Commission Minority Report (see http://www.archive.org/details/breakupofpoorlaw01webbuoft). This was both an exposition of the role of the state in alleviating poverty and also a clear attack upon the principles and practices of the COS.

For the Webbs, it was the *duties* of citizenship that were placed centre stage, although, as a reading of the 1909 report reveals, the Webbs were clearly concerned with control of expenditure and opposed to 'gratuitous treatment ... shovelled out to all who ask for it' (Webb and Webb, 1909: 567) and their subsequent comment that 'we attach [importance] to enforcing payment from those who are legally liable and of sufficient ability to pay for what they receive' (1909: 568) reveals that there were clear limits upon their universalism. Harris (2009) makes a connection between their position on the state and welfare provision and the better known (and later) Beveridge Report (1942), which was partially adopted by the Labour Party and is largely credited with being the document upon which the 1948 welfare state was founded.

The tensions between the two approaches to welfare conflicted in the Poor Law Review, and while it is not the intention to develop this any further here, one final point needs to be made. Vincent (1984) suggests that the differences between the two approaches were more a question of emphasis than subsequent history has allowed, which frequently sets the two positions at opposite ends of the spectrum. He argues for a more nuanced understanding of the position of both protagonists and argues that the COS were not purveyors of a crude individualism, and that the Webbs also possessed a claim to superiority and certainty, which would have lead to 'systematic enforcement of parental responsibility' as well as an emphasis upon the 'enforced minimum to "clean up" the base of society' (Vincent, 1984: 84).

Thus, at the beginning of the 20th century, we see clear debates being established about the nature of society and the character of its citizens in determining the nature of welfare. One hundred years later these same debates continue, albeit in a different language, and an important tool for analysis is to understand the deep-rooted nature of the debate, rather than its apparent specific nature.

Casework dominance under threat: critical approaches

Notwithstanding the Fabian position on the Poor Law, perhaps best outlined by Webb and Webb (1927), casework became a dominant methodology, as noted earlier. How this came about evidences another key tool for understanding policy, namely, that it can accommodate a multiplicity of positions and incorporate several strands. Sapsford (1993) argues that one of the key factors in the increased use of casework and an individualised approach was the rise of what he termed the 'psy-complex'. Sapsford does not concern himself with the veracity of psychology's claims, but rather argues that it represents a particular way of looking at the world (a discourse), which characterises the world in terms of individual interactions that can be reduced to 'underlying qualities or tendencies of a more general nature, the particular individual being seen as embodying a particular combination of these qualities or tendencies' (1993: 24). Sapsford builds his analysis around the developing psychologies (note that there were many forms of psychological theories, not just one) and how they explained a range of factors notably around childcare and human development. He argues that this enabled the growing body of 20th-century professionals to 'manage' behaviours that were labelled 'deviant'. We should explain that while very few (if any) contemporary welfare professionals would use the term 'deviant' to describe their service-user groups, the service-user groups of the early 21st century barely differ from those of the original 'social workers' in the 19th century, or those of the legions of welfare professionals throughout the 20th century (Price and Simpson, 2007).

Clarke (1988) argues that psychology provided a scientific rather than moral language for individualised welfare interventions. Sapsford's concluding comments about the nature of psychological approaches are significant in understanding policy development, and can be briefly summarised as follows. He suggests that the welfare professional owns no particular area of 'expertise', and that contemporary welfare professionalism has grown out of the 'friendly visiting' of an earlier age, but is now crucially legitimised by the knowledge base of psychology – yet welfare professionals remain essentially accountable to the state. The welfare professional has as their 'first concern the interests of the client' (Sapsford, 1993: 41). He points to the fact that there are individual and group psychological theories, which may even stand in opposition to each other, but that crucially:

> They share, however, a set of views about what sort of society we live in and how it is best managed.... What psychology contributes to social work and health visiting, etc., over and above a knowledge base and validation of practice, is a long-term view of society that can be rationally managed through the rational management of individuals – a Fabian utopia, in essence. (Sapsford, 1993: 42)

Utilising this argument we can begin to explain how casework (essentially a model derived from the COS and 'charitable visiting') became a central model of welfare professionalism even when the state assumed a greater responsibility for intervention post-1948. In short, while the moral individualism of the COS did not resonate with their Fabian opponents, their methodology could be readily utilised as part of a wider state programme.

Casework, however, has been subject to a clear criticism, most notably within the social work profession. The nature of the criticism is that it reinforces individualised explanations at the expense of other – structural – causes. The critique emerged in the 1970s as part of the 'radical social work' movement and its timing is pertinent since this followed the expansion of welfare in the late 1960s as a result of the Labour government's response to potential social unrest and the subsequent increase in posts for welfare professionals, many of which attracted graduates who were part of radicalised student movements (Loney, 1983). This was a criticism of both methodology and also of the nature of the welfare state, which targeted groups of people for intervention and ignored other groups – despite the universalism of the Seebohm report (Seebohm, 1968). In short, casework became seen as a particular instrument of social control in the interests of a particular form of societal organisation. Such a response was not entirely 'new' since Galbraith (1970) had proposed the view that the post-war welfare state had in fact abolished poverty, which led to a view that 'case poverty is the result of deficiencies, including the moral shortcomings of the person concerned'. Thus it was possible to 'shift the responsibility to those involved' thereby solving poverty by 'private or public charity' (Galbraith, 1970, quoted in Pearson, 1978: 153).

Pearson argued that during the economic boom of the 1950s and 1960s, casework equally 'boomed' as an ideology especially congenial to individualistic economic principles. Nevertheless, the strength of casework was that it 'stubbornly asserts the importance of individual man [sic] and of the individual small frail clusters of persons called families' (Perlman, 1970: 28).

Halmos (1965) had earlier asserted that the scientific basis for 'counselling' (and, given the nature and date of his research, it is possible to extrapolate 'welfare professional') was at least part myth, arguing that 'intervention is so much more effective when it is carried out with warmth and spontaneity' (1965: 160). Thus, the essential basis of the friendly visiting of the COS retained its supporters and to a large extent saw its *methodology* justified. Indeed, for many contemporary welfare professionals the nature of the personal relationship remains very strong, and even contemporary radical writers have underlined its importance (Dominelli and Hoogveldt, 1996; Ferguson, 2008). The 1970s' radicals knew the importance of the individual, with a focus upon being human (Hugman, 1977) and linking the individual to wider society (Bailey and Brake, 1980) – indeed, in their earlier work, Bailey and Brake had summed up the 'radical' position as not wanting to eliminate casework, 'but to eliminate casework that supports ruling class hegemony' (Bailey and Brake, 1980: 5). In other words, casework as a method is sound, but it is problematic when it is used to support a social theory, or ideology, which individualises people rather than placing them fully within a social, economic and political context. Thus, the 21st-century welfare professional will need to be able to not just understand the individual (and the associated 'psy-complex'), but also to locate this within the broader context – one of the aims of this book.

Casework, then, has been a feature of the delivery of social welfare for at least 150 years. Despite criticisms, it has flourished, partly because of its 'scientific' justification and partly because it is a method that appeals to the essential human instincts of those who are welfare professionals. Indeed, Jordan (2006) argues that it has moved from the relatively closed world of health and social care, to almost every area of modern policy (for example, the unemployed or 'job-seeker' has a personal advisor). When located in this area it is much easier to see the casework relationship as being one with the power to 'control' human behaviour and to 'manage' it to ensure that certain societal goals are attained.

The 21st-century welfare professional: providing services and doing good?

We began this section by asserting that to understand the full nature of the contemporary role, the historical background needs to be grasped so that the social location can be more fully understood. The overarching critique is that class and structure can readily be replaced by individual and character. The contemporary welfare worker is located quite clearly within the context of 'service provision' and, as will be explored in subsequent chapters, within a context dominated by managerialism and the attendant 'target culture' (Garrett, 2009).

The wider context, however, is one where debates about the nature of welfare and those who receive it are never far from the surface and, indeed, in the months leading up to the 2010 general election campaign a key theme of the Conservative Party was 'broken Britain', subsequently muted for the campaign itself. Such claims were fuelled by high-profile child death cases (for example, Baby P, Kyra Ishaq) and a case involving two young boys from Doncaster who were alleged to have 'tortured' another boy, and other stories that rested upon accounts of 'feral children' and abusing adults. Thus, the group of people who are the recipients of the services provided are widely seen as members of the 'underclass' (Murray, 1990; 2001) to whom consistent negative character traits are applied (see Chapter 11).

It is interesting that the huge gulf in wealth in Britain is not a feature of these reports, neither is poverty. The gap between the richest and poorest in some parts of Britain has been described by Dorling (2010) as being its greatest since 1854 and child poverty remains rather stubbornly at 30% of all children (Child Poverty Action Group, 2009) – yet the imagery and language used is that which focuses upon individuals and increasingly on 'character'. This trend was identified and welcomed by several commentators on the right some years ago (see Whelan, 1998). Within mainstream welfare work it remains a policy background. Yet the *character* of the welfare professional is returning to the mainstream agenda. Clark (2006) argued that this needed to be made more explicit and McBeath and Webb (2002) welcome virtue ethics (with a focus upon 'doing good') as a valuable antidote to the 'drone of modernity'. Banks and Gallagher (2009) produced perhaps the first recent textbook exploring the concept of virtue ethics that focuses primarily upon the character of the welfare professional. They are, however, careful to point out that the virtues (or qualities required) include recognising the positive qualities of those we work with. They highlight the work of Mary Richmond – a pioneer of social work (in its broadest context) – who cites the correspondence of Florence Nightingale:

> It is necessary for the safety of life that we should understand the characters of those among who we are placed. But if we are only critical, or only capable of feeling pain at differences, then blind affection 'which covers a multitude of sins' is far better. It is useless to be intelligent if we see only the defects of others, and fail to recognise the good elements upon which we might work. (Nightingale, quoted in Banks and Gallagher, 2009: 222–3)

It is, however, often the case that the role of the professional in 'doing good' remains subject to criticism. For example, see the coverage of Baby P and the criticism heaped upon social workers and health professionals in that case, or the furore over the report that one of the men who was convicted of the murder of a toddler when they were only 10 years old had been recalled to prison under licence, to see the ease at which the negative connotations of 'do-gooder' can be invoked.

The role of welfare itself then comes under scrutiny. The image of scrounger or benefit fraudster is again relatively easy to conjure up in policy terms (Connor, 2007) and the language of perverse incentives is never far removed from the surface, again reflecting the welfare debates of over a century ago. Consider this comment from a nurse in South Wales:

> I was all in favour of removing prescription charges, because I always believed that health care should be free to those who need it. But now I'm not so sure. I hear stories of people who go to their GP and are prescribed paracetamol (which you can buy cheaply in a supermarket) and of course there are all the English who claim to be living in Wales to get free prescriptions.

The context is the decision of the Welsh Assembly to remove prescription charges in 2007 and a rise in the number of items dispensed of over 5% in the subsequent year (Dobson, 2008). The controversy was further fuelled by a report that more people were registered with GPs in Wales than the official population, and it was this aspect of the story that clearly influenced the health professionals alongside their own anecdotal evidence (see Williamson, 2008).

The point here is not to engage in the debate about free prescriptions per se (although it should be noted that Scotland and Northern Ireland both plan to introduce free prescriptions by 2011, leaving England the only country in the Union where patients will still have to pay), nor to be critical of the comment, but to show how the so-called abuse of the system can lead to a focus upon those who abuse it by those who have first-hand experience of that abuse and equally know that other resources are under threat. The notion of perverse incentives has a long history. The nature of the 1834 Poor Law was to establish the principle of least eligibility (welfare should not make people 'better off' than working) and a childcare campaigner, Mary Carpenter, urged charges on those who could pay for their children's care 'lest we should confer a bonus on vice' (1968 [1851]:

6). The COS were concerned to ensure that any 'welfare' should not be abused (Whelan, 1998) and the means test has been a long-standing feature of Britain's welfare system, with few truly universal benefits ever established – child benefit being the clear exception, although, at the time of writing, there were plans for this also to be targeted at those in need.

Within the theory of welfare provision perhaps the best known proponent of welfare providing perverse incentives is Charles Murray, who argued that the provision of welfare distorts the behaviour of those who receive it and thereby offers 'perverse', that is, unwanted, incentives for behaviour. His well-known example is that of the unmarried mother-to-be who would have almost certainly married the father of the child in the 1960s; while the same situation repeated in the 1980s and 1990s, he argued, would lead to a decision not to marry the father since this would reduce welfare entitlements. Murray then goes on to extrapolate that this distortion of behaviour leads to the creation of an underclass of people who do not share the same moral codes as the rest of society (Murray, 1984; 1994). Field (1997), in an English context and from a different political position, argued that the British emphasis upon the 'means test' actually encouraged dishonesty and that positive character traits needed to be developed as a goal of policy. What both these writers share is that they connect welfare with self-interest (Deacon, 2002) and that this can have particular consequences. Equally, both claim a position that sees it as legitimate for welfare policy to attempt to shape behaviour to a desired end. A more recent example of this is the Conservative Party's plan to 'reward marriage' with tax concessions which, following some criticisms, was amended to include civil partnerships (Merrick, 2010).

What often remains absent from current mainstream debates is the extent of inequality and poverty and the impact this has upon those who receive services and the concept of welfare as a tool for redistribution and social justice (Titmuss, 1974; Craig, 2002). That is not to say that it does not feature in the programmes of political parties, but rather that the poor can easily become the targets of policies rather than policies being created to alleviate poverty. It is perhaps too easy to comment upon the haste at which the British government bailed out the banks in October 2008. The consequences, however, are that the general election campaign in 2010 saw all parties campaigning on the question of how they would reduce the deficit and this coincided with many local authorities having to make considerable 'cuts' in public services, with one estimate being that 350,000 jobs in the public sector would be lost with the attendant high level of cuts in provision (see BBC News, 2009). Thus, those who use services are often those who are subjected to increased hardship, and those who are welfare professionals operate in this context. As one West Midlands social worker commented, 'in the end it is all about resources. You try your best, but often the money is simply not there'.

In the world of service provision the welfare professional does not stand immune from wider debates that shape the way in which the public responds to 'welfare'. We suggest that, alongside this, there is a renewed emphasis upon character that has largely displaced the redistributive aspects of welfare envisaged by the 1948 welfare state allowing the focus to shift to individual traits. In this regard the debates of 100 years ago are very much contemporary.

Partnerships and collaboration: new forms of control?

The final section will explore aspects of partnerships in relation to service delivery, both in relation to inter-professional relationships and those between professionals and service users.

Crises in public provision, notably those involving health and social services, have invariably led to increased calls for closer collaboration – these were a feature of reports in the 1980s and crucially the Laming report (Laming, 2003), leading to the 2004 Children Act. Similar reports into mental health 'failures' and those in the health service, where more than one agency has been involved, had a similar outcome. It could be argued that such conclusions are tried-and-tested ways of deflecting blame, as well as offering a way forward. Frequently (though not always) social workers, as opposed to other professional groups – when they have been involved – often bear the brunt of criticism (see, for example, the media campaigns over the death of 'Baby P', especially in *The Sun* (2008), which ran a sustained public campaign for the sacking of the social workers involved). Perhaps as a response to such criticisms, there has been a considerable literature developed that deals with inter-professional working (see, for example, Headrick et al, 1998; Molyneux, 2001). Indeed, many of the early calls for greater inter-professional working originate from within the health sector along with subsequent calls for greater inter-professional education (Finch, 2000; Meads and Ashcroft, 2005).

Within the area of social work, interdisciplinary work became a key element of the 2003 social work degree and has continued to assume high levels of importance in post-qualifying awards (see, for example, GSCC, 2005). Such calls resonate with professionals who seek to promote better services, and, indeed, this movement is not contained within the UK. Munday (2007) edited a sustained overview of EU provision and the extent to which services had become integrated in different EU member states – some examples of high integration were outlined (for example, the Flemish-speaking part of Belgium) alongside examples of countries where integration continued to be an aspiration, rather than reality – although many of these were newly acceded members of the EU (for example, Latvia). Despite the authors' (and indeed other writers') enthusiasm for greater integration, a central part of the text is a review by Julkunen (2005), which reported little to no *empirical evidence* (at that time) that integrated services actually offer an improved service – though noting that perhaps they ought to. This is perhaps best summed up in the opening statement, made by the parents of five-year-old twins who both have a moderate learning disability. The parents, speaking of their experience in England, highlight the number of different professionals involved with their daughters: from teachers to occupational therapists to psychologists and language specialists, not to mention the GP and various administrators. Their experience is summed up thus: 'We're so confused sometimes. We don't understand the different roles and have so many appointments that clash. Can nobody or no system sort it out?' (Munday, 2007: 2). While these experiences call for greater 'joined-up working' to promote positive aspects of care, many other attempts have been located in creating and maintaining at least elements of supervision and surveillance, as anticipated by Scull (1983) in his study of community-based mental health provision.

Placed in the context of the historical development outlined in Chapter 1, the current emphasis upon service-user involvement and 'partnerships' should clearly act against some of the more overtly controlling aspects of an individualised casework approach. The recent history of empowerment within social care (Braye and Preston-Shoot, 1995) is located within a 'radical' agenda of welfare citizenship (see also Marshall, 1967; Esping-Andersen et al, 2002). The question for those involved in the delivery of welfare has to focus upon the authenticity of such involvement. The early formulations (Braye and Preston-Shoot, 1995; Dalymple and Burke, 1995; Martin-Crawford, 1999) primarily focused on service-user control, as opposed to partnership, seeing the former as a radical option. Indeed, partnership, and especially participation, has a far longer history, arguably as long as forms of social welfare itself, being established in parts of London (Moore, 1988) and Glasgow (Parsons, 1988) as a feature of Church-based welfare. The notion was arguably tainted, however, by de Gaulle's cynical use of participation in ending the Paris uprising in 1968 (Hobsbawm, 2007). Nonetheless, given that direct user control remains rather limited – although one example of this can be seen at the Centre of Excellence in Mental Health, Birmingham – those engaged in provision need to develop a critical appraisal of current practices.

Clarke (2004a) argues that in welfare we are now a nation of citizen-consumers, who 'consume' welfare in the way we consume other commodities and goods, yet those who actually use the services do not identify themselves as 'consumers' in this sense: 'Customer implies you toddle in, and you look at various things and you toddle off if you don't fancy it. Or you demand the most expensive, perhaps' (Clarke, 2005: 739).

Jordan and Jordan (2000) had earlier noted that service users are usually dependent upon the welfare professional's role in rationing services; bringing to mind Titmuss's definition of social policy as 'the study of social needs and the functioning, in conditions of scarcity, of human organisation ... to meet those needs' (1974: 20), surely an ever increasingly apposite definition given the plans to reduce public expenditure (*The Guardian*, 2010). Research has constantly indicated that those who use services (as opposed to the general public) want quality services and meaningful relationships with those who deliver them (Barnes and Prior, 1995; Fine and Leopold, 2001). Current moves towards personalisation and the implementation of *Valuing People* – a series of policy initiatives begun in 2001 to improve the lives of people with learning disabilities – show the limits of choice and the role of professional power in determining how services are provided, often leaving those in receipt of services ever more vulnerable (Simpson and Price, 2010). Ferguson (2008) argues that while personalisation does bring about some measure of control and independence for some service users, this is not universally so, and the use of the personalisation agenda to cover reductions in expenditure reveal the problem of the current economic organisation in Scotland and the UK. Thus, it is not the ideas that welfare professionals need to address, but, more critically, how the ideas are implemented. The welfare professional frequently adopts a socially liberal position, only to find this severely compromised by the workings of 'liberal' economic policy (Scull, 1979, 1983).

Ferguson (2008) has set out an agenda to reclaim aspects of welfare work and service delivery, and interestingly he argues for a new form of casework, valuing the relationship between the welfare professional and the service user, echoing Bailey and Brake's (1975) proposition that there is nothing wrong with casework as a method, provided it can be harnessed to an alternative 'social theory' to that which originally accompanied it (see the earlier discussion).

The radical blueprint, however, contains an irony, if not a paradox. Galper argued that a radical alternative will 'call on people [i.e. workers and clients] to grow, to risk and to change and to work hard' (1980: 13). Ferguson affirms that welfare professionals remain attracted to their work because of a desire to 'make a difference' and that 'realising that aspiration in the current situation will require vision, confidence, organisation and not a little *courage*' (2008: 136, emphasis added). To borrow the language from another era, the desire to do good cannot be left to organisation alone. In other words, the welfare professional has a responsibility to *engage* with welfare policy and this requires skills, determination and courage – one of the original 'virtues'.

Conclusion

This chapter has sought to examine the role of character and how this links to wider debates about welfare and the role of welfare professionals. A tool for understanding welfare, then, is the ability to explore the extent to which provision and policy rests (however ambiguously) upon aspects of character and to guard against becoming swept along with dominant discourses that promote negative aspects of character in people who use services, and to consider the extent to which such policies focus upon individuals at the expense of wider social and economic factors – even legitimising forms of provision that could increase vulnerability. It concludes with an examination of current practices and the extent to which those who seek to challenge them need to have certain characteristics themselves.

REFLECTIVE EXERCISES

- ➔ How far do you think welfare professionals should go in seeking to 'reform' aspects of character?
- ➔ How far do you think services should be dependent upon whether or not those who use them do so properly? An example to think of might be whether or not people who engage in activities injurious to health should pay more for health care (this is the case when health care is dependent upon insurance)?
- ➔ Consider the final comment by Ferguson (2008): if social welfare professionals are going to change aspects of welfare, why does it require 'courage'? What are the risks and how much courage will it take?

CHAPTER 3

From state-led provision to 'choice'

The two previous chapters in this section have explored the development of welfare provision from the 'philanthropic impulse' (Clarke, 1993b) to the establishment of state welfare, from the perspective of both service users (welfare 'subjccts') and also those who provided the 'services'. The development of state-led services came to be criticised as being 'monolithic' and lacking in flexibility (Thompson, 1997), ushering in a shift towards 'choice', located within a business model (Harris, 2003). This chapter aims to explore the shift away from what has been described as a monolithic, 'one-size-fits-all' approach to welfare provision, and towards the development of a more flexible person-centred or needs-led service delivery. This shift has been done in the name of improving the quality of welfare services and increasing choice for services users. The question of what constitutes quality and choice is examined in more depth. We do not question attempts to improve quality or seek to argue against 'choice' per se, but examine how these terms have come to be defined and question the mechanisms that are being developed to achieve these ends. Rather than defend or return to an alleged monolithic form of welfare provision, we examine whether or not there is a set of 'new' monolithic policies developing within contemporary social welfare.

Case study: The desire for 'choice' and quality

We begin with a dialogue from a meeting in an office:

Aisha: 'What have you done to your hand?' (Hannah raises her hand showing a bandage.)
Hannah: 'Oh, I stabbed it by accident.'
Aisha: 'Have you been to the doctor's, it looks nasty?'
Hannah: 'No, they would only refer me to A&E.'
Aisha: 'I'm no expert, but it looks like it needs stitches and it could get infected. You really should get it looked at.'
Hannah: 'No, I am not going to A&E. They treat you horrible. You don't know how long it will last and I hate needles. If I could go private I would.'
Aisha: 'Why, what difference will that make?'
Hannah: 'Because it would be like Pizza Express. They treat you nice because they have to, you are paying them. I think if you paid for health care, it would have to get better. You could choose where to go and they would have to treat you well to get your money, like Tesco's.'

In this exchange, we are interested in Hannah's description of a problem, namely, the perceived 'quality', or otherwise, of an A&E (accident and emergency) department and the subsequent solution – to go 'private'. In a sense this exchange summarises 'concerns' regarding the capacity of public services to be responsive to the needs and aspirations of a knowledgeable and diverse population of service users, or what are now designated as 'consumers' (see Chapter 1). In the early 21st century, 'choice' became a buzzword in social policy, with politicians, policymakers and practitioners keen to ensure that welfare recipients were being given more choice.

We argue that this consumerism represents a limited notion of 'choice', and that to ensure this choice, significant changes are being made to the nature of the welfare landscape. An understanding of the implications of these changes, may well lead people to question the desirability of the form of choice being made available and to seek alternatives, particularly ones that help people achieve 'control' over the nature of the services that they are engaged with and operate according to a set of values that puts the welfare of citizens, rather than their potential purchasing capacity, as their priority (Beresford, 2008).

However, the desire for choice and quality remains a central policy objective, yet the meaning of quality and choice in social welfare provision is problematic. 'Quality' in everyday life has various meanings: 'It may be a quality in the popular sense, neither more than, nor less than a certain value; or it may be described qualitatively or in terms of a numerical measure' (Jaziri, 1976: 40).

Many things have been spoken of as an aspect of 'quality': the training of personnel; reductions in waiting times; satisfaction with the service; the relative costs, effectiveness and benefits of a service; the environments in which the services are provided, and so on. We will examine the assumptions, both implicit and explicit, that underpin discussions of quality and the management and delivery of social welfare through three models: the technical, consumerist and political.

The technical model: rules, standards and 'experts'

The technical model is one where services conform to standards and rules set by peers/experts, and can be described as a 'rule-governed', bureaucratic approach to managing and delivering social welfare. The German sociologist Max Weber (1979) identified three types of authority. 'Charismatic' was based upon personal authority; 'traditional' was based upon the authority of institutions (e.g. the Church); and 'rational-legal' was based on a system of rules devised for rational reasons. Weber argued that society was increasingly based on rational-legal authority, exemplified by the development of what he described as the bureaucratic form of organisation. Bureaucracies are skilled bodies of specialists and experts, a rational form of organisation characterised by:

- Functional specialisation – tasks are divided up and allocated to people with the formally certified expertise to carry them out. Appointments and promotions are based on merit.

- Hierarchy of authority – all communications and commands would pass up or down this hierarchy without missing out any steps. Activities are controlled and coordinated by officials organised in a hierarchy of authority. A post-holder's authority derives from their appointed office and not from their person. Salary reflects a post-holder's level in the hierarchy.
- System of rules – every operating rule and procedure would be formally written down. This helps ensure calculability.
- Impersonality – the 'good bureaucrat' acts 'without anger or passion' and all decisions and judgements would be made impersonally and neutrally, without emotion, personal preference or prejudice.

In this context, quality is defined by the system and rules and is ensured and measured by the ability to follow these procedures. An influential model, bureaucracy became a widespread means by which to organise complex activities, helping to achieve effective, precise and fair procedures and outcomes. In the British context of social welfare provision, Massey and Pyper (2005) and McCourt and Minogue (2001) claim that the post-1948 work of welfare professionals was supported and enabled through a system of social administration, which, echoing the principles of bureaucracy, exhibited the following characteristics:

- Principal motivation is a sense of duty – for public rather than organisational or private interests.
- Administration is continuous and predictable – based on clearly written rules.
- Administrators are recruited on the basis of qualifications – trained professionals.
- Organisation should reflect an efficient division of labour – hierarchy of tasks and people (according to role and possibly qualifications).
- Resources belong to the organisation.
- Rational-legal authority.

More specifically, and with explicit reference to questions of quality, Donabedian (1980) concentrated on the characteristics of quality, proposing that three aspects of health care were amenable to evaluation: structure, process and outcome. Maxwell (1983: 13), by contrast, identified six dimensions of quality:

1. Appropriateness – the service or procedure is one that the individual or population actually needs.
2. Equity – services are fairly shared among the population who need them.
3. Accessibility – services are readily accessible and not compromised by distance or time constraints.
4. Effectiveness – the services achieve the intended benefit for the individual and for the population.
5. Acceptability – the service satisfies the reasonable expectations of patients, providers and the community.

6. Efficiency – resources are not wasted on one service or patient to the detriment of others.

In the technical model, the judgement of the expert is privileged. The judgement required, which can also be extended to the nature of the evidence and means by which such judgements are made, may often lead to rather obscure and opaque-looking procedures to the non-expert. Within this model, then, 'quality' is guaranteed by the organisational structure. There have been numerous critiques of this technical approach. Leibenstein (1966) argues that in the organisation there will be an assumed failure to achieve efficiency, a phenomenon he termed 'X-inefficiency'. Mooney and Law in their overview point to those who suggest that it is the absence of pressures from a competitive environment (notably in the public sector) that generates such alleged 'X-inefficiencies' (2007: 28). Merton (1957) had earlier argued that within bureaucratic organisations employees follow the rules to the letter as a mode of self-protection and career advancement. The result is that rather than seeking more efficient ways of meeting the organisation's aim, a slavish following of procedures will result in X-inefficiencies. Critics of professions have further suggested that they tend to reflect and pursue their own interests, at the expense of the service user and the efficiency of the organisation as a whole. It is suggested that within state welfare organisations this tendency is pronounced as in effect a 'monopolisation of trade' results. It is argued that this monopoly means that professionals are not accountable to anybody but themselves. Consequently not only is there no incentive for making services and practices more efficient, but there will also be a tendency to artificially restrict the supply of services (Mooney and Law, 2007: 32–3).

There has also been a questioning of the authority traditionally attached to professionals or other experts and an awareness of the significance of lay and experiential knowledge in both decision-making about individual service use and in shaping public policy (see Chapter 1). This can be seen in discussions and the equivalence that has been drawn between state-led provision and 'deinstitutionalisation'. Some service-user groups were subject to provision that saw them warehoused in large institutions, run by either the NHS or social services departments in local authorities, although significant numbers remained with their families (Rolph et al, 2005; Hreinsdóttir et al, 2006). These groups included people with learning and other disabilities and those who experienced mental ill health, and as such they were segregated and/or excluded. Oliver (1990) set this trend within the context of capitalist development, while Ryan and Thomas (1987) emphasised the role of 'social Darwinism' (survival of the fittest). Large-scale institutions – 'subnormality' hospitals, mental health 'asylums', large-scale 'approved' schools for youth offenders – were the main thrust of policy until the 1980s, with the main policy directions emphasising 'exclusion' and 'segregation' (Simpson and Price, 2010). Movements within disability groups, for example, the normalisation and social role valorisation movements that began in the 1960s and 1970s (Wolfensberger, 1992), and the 'decarceration' of those with mental ill health (Scull, 1979) began to present a challenge to these types of 'service'. Part of the current narrative is that contemporary organisation is 'empowering' and thus, by implication, what went before was 'disempowering'.

Although other services were not so focused around the large institution, there was a sense in which they too were 'institutionalised' in that the local authorities, education authorities and health services were the providers of services they funded 'in-house' (to use current terminology), that is, the state had the monopoly on how services were provided and delivered. It was the 1990 NHS and Community Care Act, ideologically driven by the Conservative government, which created a legislative framework that separated 'providers' and 'purchasers' and set the business model of welfare delivery in motion (Le Grand, 1990; Harris, 2003). Even though the Act was firmly located in the politics of the free market exemplified by its forerunner, the Griffiths report (Griffiths, 1988), many aspects of it were welcomed by some progressive voices within the field of social welfare.

Technical discussions of quality tend to neglect the fact that any evaluation of a policy or service will inevitably require political choices regarding which facts will be valued as indicators of success and which interpretations of facts will serve as a basis for judgement (Aspect, 2009). Both those who work in and are on the receiving ends of bureaucracies, therefore, may report what is described as an 'iron cage of rationality', a concept originally developed by Weber (1922) and which underpins the work of Ritzer (1995) and, in relation to social care work, Dustin (2008). Put simply, this is the sense of being 'a little cog in a big machine', where impersonality, rather than being seen as a guarantor of equitable treatment, is seen as dehumanising – a common view among many welfare workers. People may be willing to accept a degree of control, but the constraints of a bureaucracy offer little opportunity for creative approaches. A combination of these critiques has also led to the suggestion that bureaucratic forms are unsuited to uncertain and fast-changing environments, particularly where the needs/wants of the recipients are becoming ever more complex and diverse.

The consumerist model: rights to information and choice

Chapter 1 focused upon service users as 'active' rather than 'passive' welfare recipients and as such they have attempted to make services more responsive, and some of these ideas were explored briefly in Chapter 2. Here, we move on to the consumerist model, which emphasises consumers' rights to information, access, choice and redress in an economic sphere, for while consumer sovereignty is paramount, individuals' rights are enacted through the rational exercise of exit and choice. *Homo economicus*, or the 'rational actor' (Houston, 2010), assumes that an agent is rational in the sense that they will be driven by 'economic' motives, that is, by the intention of making the maximum possible (material or monetary) utility or benefit. This is best reflected in an oft-cited quote from Adam Smith:

> Give me that which I want, and you shall have this that you want … it is in this manner that we obtain from one another the far greater part of those good offices which we stand in need of. It is not from the benevolence of the butcher, the brewer or the baker that we expect our dinner, but from regard to their own interest. We address ourselves, not to their humanity but to their self love, and never talk to them of our necessities but of their advantages. (1976 [1776]: 118)

The rational *homo economicus* – a long-standing paradigm in economic theory – examines choices and will choose the most preferred alternative, one that will maximise utility. Services users, purchasers and providers merely make a series of rational choices in their own interests and by acknowledging the existence of self-interest in this way, the market (i.e. the range of service providers) makes the necessary adjustments as part of a rational calculus. The extent to which this applies in, for example, the retail industry is neither straightforward nor without its critics (Adburgham, 1989), but how far can it be extended to attempts to understand social interaction and society as a whole, and for our purpose here, the provision of welfare services?

The economic basis of consumerism (and by extension at least some aspects of the focus upon service users) is located within mutual self-interest. Social interaction needs to be understood as a process of social exchange, where parallels, if not quite equivalences, are drawn between the exchange of goods and services that one might find in a market and the 'exchange' of approval and other valued behaviours that one may find in social relationships (Homans, 1961). These theories, however, have difficulties explaining the cooperation of individuals in different forms of collective action and also the norms, morality and the construction of what counts as 'interests' (Duncan, 2000). Social relationships are not equal, but are influenced by a range of dynamics including power (Amin, 1998). What is not in doubt is that consumerism, as an approach to social welfare, introduced and sustained a significant change in the way that welfare work is undertaken. On the one hand, there are those who would point to the creativity of 'new approaches' generating 'positive outcomes' for service users (customers) (Duffy, 2008). Against this are the cautionary warnings that the market distorts social relationships, leaving the vulnerable even more exposed (Ferguson, 2007).

Nevertheless, within a service-user-as-consumer model, the consumer is empowered through their ability to purchase services and, subsequently, providers are required to be more responsive to their needs. Proponents of such a model argue that the net result is higher 'quality' services for all users. Glennerster (2009) identifies the assumptions underpinning a consumerist approach as follows:

- self-interest is more consistent and reliable than goodwill;
- dynamic efficiency and the profit motive;

- consumer sovereignty (allocative efficiency) – or, more colloquially put, 'the customer is always right';
- productive efficiency.

Providers are expected to identify and be responsive to the needs of the customer and it is this orientation that is considered the key to commercial success (Peters and Waterman, 1982). The motivation for providers to engage with consumers is financial. Consumers' views are sought to ensure that services more accurately reflect their needs and thereby enhance market competitiveness. Proponents of a consumerist approach point to the impact this can have on the productivity of social welfare services.

Productivity measures offer a way of comparing the cost of something to its benefit. In a manufacturing context this can appear quite clear-cut. For example, output would refer to how many units you can make in a given period of time, against how much it 'costs' to produce those units. There have been attempts to apply productivity measures to social welfare. As part of the Office for National Statistics (ONS), the UK Centre for the Measurement of Government Activity publishes a range of data on public service productivity (ONS, 2010a). In what is described as a very complex task, the ONS calculates the productivity of public services to assess whether 'taxpayers' are getting 'value for money'. Recent figures have suggested that productivity has fallen, and that productivity in the public sector is poor when compared with data from the private sector. These observations are used to support the argument: (a) that improvements in public services will not be achieved by increasing spending; and (b) that there is something inherent in public services that makes them unproductive (see the earlier discussion about bureaucracies). We suggest that the results should be treated with some caution. First, productivity should be considered *a* measure, rather than *the* measure, for assessing an organisation's performance. Second, welfare professionals frequently ask a number of questions as to the extent to which their activities can be measured in terms of productivity, for example:

- How should the qualitative aspects of a service, those that can define the nature of the relationships and care provided in social welfare, be measured?
- Over what timescale is the effectiveness of an intervention to be measured?
- While it may be relatively straightforward to measure outputs, what value can be placed on improvements in the education, health or well-being of the population?

Third, while proponents of productivity measures may concede the above points, their suggestion that those activities that can be measured should be measured can give rise to the danger of perverse incentives. This was summed up by a social worker who, upon noting that their local authority had recently improved their star ratings, commented that 'managers had merely become better at filling in the forms and focusing upon their "targets"'.

The consumerist approach (as exemplified in the exchange between Aisha and Hannah at the start of the chapter) rests upon the view that the market will deliver. Seldon (1977) summarised its strengths:

- 'choice' for the consumer;
- a service led by the consumer rather than by the professions;
- more efficient services at lower costs (because this increases profitability);
- responsiveness to need (because their profit depends on it);
- the education of people as to the implications of their choices.

However, markets 'fail', not only in terms of collapsing 'demand' or credit bubbles, but they also fail if people do not have the choice and crucially do not bear the costs of the actions themselves. Several writers in relation to social welfare argue that the market-based economy of welfare will lead to the exclusion of people with extreme needs and those considered to be a 'risk' (Titmuss, 1970a; Esping-Andersen et al, 2002; Jordan, 2006). The response to individual preferences in social welfare may end up failing to meet wider social needs (Esping-Andersen, 1990, 1999; Mooney and Law, 2007). Finally, the market produces alienation and recent analyses have shown how this can be extended to the field of social welfare (Ferguson and Lavalette, 2004). Summarised more simply with reference to the case study: the A&E department is not established on the same principles as Tesco's (or any other supermarket retailer for that matter)!

Political approaches: the state, power and struggle

A recurrent theme in this book is that developments in social welfare need to be understood within the context of Bryson's comment that 'the state with its institutionalised power relationships represents one site for struggle' (1992: 15). Morgan (2006) argues that one of the origins of the idea of politics is that where views and interests are divergent, society should provide a means of allowing individuals to reconcile their differences through discussion and negotiation. It is argued that politics provides the means of creating order out of this diversity and conflict, while avoiding forms of totalitarian rule. Questions of 'quality' in social welfare are rarely cast in these terms, and yet Morgan clearly reflects a common experience for social welfare professionals:

> Most people working in an organisation readily admit in private that they are surrounded by forms of 'wheeling and dealing' through which people attempt to advance specific interests. However, this kind of activity is rarely discussed in public. The idea that organisations are supposed to be rational enterprises in which their members seek common goals tends to discourage discussion of political motive. Politics in short is seen as a dirty word. (Morgan, 2006: 154)

In sharp contrast to the technical and consumerist approach to 'quality', individuals are not only considered as the recipients of public goods, but as citizens, engaged in the formulation and implementation of policies. In a political approach it is assumed that people will have different interests. The value of a political approach is that it helps make explicit the role and nature of power in policymaking and practice in that discord will be found whenever interests collide. In the technical model conflict is seen as dysfunctional and attributable to some unfortunate or resolvable circumstance or cause (a personality clash, insufficient training and communication problems). In a political approach, however, conflict is considered to be an inherent part of social life and, in social welfare, a conflict that is heightened over the distribution of scarce resources. While there may be a number of means available for resolving these conflicts, in a political approach it is 'power' that is the medium through which conflicts of interest are ultimately resolved. Power will influence who gets what, when and how. A range of sources of power are available, including: the role of formal authority; the control of scarce resources, knowledge technology and decision making; alliances; and, most critically, structural factors, which define and shape the stage of action. These sources of power provide organisational members with a variety of means for enhancing their interests.

In British social welfare the political approach to organisations is most clearly expressed through the distinction that is drawn in central and local government between politics and administration, that is, a role distinction between political leaders – councillors and MPs – who are accountable through elections, and officials – civil servants, policy officers, administrators and professionals – who are appointed. Within this system the practices and policies of social welfare are made accountable through the electoral process.

A political approach addresses the legitimacy of services by enabling citizen users to challenge and force those in power to consider and justify their practices. In this respect, a strategy adopting an explicitly political approach can be seen as a force for democratic renewal. This should be seen in the context of the previous two chapters, with reasons for political forms of involvement in provision including: the desire to achieve better public services; increasing the legitimacy of decision-making; revitalising; creating responsible citizens; and resolving major policy problems. There has been consistent pressure from variously constituted groups, including New Social Movements (Touraine, 1985; Habermas, 2005), to make themselves heard and influence policy from outside (again, see Chapter 1). As a consequence, the professional paternalism that traditionally characterised public experiences of the welfare services now appears outmoded (Milewa et al, 1998).

A political approach to quality has come to be associated with attempts to enhance and increase the involvement of service users in the provision of services, in what has been termed participatory democracy – an early articulation of this being Arnstein's (1969) ladder of participation. The benefits claimed include:

- making public services more responsive;
- making decision-making more transparent;

- highlighting the challenges facing public services while also opening up the 'pool of resources' available for addressing such challenges;
- enhancing the legitimacy of public services.

These 'democratic' approaches place an emphasis on 'development', where individuals and groups are empowered to influence the pattern and delivery of services. The process of participation in itself is valued for broadening citizens' experiences, facilitating inclusion and developing 'citizenship'. Such notions lie at the heart of many of the service-user movements and empowering practice in welfare work, as identified in the earlier chapters, and have been termed 'radical' (Braye and Preston-Shoot, 1995). Such approaches should indeed be welcomed, but they are not beyond critique. One possible critique is whether or not the correct method or tool is being used to achieve the stated aim, that is, are people able to access the forum, and are the consultative exercises of 'participants' representative of the population as a whole?

A more theoretical critique is whether the assumptions being made when employing democratic approaches are correct. In the British experience, they tend to reflect a pluralist perspective, which assumes that those with power are happy to share this power and that the decision-making process is open to influence through deliberation, rationality and evidence. Yet, as noted by Arnstein (1969), participatory efforts can remain tokenistic, or even manipulative. Rather than seeking to achieve their stated aims, participatory approaches have the potential to be misused as a social technology of legitimisation. Authorities, in the form of organisational or individual practitioners, have recognised the political capital to be gained from public involvement in needs assessment and priority-setting exercises. This is what has been described as a social technology of legitimisation, in that institutions have been able to limit public influence over service planning by using the issue of representation to 'delegitimise' user views. Public influence has been constrained by the public's role being advisory and their decisions not binding. Public engagement activities enhance the credibility of commissioning organisations without devolving decision-making power to users. Thus, in the more radical accounts of service-user empowerment, 'participation' is regarded as 'traditional', while user-control is considered 'empowering' (Braye and Preston-Shoot, 1995).

This form of organisation, referred to as 'deliberative democracy', creates what is termed a 'delivery paradox'. This refers to the trend for service-user satisfaction levels to plateau or even decrease despite what appear to be substantive improvements in the provision of services (Blaug et al, 2006). Interestingly, perhaps, the solution appears to be a higher quality of engagement by 'public managers to interact with the public to design, plan, provide and evaluate service provision to ensure that services are responsive to citizens' needs' (Horner et al, 2006: 8). This 'solution' highlights a further difficulty with some variants of the political/democratic approach, namely the neglect of public-sector staff in decision-making regarding the delivery of services. For practical purposes, the absence of social welfare professionals in deliberative processes means that insights into how the delivery of services can be improved are missed. There is, however, a long history of attempts to develop worker- and user-controlled organisations, ranging from cooperatives to workers' councils, which are arguably a more radical response located within a political analysis (Amin, 1998) and seek to achieve the democratic and collective control of the production and distribution of resources. Within the field of social welfare, recent developments with non-affiliated service-user groups can also provide greater levels of influence, if not control (see for example, *Suresearch*, a service user organisation in Birmingham).

Political approaches to quality in public provision have clear strengths, nonetheless, in that they recognise the importance of power, place policy and practices in a wider socio-political context, and recognise that strategies need to be developed in order to secure resources and services. Furthermore, they explode the myth of rationality, and demonstrate that tensions and conflicts are inherent and legitimate rather than the result of 'problematic' differences. By contrast, the limitations are that in some instances the pursuit of power is its own end and this may create a climate of 'mistrust'. As with everything relating to a political perspective, the question has to be asked as to what extent the analysis adopts a plural or critical stance.

We have tried to separate out these strands, but as seen in the discussion of the mixed economy of welfare, in reality, the management and delivery of social welfare has involved a combination and/or compromise between these different mechanisms. This theme will be addressed in subsequent chapters to help make sense of how and why these compromises occurred and their impact. What can be stated with more certainty is that the particular combination of technical and consumerist approaches that has come to predominate in contemporary policy and practice has led to an attempt to depoliticise social welfare. One can understand a desire to seek a model for resolving disputes over access to finite resources without recourse to 'conflict'. However, a failure to view the provision for social welfare as a political system, that is, as a series of shifting coalitions of sectional groups, each with its own objectives, has led to a number of erroneous assumptions based on an image of the provision of social welfare that stresses consensus and harmony (Hunter, 1980). Not only does this provide a rationalisation and veneer for the inequalities that exist, but it also casts those who seek to highlight these inequities as in some way 'irrational' or attempting to deny individual service users 'choice'.

Conclusion

In this chapter, the notions of technical, consumerist and political approaches to 'quality' have been examined. These ideal-types do serve to highlight the different mechanisms that can define and are considered to improve quality:

- 'Technical' model – underpinned by an evidence-based, procedural and rule-governed mechanism (rationality).
- 'Consumerist' model – underpinned by 'economic' mechanisms and another form of economic rationality.
- 'Political' model – underpinned by political forces.

We argued that improvements in social welfare have increasingly come to be seen to be secured by a hybrid of a technical and consumerist model. A desire for choice can appear to be self-evident since, surely, increased choice is a better proposition than less choice, or no choice at all. To argue against measures to deliver more choice appears to be suggesting that individuals should have less choice. In this way, 'choice' is used as a warmly persuasive term, casting a soft glow across measures or practices that extend the market into social welfare. One of the appeals of this model is that it rings true with people's everyday experiences. In this respect a consumerist model is one that appears to be a common-sense, if not natural, solution to the oft-cited problems facing the management and delivery of social welfare. What this chapter attempts to do is show that the consumerist model represents just one of a number of models for improving the quality of social welfare.

We suggest that, contrary to the claims made by proponents of these perspectives, rather than putting the consumer at the centre, both the recipients and providers of welfare are ill served by these approaches. Choice is limited to that expressed by the consumer – but also by what is made available – hence choice becomes the 'new' monolith of social welfare, but is limited, as all consumers know, by what is stocked in the shop!

We end this chapter and section with the fulcrum point of much of what follows: social welfare is shaped and constrained by political choices. We suggest that an important tool for analysis is to understand the 'to and fro' of the management of social welfare as a struggle for control, and that struggle includes contests over the meaning of the terms and labels used to describe and define 'quality', 'service users' and the means by which to improve services and the allocation of resources (Pollitt, 1993: 162). A lack of agreement about definitions and concepts is driven by struggles for 'turf', where different groups are seeking to gain an authoritative and definitive position on issues of quality. Control over what counts as quality can lead to control over what happens in services as a whole. The tensions between these groups can be seen to be influencing the development of policy and practice in social welfare. The value in recognising the political nature of the choices being made is that it makes explicit that a choice has been made. For a choice to be made, alternatives need to be available from which to make this choice. So is there an alternative to the current trend in the management and delivery of social welfare services? The following chapters will explore other important factors and develop our position that provides the answer: yes, there is.

REFLECTIVE EXERCISE

This one is slightly different to the earlier exercises, but still draws directly upon the material in this chapter.

- ➔ If you, a friend or relative feel as if you have been treated badly (do not make something up) you should make a complaint. First find out what your rights are, confirm that you have a case to be considered and forms of representation are available to you. It is at this point that you may want to consider the different mechanisms and forms of redress across different institutions. Conversely, when you think you have been particularly well treated, give some thought as to why this may have been and how you would provide this feedback.
- ➔ During the course of this, think about the different models of quality in the chapter and how they may apply. Even if you are not in this position, as a welfare professional (current or future) you may well be at the other end of a complaint. Consider how the models of quality are used from this perspective.

Part Two
Working in society

CHAPTER 4

The mixed economy of welfare and political priorities

In this chapter we show how the delivery of services is in essence something that comes out of political priorities. In this respect we move from understanding how policy impacts upon the personal relationships that characterise much social welfare work to enabling social welfare professionals to contextualise these practices in a more overt policy context. To this end we examine what is described as the 'mixed economy of welfare', where the logic and mechanisms that underpin the institutions that constitute a mixed economy, 'civil society', the market (or what we prefer to describe as the 'for-profit sector') and the 'state', are examined. How policymakers should guide, manage and oversee the provision of social welfare is a question that lies at the heart of contemporary debates about government and public administration.

Case study: David Cameron and the 'big society'

'Because we believe that a strong society will solve our problems more effectively than big government.... Our alternative to big government is the big society. But we understand that the big society is not just going to spring to life on its own: we need strong and concerted government action to make it happen. We need to use the state to remake society. The first step is to redistribute power and control from the central state and its agencies to individuals and local communities. That way, we can create the opportunity for people to take responsibility. This is absolutely in line with the spirit of ... the post-bureaucratic age.... Our plans for decentralisation are based on a simple human insight: if you give people more responsibility, they behave more responsibly.' (Rt Hon David Cameron MP, Speech on the 'big society', Hugo Young memorial lecture, 10 November 2009)

Questions regarding the governance and organisation of social welfare are linked to wider conceptions of society and the relationship between the state, institutions and individuals. Therefore, rather than particular strategies being seen as inevitable or 'technical' responses to a set of circumstances, they are better seen as reflecting particular political choices. As each of these political choices reflects and constructs a particular set of relationships and underlying mechanisms, those involved in the field of welfare should be able to engage critically with such policies and competing policy formulations. This is why we argue that an essential skill that social welfare professionals should develop is that of understanding aspects of governance and political priorities through an examination of the state in social welfare. Through nurturing these skills, those engaged in social welfare will be in a stronger position when it comes to engaging in debates and changes in the governance and organisation of social welfare.

The mixed economy of welfare

As noted earlier the provision of welfare can be analysed through what is known as the mixed economy of welfare (for example, Esping Andersen, 1990; Mayo, 1994). Powell (2007) offers an expanded account of the mixed economy of welfare. However, for the purposes of this chapter the focus is on exploring the constituent parts of the 'mixed economy', namely: civil society; for-profit organisations; and the state – central and local government.

Civil society: family, volunteers and 'not-for-profit' organisations – complex interdependency

For the purposes of this chapter, and for analytical purposes, the term civil society is used to describe and include the community, the informal sector, non-statutory sector, third sector, voluntary sector and the 'family', but exclude the market. While distinctions can be drawn between these components they all share, in theory at least, an underlying mechanism of reciprocity. Throughout history and across a number of different societies, it can be argued that what can be described as civil society, rather than the state or the market, has been the main source of provision for social welfare. And yet, within the study and practice of social policy, the role of civil society in the provision of welfare continues to be relatively neglected. This does not reflect the value and importance of informal care. Buckner and Yeandle (2007) estimated that the value of the support provided by carers in the UK was £87bn a year (i.e. 'carers' saved the country around £15,260 a year each) while NHS spending in 2007 was £82bn. Hirst (2001) argues that the proportion of the population providing informal care has increased, while demographic trends suggest that the demand for future care will be greater than the number of people who are able to provide it (Karlsson et al, 2006; Pickard, 2008a, 2008b, 2008c). Informal care is more likely to be provided by a partner or spouse, a parent caring for a child or a child caring for a parent. The significant trend appears to be for the intensification of informal care, with increasingly heavy demands being placed on the carer (Hirst, 2001). It is clear that informal care comes at a cost, particularly to those providing the care. With or without the relevant support, providing informal care can have an impact on the physical and mental health of the carer and a significant impact on both the opportunities and income available to the carer. Many of those providing informal care remain isolated and unsupported, and it is estimated that one in five 'carers' gives up work to provide informal care every year (Buckner and Yeandle, 2007).

The importance of this for civil society is that it is constituted *by* and *through* individual members and sectors that have a variety of distinct characteristics and interrelationships (Thompson et al, 1990). Individuals may belong to multiple communities at any one time, but of particular interest are the specialised functions, activities or interests that individuals may hold within civil society, and the relationship of civil society to the social and political organisations that constitute society as a whole.

A concept that is closely associated with civil society is 'social capital', which describes the pattern and intensity of networks among people and the shared values that arise from those networks. The theory is that the greater the interaction between people, the greater the sense of community spirit. Definitions of social capital vary, but the main aspects include citizenship, 'neighbourliness', social networks and civic participation (Cote and Healy, 2001). Measuring social capital is complex, but a common focus is levels of trust within a neighbourhood, membership of clubs and social groups, and other networks (including the family). Woolcock (2001: 11) notes that those with extensive networks are more likely to be 'housed, healthy, hired and happy' (a typical question bank can be found at: www.ons.gov.uk/about-statistics/user-guidance/sc-guide/the-question-bank/index.html).

Thus, civil society is not as straightforward a concept as can be suggested and we have briefly noted some of its features. We have focused our definition upon relationships and actions, a key concern for the welfare professional. Within an informal setting, Qureshi and Walker (1989) provide a useful starting point when they suggest that reciprocity is central to understanding the caregiving relationship, that is, the implicit or explicit understanding that any care given will be returned (Finch and Mason, 1993). As informal care is normally derived from kinship relationships, friends and neighbours, or people experiencing similar issues, there is no doubt that reciprocity plays its part, but one also needs to consider questions of obligation and duty (Arksey and Glendinning, 2007). That is an extension of the belief that looking after a friend, neighbour or family member is the 'right thing to do' (Williams, 2004). Finally, people may be 'caring' because, for a variety of reasons, they are left with little alternative – 'enforced altruism' (Davis and Ellis, 1995).

Civil society: all things to all people?

What is interesting about the notion of civil society is that it appears to garner support from a number of different perspectives and for a variety of reasons. For example, it is the potential civil society has for facilitating innovative, non-hierarchical, autonomous and participatory structures that the concept and related terms are embraced by radical critics of authoritarianism, particularly those who stress the importance of grassroots activism and welfare service provision. In a similar vein, advocates of a civil society perspective suggest that communities provide the key to social change. There is a significant radical history of such efforts in British society (Annetts et al, 2009). In a more conservative perspective, at least of the small 'c' variety, Etzioni's (1995, 1998) communitarianism argues that individuals' principal responsibility should be to attend to their children, and vulnerable community members. By engaging in such activities, he suggests that people from different backgrounds will be brought together, work together, build communities and foster mutual respect and tolerance. In this context, civil society provides the networks that improve individuals' lives (Misztal, 2000). It is argued that this is because working at a community level not only enriches and releases people's potential, but offers individuals and groups real opportunities to be equal partners, create new forms of governance and redress imbalances in power. Notably, the formation of the Conservative–Liberal Democrat coalition in May 2010 has as one of its joint projects this notion of 'localism' or, as identified earlier, 'the big society'.

Taylor (2003) highlights a range of criticisms of a civil society perspective. It is argued that, although laudable, the expectations placed on communities to promote social welfare are, at best, misplaced and, at worst, a subtle form of victim-blaming. Explaining the interest in civil society, particularly from policymakers, critics point to the role that civil society initiatives have in propping up capitalism and legitimising cuts in public services. In effect it becomes a mechanism by which the 'excluded' are 'enabled' to manage themselves, leaving the main beneficiaries of 'civil society' the established interests and the professionals, consultants, advisors and practitioners who are now able to make a living out of a burgeoning civil society industry. Social welfare tends to be driven by funding, fashions and government agendas rather than an analysis of what is required (see Shaw, 2004). Extending this argument, it has been suggested that the problem with civil society as a concept and practice is that in reality participation is no more than a cost-cutting and legitimating exercise.

Terms of participation are defined by the powerful so that civil society organisations are co-opted to legitimise existing agendas. In this way, it gives capitalism and market-based policies a human face. Even those efforts that are considered to sidestep this co-optation are considered to be limited as they fail to address the logic of global capitalism, that is, that the problems created by capital cannot be addressed through a patchwork of civil society-based regeneration (Mayo and Craig, 1995).

In what Taylor (2003) describes as a pragmatic position, it is argued that by working with and through civil society, spaces and initiatives can be developed that may be able to foster and sustain resistance and provide opportunities for small footholds of change and power. Within the complex of paradoxes, balancing acts and tensions that is policymaking, it is argued that working with and through civil society equips communities to make the most of those opportunities that do arise. It is argued that this pragmatic approach makes it possible for work to take place within and across civil society over the long term, identifying and enabling innovative ways to move forward and create new political spaces.

For-profit organisations: the market at work

One of the most influential writers on the theory of the free market was the Scottish economist and philosopher Adam Smith (1723–90). In his major work, *An Inquiry into the Nature and Causes of the Wealth of Nations* (1976 [1776]), Smith noted the benefits of the division of labour (specialisation) and examined and outlined the workings of the market mechanism (price system). Smith was highly critical of the economic orthodoxy of his day – that is, mercantilism. This held that the nation's 'wealth' could be measured by the stock of gold and silver available in the national vaults. Subsequently, a rather skewed view of trade was evident: imports were considered damaging to the nation's wealth, while the ability to export goods was considered good, because this brought 'wealth' into the country. A consequence of this was protectionism, restrictions on local craftspeople and the desire of merchants and manufacturers to seek monopolies.

Smith argued that trade should be considered as beneficial to the nation's wealth as manufacturing and agriculture and that a nation's wealth should be measured by the total of its production and commerce, not the quantity of gold and silver in its vaults. Smith argued that through free trade, both sides benefit. The logic was simple, why would people trade, unless both parties, the buyers and the sellers, benefited.

Smith describes the capacity of the market to guide economic activity as acting like an invisible hand allocating resources. Prices would be the main means to do this. Prices would rise when there was a shortage of something and fall when it was plentiful. This is what is described as the price mechanism:

> a system where the economic decisions in the economy are reached through the workings of the market: changes in the relative scarcity of goods and services are reflected in changes in prices and these price changes produce incentives for producers to reallocate available resources towards reducing market shortages and surpluses. (Beardshaw et al, 2001: 8)

For this price mechanism to work, a successful market requires certain conditions to be met. Competition ensures that individual providers bring prices down to their lowest possible levels (making minimal profit) as producers try to outsell each other in order to increase profits. If there is not (enough) competition, a small number of producers (a monopoly) would make more profits. However, these providers would no longer have an incentive to increase the efficiency of producing the required goods or services, whereas in a free and open market, the opportunity to make a profit provides enough of an incentive for new providers to enter and compete in the marketplace. This is termed 'dynamic efficiency'. Producers also need to be sensitive and responsive to the demands of consumers. If consumers do not have the ability to choose which providers they purchase a given good or service from, they are left with no choice and the provider has no incentive to respond to any change in demand – in crude terms, it is 'like it or lump it' (in welfare terms, the one-size-fits-all approach outlined in Chapter 3). However, in a competitive marketplace, where consumers can express a choice, providers now need to convince the consumer that they meet their demands better. The ability of markets to meet consumer preferences is described as 'allocative efficiency'.

The market: a mechanism for welfare?

Exponents of the free market argue that all goods and services, including those to promote social welfare, should be delivered using the market mechanism, as opposed to state intervention, as only the market is able to respond to the changing demands of the public and thereby organise production and distribution to suit their needs. If this is so, it is worth asking why the state needs to get involved in social welfare at all. Within market theory, there are limits to the applicability of markets. Glennerster (2009) notes that there are situations where markets may not deliver on their promise of efficiency; these include: situations characterised by information failure, where there may be either a lack of knowledge or uncertainty as to the future behaviour of people and therefore the provision of goods; situations where people do not behave rationally, in the sense of maximising their satisfaction; and, most notably, situations concerning the question of private and public goods.

Public goods are typically described as possessing two distinct qualities. The first is that once the goods are provided, it is not possible to exclude people from using them even if they have not paid (people rather disparagingly described as 'free-riders'), or that it is not possible or practical to charge a consumer for the use of the good (that the good is 'non-excludable'). The second quality of public goods is that the consumption of the goods by one person does not diminish the amount available for the next person (that they are 'non-rival' goods). A widely cited example of a public good is clean air – recognised as important for social welfare since the introduction of legislation in the 1950s as it provides a considerable step forward in increasing the quality of life and life expectancy. If clean air is provided, then it is not possible to exclude people from benefiting from these goods. At the same time, one person's consumption of this good does not diminish the amount available for the next person, so it is a public good in that it is non-rival and non-excludable. Consequently, it is argued that public goods are goods that would not, and therefore should not, be provided in a free-market system, as providers would not be able to adequately charge for them. In this respect, public goods are used as an example of market failure and an argument for collective intervention in the economy. Debates in social welfare can rest on the degree to which a particular good can be defined as private or public. A good example of this is education and health. Although individuals benefit from the provision of these 'goods', it is also true that society as a whole can benefit from an educated and healthy population. However, one should not overstate the evidence-based nature of such debates. It is not as if goods are categorised and 'for-profit' or 'not-for-profit' services developed after the fact. Rather, in practice, the definition of goods and services tend to be as a result of political choices. Returning to the example of health and education, this can be seen in what is described as the 'marketisation' of these services (see Chapter 5).

What is the state?

The state is a term normally used to describe the sum total of the institutions, agencies and procedures related to government. We argue that the defining mechanism of the state, particularly when compared to civil society and the for-profit sector, is the role of power and politics (see Chapter 3). State institutions can be located at different levels, for example, national (central) and local government. Considered to extend and endure beyond any particular 'government', the state can be defined in terms of its institutions and/or the functions these institutions perform (Ham and Hill, 1984). In a British context distinctions can be drawn between the executive, legislative and judicial institutions and functions. However, rather than focus on the 'nuts and bolts' of these institutions (for an extensive discussion of local government in the UK, see Wilson and Game, 2006; and for resources on what parliament does and its role in UK politics, see http://www.parliament.uk/about/how.cfm), attention is paid to examining different theories regarding the role the state does and should play in society and related assumptions about the nature and workings of society as a whole. We will explore briefly two contrasting theories of the state, pluralist and Marxist, and the implications these different theories have for the role the state can and should play in the provision of social welfare.

Pluralism

The state is frequently portrayed as a neutral body that seeks to represent a combination of classes and interests in pursuit of the common good or national interest. The essential characteristics of such a pluralist theory emanate from the notion that society contains a number of diverse groups, for example, businesses, professional bodies, trade unions, social movements, community groups, political associations and religious groups, and that, therefore, power is widely shared, derived from and through many different sources. Central to a pluralist perspective is that no one group is or should be dominant, as with a variety of sources of power, no one group can hold a monopoly over power (Parsons, 1959, 1966; Dahl, 1961). It is for this reason that the state is considered to be an essential element in the provision of social policy, for it is argued that only the state has the capacity and legitimacy to act on behalf of all citizens (Alcock, 2008). This is summed up in the motto of the USA '*e pluribus unum*' ('One from many'). This is based on the assumption that the different parties will share, or at least accept, the procedures and principles of a political framework that will need to involve bargaining and compromise to ensure that all groups are given the opportunity to influence the make-up and running of the major institutions and government policy. Democracy is thought to provide the necessary framework and process for the different interests to compete over the nature and direction of society.

Within this pluralist conception of the state and society, individuals with common interests are encouraged to exert influence on decision-makers by collective action. The political process is constituted through a variety of groups of different sizes and an individual may be a member of a number of different groups. Each group may have very different views on a particular issue, but there is not one all-powerful group agreeing or making decisions on all the issues, in the absence of others challenging this authority. Any individuals who do not believe their interests are being represented are encouraged to identify others who have a similar perspective and begin to organise and form their own group. The state represents institutionalised power and authority and, in pluralist theory, is the referee or mediator between these different groups, in effect representing all and no particular interests. Pluralists suggest that the functions and power of the state should be separated out into different branches. Not only is this considered to reflect the pluralist nature of society and reduce the potential of the state to establish a monopoly of power, but it also gives individuals/groups different points of access to the policy process.

The role of the state in reality is contested within pluralist theory. There are those who believe that although interests are diverse, it is possible for the state to promote harmony, develop consensus and coordinate the major institutions. By contrast, the interests in society may be deemed so diverse and incommensurable that the state needs to assert authority in order to police the competing groups. In this respect the primary role of the state is to maintain the security of society through the establishment and preservation of law and order. In essence, these two positions represent a tension between attempts to provide central coordination, on the one hand, while ensuring that there is a relatively equal distribution of social powers, on the other. They also reflect a tension between the view that the state is and should be constituted through and by the people and the view that the state has to be autonomous and in some way stand above and away from the society it seeks to represent.

Pluralist theory is criticised for believing that the state can remain disinterested and independent. While this may be a laudable aim, it does not reflect the nature of society or how the state actually works under capitalism (Hirst, 2001).

Marxist theories of the state

There are a number of different interpretations of Marxist theory as a whole and this is also true with regard to Marxist theories of the state. However, they all have their origins in, or are at least oriented towards, arguments that society needs to be understood in relation to the mode of production, that is, that the dynamics of society originate in its economic activity, which is essentially the production of material life – food, clothing, shelter and so on – and culture arises out of this process of economic activity. A Marxist theory of the state argues that power flows from these economic and social relations, and, therefore, that political power is not centred in the state, but in the nature of class relations, that is, who owns and controls the means of production (Gough, 1979).

Economic dominance is translated into power in all other societal realms, especially the state. In sharp contrast to the pluralist perspective, the state is not considered independent or disinterested, but rather plays an important role in maintaining and reproducing the capitalist system and its class relations by helping to establish and sustain the conditions necessary for capital to continue to accumulate capital (Marx, 2005). The actual nature of these conditions may change according to the needs of capital at any one time, but generally they are considered to include: protecting the system of property relations; propagating dominant values in schools, the media and other social institutions; and fostering a dominant ideology to assist in the reproduction of a suitable workforce and legitimate existing social relations. Althusser (1971), in his structural Marxism, argued that the state is a kind of governmental formation that arises with capitalism and is formed to protect its interests. He identified two major mechanisms for ensuring that people within a state behave according to the rules. The first is what is described as the repressive state apparatus (e.g. the police, armed forces and criminal justice system); and the second is the ideological state apparatus (e.g. schools, religions, the family and legal systems). The ideological institutions generate ideas and values that we as individuals and groups internalise. Gramsci (2003) developed the concept of cultural ideological hegemony, where the ideological hegemony of the ruling class operates through the state itself. It is argued that the ruling class controls and shapes the ideas and, hence, consciousness of the masses, the dominant class uses its political, moral and intellectual leadership to establish its view of the world as all-inclusive and universal, and to shape the interests and needs of subordinate groups. In an English context, Hall (1987) broke with conventional Marxist thinking and suggested that the relationship is not a straightforward 'them and us' dichotomy, but a more subtle form of hegemony, which will change over time, since we do not all necessarily share 'dominant' ideological views, particularly in the private, family sphere.

The dominance of capital is not to suggest a conspiracy theory where a small number of individuals seize control of society and the state. Rather, following Poulantzas (1973), it is the logic of capital accumulation, where attempts to achieve the conditions that best serve capital's interests, which are also taken to be in everybody's interest, inform the practices and policies of the state, even in the absence of direct control of the state. Put more simply, this refers to the commonly held view that the viability of the state is dependent on a healthy economy. Marxist theorists define this as the accumulation of capital involving the extraction of surplus and therefore requiring the reproduction of capitalist relations – in short, the exploitation of groups of people to create profit. State leaders, including those who seek to employ policies that appear to be against the interest of capital, believe that for the state to play its 'independent role' it needs to act in accordance with the interests of 'big business'. This also accounts for the fact that capitalists seek to exert influence on political officials and institutions, thereby maintaining the appearance of state impartiality. The challenge for the state is that its institutions and practices must somehow maintain the appearance of class neutrality while at the same time effectively excluding anti-capitalist alternatives. This can help explain why '[s]tate welfare was and remains a deeply contradictory experience: providing for essential needs, but in ways which are often felt to be alien and oppressive and over which they have little say or impact' (Jones and Novak, 1993: 50–1).

The nature of care

These ideas will be discussed in more detail in Chapter 7, which focuses upon understanding the economy, a crucial factor in the daily working lives and practice of many welfare professionals. For the moment, though, we focus on the implications of the dynamics underpinning the institutions of civil society, the for-profit sector and the state for accountability and change.

Case study

'After being diagnosed with a long-term illness, my mother received care at home and in hospital. On the one hand, I was grateful and appreciated the fact that my mother was able to receive treatment and that a 'care plan' had been put in place. My family and I could not do this on our own, so to have this type of support was invaluable. However, when I visited my mother, I was distraught at how distressed she appeared, the nature of the conditions and the way that she was treated by some members of staff. There was nothing that could really be called care in evidence. With some notable exceptions, the doctors, nurses and social workers just did not seem to get what the problem was. The only people who seemed to be prepared to listen and act were the health care assistants and I will always be grateful to the help they provided to my mother and family. I was left angry, frustrated and powerless to do anything. I felt ashamed.' (Carer in the West Midlands, 2010)

Thinking about this case in relation to the chapter as a whole we can ask whether these feelings are an inherent part of the situations that social welfare services are designed to address, that is, does this experience just reflect those times in our lives when we need to arrange care for ourselves, friends and relatives? Are these feelings nothing more than internal frustration and anxieties being transferred on to others? Are expectations too high? Or is it that there is something that can and should be done in the way that social welfare is organised and delivered so that, in the words of Jones and Novak, the services we all receive are not so alien and oppressive? Thus, through a short, and unfortunately not uncommon, experience we can utilise theories about the state, civil society and how the mixed economy of welfare is organised to analyse the nature of the experience.

In the rhetoric, and at times reality, of social welfare, the response appears to be that if the provision of state welfare is alien and oppressive, then the solution is for the state to minimise its involvement in the provision of these essential needs. It is precisely this kind of criticism that has been levelled at the 'post-war welfare state', and the early 21st-century response is that the for-profit sector and civil society are considered to provide the solution to these alleged deficiencies. Extending the logic of consumerism (see Chapter 3), in the 'for-profit' sector the choices and line of accountability are 'exit' and 'voice'. That is, either leave and take your 'custom' elsewhere, or make a complaint. The provider's motive for being responsive is to maintain a profit. In civil society the line of accountability is more blurred. Essentially you are reliant on 'agencies' and individuals doing the 'right thing', because of the soft form of reciprocation and duty that underpins civil society. There is the option of voice when attempting to highlight that the 'right thing' is not being done, but there is no formal sanction or easy exit, particularly with reference to area-based civil society agencies. With the state the formal line of accountability is through the political or, more specifically, electoral process, that is, contact is made with either your electoral representatives, or those elected members charged with managing social welfare services (at a national or local level). At this point none of these options appear in themselves to provide the remedy. Yet, we suggest that there is nothing inherent in the provision of a state service that makes it 'alien and oppressive', nor is there any guarantee that other social welfare configurations will be less so, since Jones and Novak are more accurately describing a process or organisation of services. If the problem with bureaucracies lies in their lack of responsiveness or accountability, does the 'for-profit' sector and the promise of choice really give control over the provision of social welfare? This is not an argument for the status quo. Rather, what the state perspective offers (even if this has been lost in recent years and requires a reconfiguration) is an explicit politicisation of welfare – a politicisation that tends to be denied by the institutions of civil society and the for-profit sector.

Conclusion

The chapter has explored the mixed economy of welfare focusing upon the relationship between the for-profit sector, civil society and the state. We have taken time to present some theoretical positions and connect these in the final analysis to the role of the state and, thereby, to the political choices that are made. The importance of these concepts for social welfare professionals is that they remind us that an examination of social welfare goes beyond a focus on 'the welfare state' and it is necessary to examine other elements: private, voluntary and informal alongside the occupational and fiscal, all of which form part of the contemporary 'welfare state' (Titmuss, 1970b) or, following Clarke (1993b), the current 'welfare settlement'. This type of analysis allows us to consider claims of rolling back the state. As the general election campaign of 2010 and the subsequent elevation of the 'big society' reminds us, the nature of the balance within the mixed economy of welfare can, and is likely to, change. We have argued that although there are arguments for supporting a far more enhanced role for civil society in the provision of social welfare, the 'big society' is essentially part of a strategy to undermine collective social welfare service provision and usher in a far more prominent role for the 'for-profit' sector in social welfare. In practice there is an increasing blurring of the edges between the institutions of the state, civil society and the for-profit sector. Any partnerships become difficult in a context where there are competing and contradictory interests. Tellingly, even institutions that are nominally state institutions are expected to behave as if they are 'for-profit' agencies (a theme developed in Chapter 5).

For these reasons, questions need to be raised as to the extent to which the 'big society' and civil society are being used as apologias for the encroachment of the for-profit sector in social welfare (Meiksins Wood, 1990; Lavalette and Ferguson, 2007). As such, questions of non-intervention by the state should also be subject to analysis, even if this is restricted to the question of who benefits (Bryson, 1992: 5). If those in social welfare are able to develop an awareness of the constraints on practice, then it is possible not only to change the way we think about things, but also to articulate the changes that can be made in the short term, which may then lead to further changes in relationships and the flow of resources (Healey, 2006). Future debates and policy shifts will focus on aspects of the 'public good' and the role of the state and civil society in promoting this. By developing a knowledge and critique of the mechanisms that the different institutions that constitute the mixed economy of welfare operate by, those engaged in social welfare will be able to consider the implications of shifts across the mixed economy of welfare. The ability to undertake such an analysis is important because what will become even clearer is that these debates are not confined to theoretical discussions, but are constantly mediated through political priorities.

REFLECTIVE EXERCISES

➔ Think about the nature of civil society, profit-making organisations and the state. Drawing on what you have read here and your own experience, either as an (aspiring) welfare professional or someone who is receiving or has received services, what do you think are the advantages and disadvantages of the different organisations as providers of care and welfare?

CHAPTER 5

Social inequalities and the welfare professional

In this chapter, we focus on the question of social inequalities. In much social welfare work, professionals are engaged with people who experience poverty, exclusion and inequality. Here we discuss 'inequality' as distinct from, but related to, poverty and explore in more detail the relationship between inequality and political choices (as introduced in the previous chapter) and their significance for the welfare professional. It is argued that there has been an enduring and increasing tension in much social welfare work, that is, that although a great deal of laudable work may be undertaken addressing the symptoms of inequality, both the policy and practice of social welfare are moving away from attempts to address the structural causes of poverty and exclusion. At best, aspects of social welfare work can be seen as well-intentioned, but misplaced. At worst, it can be argued that large swathes of social welfare work are complicit in securing a social order that goes against the interests of those social welfare claims to serve. It is argued that those engaged in social welfare need to become aware and critical of such an ordering, before moving on to articulate and develop policies and practice that seek to address social inequalities.

Understanding social inequality

There are growing calls for the gap between rich and poor to be seen as a social problem in its own right, as distinct from poverty (Orton and Rowlingson, 2007a). A wide variety of economic and social trends have been associated with rising income inequalities (Wilkinson and Pickett, 2009). The specific degree of inequality can vary according to the measure of wealth being used. Reflecting a consistent and enduring pattern, however, data from 2006–08 on wealth, which include pension wealth, showed that while the wealthiest 20% of households had 62% of total wealth, the least wealthy half of households in Britain possessed only 9% of total wealth (ONS, 2009). One way of measuring inequality is to use a Gini coefficient. A Gini coefficient of 0 corresponds to perfect income equality and a Gini coefficient of 100 corresponds to perfect income inequality. In the UK, the Gini coefficient of net disposable household income rose from 27 in the late 1970s to 34 in the late 1990s. The increase in top-earner incomes has also had a major impact on the distribution of income – with the top 10% in the UK having nearly seven times the disposable income of the bottom 10%, up from only three times in the mid-1970s.

Wilkinson and Pickett (2009) illustrate that inequalities are pivotal in determining not only the health and mortality of any society, but also the prevalence of a host of other social problems, including mental illness, obesity and homicides. They demonstrate that a wide range of 'social problems' are not only more common at the bottom of the social ladder, but, significantly, are more common in more unequal societies. In other words, it is less the overall income of a society, and more how that income is distributed, above all other factors, that provides us with a measure against which we can assess the overall welfare of any given society. The importance of social inequality for welfare professionals, who routinely deal with such 'social problems', becomes clear.

'What's the problem?'

A number of competing claims as to the nature, extent and underlying causes of 'social problems' are available. An extension of this position is that a 'social evil' cannot be viewed independently of the efforts of individuals, groups and institutions to make claims as to what phenomena prove the greatest threat to people's welfare. As such, any attempt to identify what constitutes the 'common good' is in dispute, as is any attempt to establish the means by which 'social problems' are to be remedied. Such a pluralist perspective may be considered healthy; however, what is also implicit in such a 'subjectivist' outlook (Best, 2008) is what Bacchi (1999) describes as a 'What's the problem?' approach to policy analysis. Rather than start from the assumption that policymaking reflects a 'rational' response to pre-existing givens, attention is paid to how a 'problem' is fabricated and how a particular response to a 'problem' is legitimated. A particular definition will carry with it a number of assumptions, not just about the topic concerned, but also about the wider workings of society and questions of 'agency'. The importance of definitions, and why so much effort can go into trying to establish a particular definition, becomes clearer when one considers that they can not only determine the scope of the response, but also 'betray' a political and/or ideological element. Thus, what is *considered* a problem is to a large extent a political act. So, in earlier chapters we saw how the Victorians in particular focused upon the lack of moral character as a 'problem' and then sought to address it through voluntary means. Box (1983) and Cook (1989, 2006) have shown how the economic 'crimes' of the poorer socio-economic groups, such as benefit fraud, are foregrounded and constituted as 'problems', while those of the rich, for example, the illegal non-payment of income tax or the breaking of minimum wage legislation, are seen, by authorities at least, as less problematic, and are therefore under-resourced and less well policed. Initially, the essential skill for the welfare professional lies not in 'deciding' what the problem is, but rather in recognising how the way a problem is defined carries assumptions and determines the scope of the response.

Returning to the question of social inequalities, drawing heavily on the work of Byrne (2005) we outline three different positions for explaining inequalities: the behaviour of individuals (possessive individualism); the failings of the institutions (system failure); and the wider operation and structures of society (exploitation). The welfare professional, we argue, cannot remain neutral in such debates.

Possessive individualist explanations

Do people 'fall' to the bottom as a result of their lazy or feckless behaviour and others rise to the top because of their hard work and moral character? Can inequalities be explained through differences in attitudes, values, behaviour or genetics? Are parents/guardians, peer groups and communities to be blamed for the transmission of negative cultures and behaviour? As Byrne (2005) notes, a possessive individualist perspective answers 'Yes' to some if not all of these questions and argues that the condition of those in poverty derives in large part from their stubborn refusal of 'poor work'. Such individualist positions can be seen as emanating from a classical liberal tradition. Byrne (2005) draws a distinction between a utilitarian position, which argues for unfettered markets on the basis of optimising efficiency and the greater good (Friedman, 1962), and what can be described as philosophical or 'ethical' individualism, which asserts the absolute primacy of negative liberty (Nozick, 1974). What both these positions share, though, is a commitment to non-intervention in the affairs of individuals (Crouch and Marquand, 1989). As the name suggests, individualism is 'inherently anti-collectivist' and draws on a particular strand of liberal thinking where society is described 'as networks of voluntary exchanges between autonomous individuals with their own interests and situations' (Silver, 1994: 542). Historically, individualism carries with it a radical connotation, as it emerged as a challenge to conventional feudal social ties and, as Judt (2010) argues from a collectivist perspective, was an unfortunate feature of some 1960s radicalism. In that regard the ideas of individualism are an important part of modernity, and are part of early 21st-century social and cultural hegemony.

Individualist perspectives argue that inequalities can be explained in terms of the hard work and endeavour of the rich and the recalcitrance and idleness of the poor. Notably, from a possessive individualist perspective, inequalities not only reflect legitimate differences, but are also necessary to provide the motivations necessary for a 'market' society, that is, that hard work will lead to rewards and laziness should lead to failure. In other words, the inequalities that exist are in part a reflection of a *meritocratic society*, which places emphasis on the choices made by individuals. For instance, unemployment is seen as a voluntary choice, since it is argued that jobs are available, but that those who are unemployed are unwilling to accept lower wages, less attractive working conditions or longer journeys to work, or transfer to other occupations, industries and locations in order to find a way back into work. Insufficient flexibility results in unemployment 'by choice' – or unemployment is a result of government policies that provide incentives to workers to remain unemployed (an example of the perverse incentives discussed in Chapter 3; see also MacKay, 1998: 50–1). This perspective also finds expression in notions of a 'culture of poverty', 'problem families', 'cycles of deprivation' or the 'underclass', when the poor's own attitudes and values are identified as the source of their poverty (see Welshman, 2006).

Consequently, individualist perspectives may argue that not only is society under no obligation to address the concerns of those in poverty, but that any intervention undermines society's system of incentives and sanctions and creates a culture of dependency. However, recognising the political, social and economic risks associated with inequalities, a possessive individualist position accepts that there is a requirement for social welfare work, but argues that this should be done through civil society, that is, the market, community and voluntary and family associations. One of the implications of a possessive individualist perspective is that unemployment and its consequences for the community, including inequalities, are depoliticised. Questions as to what should cause changes in the labour market and wider social conditions are not even asked, never mind answered.

System failure

A system failure perspective, also described as a non-transformational or reformist collectivism, is one that recognises the value of collective action, the importance of social order and the rights and obligations all those who are members of the collective owe to the social order. Exponents of this reformist position argue that capitalism, despites its failings and excesses, particularly with respect to the creation of inequalities, is essentially a corrigible system (Byrne, 2005), that is, that capitalism can deliver in terms of collective social goals, but that the 'market's' failures must be addressed through the development and actions of social and political institutions. In this respect, a 'reformist' position recognises, and seeks to make explicit, the interdependence of society, the state and the economy. State power is to be used both in order to regulate the economic system so that it does not challenge social goals, and, in the context of this chapter, to reduce inequalities. An extension of this is that any inequalities to be found can be explained in terms of the failure of the state to act sufficiently and/or through the discriminatory actions of institutions, such as the active exclusion or inability of certain groups to access the resources and services on offer. A classic policy example of this is the belief that the post-war welfare state had effectively eliminated poverty and that those who remained 'poor' were simply unable to take advantage of what was on offer (Galbraith, 1983). The rediscovery of poverty in the 1960s in the UK formed part of the background to the Seebohm report (Seebohm, 1968), which outlined the fifth social service (after health, education, public housing and social security, as outlined in the Beveridge report [1942], which informed the development of the post-war welfare state in 1948). The report provided the basis for a national expanded social work service, which was to move from the 'specialist' to the 'generic' social worker who would be 'capable of grasping the variety of human experiences, assessing individual and family needs and offering services to meet them' (Langan, 1992: 50). Crucially, the report set social workers a brief to 'enable the greatest possible number of individuals to act reciprocally, giving and receiving a service for the well-being of the whole community' (Seebohm, 1968: para 2). Utilising the material from earlier chapters we can see how this was a 1960s' attempt to help create and sustain a new form of welfare settlement and most importantly to militate against 'system failure'.

In general, system failure perspectives recognise that, if left unfettered, capitalism can lead to the creation of inequalities, but that these can be addressed and ameliorated through the collection, regulation and management of macroeconomic policies and the provision of services and resources within a mixed economy of welfare. This perspective has much in common with what has been described as a social administration perspective. Social administration is the science of reformism, of administrative interventionism and piecemeal social engineering, underpinned by values of compassion and social justice as well as efficiency. Social administration traditionally has almost exclusively focused on government policies and the operations of statutory services in particular. Efforts are directed towards measuring the dimensions of a problem, evaluating past policies and proposing recommendations for future action (Mishra, 1977). In this regard the Seebohm report (Seebohm, 1968) represents a distinctly reformist agenda, in that the advancement of welfare, rather than the accumulation and refinement of a body of tested knowledge, is the central concern. Given this concern with amelioration – with the improvement of conditions – social administration is likely to concentrate on the practical problems of social policy. It is argued that a great deal of social welfare work, particularly after the Second World War, can be located within this perspective. Emphasis is placed on developing social cohesion and a sense of reciprocal fraternity, if not solidarity, within which a level of inequality is considered permissible.

There are also differences within a system failure perspective both as to the nature of the system and its failings. For example, more recently efforts have focused on reining in the bottom level of society rather than curtailing any excesses at the top. This has taken the form of directing efforts towards securing integration into society by ensuring access to opportunities for paid work (Levitas, 1996; 1998; Byrne, 2005). This perspective can differ in the degree to which this integration is to be achieved by ensuring the right to work, or a duty to work. At the same time, the social and political institutions that were intended to tackle poverty and inequalities (that is, the post-war welfare state) are not only being criticised for their inability to undertake such a task, but are also being cited as the cause of social problems.

It can be argued that for those who seek to reduce inequalities, there is a great deal that a 'system failure' perspective has to offer and, in historical terms at least, has achieved. However, this depends on how the case of social inequalities is defined in the first instance and the degree that the capitalist system can be fettered. For example, a further line of criticism of the system failure perspective argues that some of the measures that are intended to alleviate or reduce inequalities can actually have the effect of extending not only the experience of inequalities, but also the conditions for their continuation. In this respect, inequality, and what has come to be described by some as 'exclusion', needs to be understood as a consequence of exploitation, rather than domination, that is, that inequalities are the result of particular sets of economic relations. It is to this explanation that we now turn.

Exploitative explanations

An exploitative explanation of inequality is based on the idea that the advance of capitalism is characterised by the creation of wealth at one end of the economic spectrum and a downward pressure on incomes at the other. The creation of relative poverty at one pole of society is seen not just as an inherent by-product of capitalism, but as a necessary condition for the continued accumulation of capital. It is argued that a 'surplus' or what has been described as a 'reserve army' of labour is necessary for the disciplining of the population as a whole during periods of relative prosperity and the restructuring of production during crises (Marx, 2005). The discipline comes from the alleged threat the surplus population poses to 'hard-working families'. This can be symbolic, as witnessed in the labels that become attached to the unemployed (vagrants, paupers, indigents, the feckless or the underclass – all terms that have been used throughout history), but also material, as in the way a 'surplus' can weaken the bargaining position of those in work.

For example, in a recession, people lose their jobs. This not only reduces the incomes of those people out of work, but leads to calls for those still in work not only to forgo any future pay increases, but also to consider a freezing of, if not reduction in, their pay and conditions in an attempt to secure their work. In this way, the early stages of economic crises permit capital to exert a downward pressure on incomes and enable a wider restructuring of 'production' (new technologies, practices and forms of organisation and management) in what is considered to be a necessary condition for 'economic growth' (O'Connor, 1981; Byrne, 2005). The call for public sector pay restraint in 2009 as a response to the financial crisis and the policy of the Conservative–Liberal Democrat coalition in 2010 of a public sector pay freeze are all too familiar examples of this for welfare professionals.

The added bonus for those in a dominant position is that the behaviour of the 'created surplus' becomes a useful way of explaining the social problems associated with increasing inequalities – hence a focus upon the behaviour of the so-called 'underclass' in tabloid newspapers and subsequent legislation to regulate this part of the population. Even as the economy expands, a surplus, which becomes increasingly marginal, is necessary in order to maintain discipline and continue to exert a downward pressure on the cost of labour. From this perspective, if inequalities and a 'surplus' population were not an inherent part of capitalism, it would be necessary to create them. In this respect an alleged 'surplus population' is to be understood as a population created by and essential to society, but then rejected (Auyero, 1997). Thus, increasing inequalities do not represent a broken society with a marginalised poor distinct from an integrated 'mainstream'. Rather, the wealth at one pole is clearly dependent on the creation of the poor at the other. As such, poverty, exclusion and inequalities are essential to contemporary forms of exploitation (Byrne, 2005). In this respect, it should be noted that attempts to get tough on the recipients of welfare are only the first and most visible attempts to exert a downward pressure on the majority of people's wages.

Based on this analysis, it is argued that any efforts to reduce inequalities within capital relations will be limited. As inequalities are seen to stem from a particular set of economic and social relations, it follows that attempts to reduce inequalities require attempts to transform the social and economic conditions of society. Furthermore, as the origins of exploitation are 'economic' and cast along class lines, it follows that attempts to overcome this exploitation need to follow this economic fault line and be expressed as a rejection of the ascription of human beings as resources to be exploited and to end the separation of producers from the product and the meaning and control of their labour.

A historical case study

So far in this chapter we have examined three different perspectives for explaining and responding to questions of social inequalities. At this point we seek to examine how these perspectives have informed and been drawn upon in social welfare policies. An examination of the full development of the welfare system in England is not possible in a text of this nature, yet a brief study of the Poor Law Report and the 1834 Poor Law Amendment Act (New Poor Laws) is possible and relevant to a discussion of social inequalities in contemporary social welfare for three reasons. First, the establishment of the New Poor Laws represents a significant milestone in the history of British social policy. Its legacy is not just to be found in that, in large part, its operations remained in place until the foundation of the 'welfare state' in 1948, but also that the logic, principles and practices developed in the Poor Law Report continue to ebb and flow in social welfare. Second, it illustrates how the definition of a problem, largely reflecting a particular perspective, comes to shape subsequent policies and practices. Third, the New Poor Laws provide an instructive example of how the interplay between economic, political and ideological mechanisms results in policies and practices that, although purportedly operating in the national interest, serve some at the expense of others. In this respect, the form, language and content may change, but the dynamics informing these policies are still in play and should be part of any attempts to understand development in social welfare.

Case study: The New Poor Laws (1834)

'There are two general enquiries to which each specific enquiry may be made subservient. One is the great question how far the law which throws on the owners of property the duty of providing the subsistence and superintending the conduct of the poor, has really effected its object; how far the proprietors of land and capital appear to have the power and the will to create, or increase, or render secure the prosperity and morality

> of those who live by the wages of labour.' (Instructions from the Central Board of Poor Law Commissioners to Assistant Commissioners, 1837: 425, cited in Higgins, 1981: 35)

In 1832, in the context of significant economic, political and social changes, a Royal Commission, chaired by a Tory Bishop of London, Charles Blomfeld, was established to investigate the existing provision of poor relief. The Royal Commission included eight other commissioners and 26 assistant commissioners. The most well-known and arguably most influential members of the commission were Nassau Senior and Edwin Chadwick. Early Poor Laws (1597 and 1601) and successive pieces of legislation had imposed some regulation upon the distribution of poor relief. The final report became known for its criticism of the Old Poor Laws, both in terms of its system of administration and effects on the population. Central to the report were criticisms of the parish allowance schemes, which demoralised and 'pauperised' the labouring class and had an adverse effect on the free market. In essence, the authors of the Poor Law Report believed that the existing system undermined work incentives and encouraged idleness. It was suggested that everything should be done to ensure that the indigent (i.e. the 'deserving') were distinguished from the (able-bodied or 'undeserving') poor. The report suggested that the best way to achieve that aim was to end the provision of outdoor relief and to ensure that relief was only made available to 'eligible' recipients to be established and provided through and by the workhouse. It was suggested that poor relief was to be set below the pay of the lowest-paid workers. Poor relief would be a last resort and the recipients of poor relief were to be in a less eligible position than those in employment. The appeal and simplicity of such a proposal lay in the suggestion that there would be no need of any further (costly) regulations, appeals or procedures.

On the surface, the work of Chadwick and others appears to represent a fledging social administration tradition, where the systematic and impartial collection of evidence was undertaken in order to provide a sound basis for the development of good judgement on policy matters (Baptist and Bricker-Jenkins, 2001). Subsequent analysis has argued that the prime movers of the Poor Law Report (notably Chadwick) had used the available evidence to fit their preconceptions about both the poor and the need for a regulated workforce in the emerging industrial capitalist era (Bryson, 1992). The focus on 'less eligibility' in the rhetoric and practice of the New Poor Laws met the demands of the day. Notably, despite all the 'social problems' created by this 'surplus population', this growing pool of 'free' labour provided a necessary precondition for the development of capitalism. The labour that was required was relatively unskilled and plentiful, thus the main aim was to ensure that new work habits and ethics among the workforce were established and maintained. In this respect, the development of the Poor Laws should not primarily be seen as concerned with the relief of hardship, but rather, as Piven and Cloward (1977) argue with reference to the development of 'social security' more generally, as a form of social control. For example, the subsequent

Poor Law Amendment Act included a workhouse test. Those in receipt of the 'relief' were to be compelled to enter the workhouse. Men and women would live in different quarters and a basic diet would be provided. Claimants were to wear a uniform and undertake arduous and monotonous work, and the voting rights of those who had them would be forfeited. These measures were designed to dissuade low-paid workers from claiming relief as it was hoped that the harshness of the new scheme would deter all but the most desperate from claiming assistance. Indeed, such was the supposed tyranny of the workhouse that it was freely available to all who knocked – safe in the knowledge that few would (Englander, 1998).

Reviewing the New Poor Laws, the focus on 'dependency', the requirement to establish the 'eligibility' of recipients and the suggestion that poor relief should be the last resort and set below the pay of the lowest-paid workers not only reflects what has been described as a possessive individualist perspective, but also can be found in the rhetoric of contemporary welfare reform. And yet, both in contemporary accounts and the New Poor Laws, there are elements that appear to undermine this possessive individualist account, for a second legacy of the New Poor Laws was the proposal for the system to be overseen by government and government officials. In this respect, the New Poor Laws proved to be instrumental in laying the foundations of the modern (welfare) state. The New Poor Laws helped establish and extend the infrastructure and principles through which 'the modern British state's power was itself built and extended' (Novak, 1988: 35). Yet this would appear to be anathema to any self-respecting possessive individualist. It is argued that this represents one of the primary contradictions of the possessive individualist approach: that, on the one hand, it supports a capitalism that both requires and produces significant social changes, while at the same time values and requires the social fabric provided by civil society that is all too easily torn apart by the operation of a dynamic capitalist economy (Roche, 1992). To square this circle, those espousing a possessive individualist position have found it necessary to intervene in social and human affairs. The report also recommended that any number of parishes could become incorporated (combined) in the provision and management of a workhouse and, most significantly, sought to replace the localised administration of poor relief through the appointment of a central board, which would have the power to regulate and enforce the implementation of the Poor Laws. The creation of a central authority and Poor Law Unions proved to be one of the most enduring influences of the Royal Commission. The Poor Laws also led to the expansion of the voluntary forms of 'social work' identified in Chapters 1 and 2, and paradoxically to their ultimate demise as the state gradually took over the functions of these 'welfare providers' – demonstrating the paradox at the heart of the problems of inequality endemic within industrial capitalism and the growing recognition of the limitations of philanthropy, voluntarism and the market to address the needs of the age – a theme developed throughout the 19th century.

Consequently, it is this contradiction that helps explain why those who appear to value the liberty and freedom of individuals find themselves developing and supporting policies that require greater interventions, particularly with respect to efforts to control and regulate large parts of the population. As noted earlier, the establishment of the New Poor Laws were in large part a response to substantial social changes and social unrest around the turn of the 19th century linked to the development of industrial capitalism. It is in this context that one needs to understand the development of the Poor Law Report of 1834 (Thompson, 1963; Harris, 2004) and its successive social welfare policy reincarnations, albeit in different guises, during the 20th and early parts of the 21st centuries.

Alleviating poverty or regulating the poor?

Wilkinson and Pickett (2009: 213) argue that, 'for several decades, progressive politics have been seriously weakened by the loss of any concept of a better society'. Given the evidence of the impact of inequality on a range of health and social measures, such increases in inequality would be highly dangerous. If that inequality affects every aspect of social life, as an increasing body of evidence continues to suggest, then surely any vision for the future needs to be assembled around the notion of a more egalitarian society. This chapter has begun in part to outline an answer to the question of how to achieve a more egalitarian society by demonstrating that the way that a problem such as social inequalities is defined, in large part can determine the solutions that are proposed (i.e. policies). This is because a definition of a problem can determine what issue is to be addressed, who or what is responsible, what group or area should be targeted, the level of resources to be employed, the actions we should take and what counts as success. Welfare professionals need to develop this analytical skill and then examine what they can do to bring about change at a number of levels.

We argue that, historically, social welfare policies have played a significant part in strategies to help create and sustain a market in human labour, that is, a class of people – a 'working class' – who had no means of survival other than selling their labour, and no alternative other than to do so. It was to take many hundreds of years for this transformation to be effected, for the peasantry to be uprooted from the soil and made dependent upon waged labour for survival. Despite the clear differences in the specific policies and practices of the past and the present, a notable continuity is that society is still driven by the fundamental processes of capitalism, namely, a competitive search for economic advantage or political dominance (Nelson, 1995).

It is for this reason that we argue that an examination of the Poor Laws can offer an insight into a number of contemporary trends in social welfare and the predominant characterisation of social inequalities in particular. For example, questions such as what the effects of benefit levels are on economic performance, wage levels and the motivation of individuals, and whether the funding and provision of services should be left to local bodies or whether central government should take a leading role on grounds of equity and fairness, continue to be posed by policymakers and academics alike. Answers to these questions find expression in those policies that continue to seek to ensure that the recipients of benefits such as the unemployed receive less than those undertaking paid work and/or that those in receipt of benefits be required to be actively seeking work (see Chapter 9). The emphasis we have placed on economic inequalities and an exploitative explanation should not be taken as a suggestion that other forms of inequality are not important or that inequalities cannot be understood in relation to questions of ascribed, essential or self-chosen identities. The enduring presence of a number of different forms of discrimination is all too clear. However, there has been a tendency, at least until recently, for a number of writers to almost neglect the 'poor', never mind class relations. To urge a closer analysis of and engagement with class relations should not be taken as an attempt to erase other perspectives. What we are arguing is first, that, although far from exhausted, there are limits to the degree social inequalities can be reduced or liberation achieved within capitalist social and economic relations. Second, and more immediately, any attempts to reduce inequalities in any form can and will gain significant ground when attempts are made to articulate an analysis and practice in conjunction with those resisting economic exploitation. For these reasons, it is argued that part of the welfare professional's toolkit for understanding society, policy and practice is the ability to engage with and discuss class analysis in conjunction with other forms of analysis and practice (see Chapters 8 and 11).

Conclusion

The main purpose of this chapter has been to explain and illustrate the importance of the definition of a social problem and its role in helping to determine the scope of the policy response. In this respect, we have tried to argue and illustrate that the different perspectives on understanding inequalities are not merely intellectual abstractions, but continue to inform social welfare policies (Byrne, 2005). The analysis we have attempted to outline poses a significant challenge to many of those engaged in contemporary social welfare. Essentially it is argued that if an exploitative position is to be taken seriously (and we are suggesting that it should), the historical and contemporary forms of social welfare, despite the advances that have been made, can be seen as not only ultimately ineffectual when addressing poverty, but (increasingly) complicit in the reproduction of social inequalities.

REFLECTIVE EXERCISE

- ➔ Think about the different explanations offered here for inequality in the context of your own life and also the lives of the people you come into contact with as a welfare professional. How far do the different explanations help you to understand both your own biography and theirs?

And moving on ...

- ➔ Reflection, or thinking about something, obviously helps develop your understanding and skills of critical analysis. This is necessary, but some writers move this forward into the more important area of 'action', creating a cycle of thought–action–thought. So, to develop your skills in action you could join or support a community group/service user organisation/campaign.
- ➔ A quick search of the internet quickly reveals the range of groups and campaigns that are available. It may be something as relatively modest as starting or signing a petition or writing an email or letter to an MP/local councillor. It can also include organising public meetings and taking part in protests. Apart from seeking to achieve your organisation's/campaign's goals, give some thought to your experiences and ask questions about how the organisation/campaign works.

CHAPTER 6

The decline of the 'union' and the rise of the 'manager'

In earlier chapters we have examined the mixed economy of welfare and political choices, especially around the role of the state. We have also explored inequality, offering theoretical explanations for this that culminated in an emphasis upon Byrne's concept of inequality as a consequence of exploitation. Previous chapters have focused upon questions of agency both in the receipt and development of services. We turn now to examine the demands for welfare from the working class through organised labour, as well as the subsequent role of trades unions in defending welfare gains. The local context of service provision and delivery is often referred to as managerialism. In this chapter we examine the rise of managerialism, linking it to experiences within the welfare professions, and we set this alongside the general decline of trades unions. The aim is to enable welfare professionals to see that social welfare in the political sphere has resulted from organised labour and pro-welfare organisations, while the recent trends have seen a rise of individualistic policies and the decline of 'collectivism', frequently in the name of 'choice' and 'rights'. To some extent this has been offset by 'new social movements', and we encourage welfare professionals to explore the nature of organisations in promoting welfare and engaging in processes of change.

The demand for welfare? The historical context explored

Until now, we have focused upon aspects of individualised welfare provision, either from the provider/service user perspective or within the political arena of the state and civil society. At this juncture we offer the view that welfare was not provided as an act of largesse by those in power, but rather that it came about as a result of 'struggle' and 'collective action', even if this was merely to offer a 'sop' to the working class (Saville, 1957).

Chapter 5 closed with an exploration of exploitation along class lines and it is generally the case that trades unions have promoted the interests of the working class against the interests of capital. There was an early realisation that to achieve any sense of progress, workers needed to organise or 'combine' and this very act itself became a site of initial struggle. The 1799 and 1800 Combination Acts led to a 'fast track' of punishment for illegal combinations to limit trade, especially during the Napoleonic wars. The Acts were repealed in 1824 following significant social unrest, including the Peterloo massacre, but even so, restrictive legislation remained even though trades unions were legal, with the most well known prosecution being brought against six farm labourers from Tolpuddle under the 1797 Unlawful Oaths Act. Thus, there has been a long-standing antipathy towards collective organisation, both because of its potential strength and also because of its oppositional stance to hegemonic individualism (Thompson, 1963; Hobsbawm, 1987).

Much trades union activity was directed towards expanding voting rights (the Chartist Movement) and securing better wages for their members. In this regard, trades unions were not fully engaged in a struggle for 'welfare' per se. This was not confined to the UK. Writing about the German trades unions and socialist movements, Reidegeld (2006) argues that they were active in work-based reform, for example, safety at work legislation and, to a lesser extent, pensions, but their major focus was upon ensuring decent wages to avoid or at least minimise exploitation. This focus brought working people into direct conflict with factory owners, who were intent on preserving their profit and averse or even hostile to increased wage demands. However, increasing mobilisation of the working class fuelled fears of a proletarian revolution. Stedman-Jones (1984: 316), writing of trades union activity in London in the late 19th century, observed that through the match-girls' strike led by Annie Besant, and the dockers' strike led by Tom Burns in 1889, 'trades unions were no longer seen as the harbinger of class conflict or fetters upon the market, but primarily as agents of "self-help" and moral improvement'. In short, they came to reflect, in part, the dominant Victorian emphasis upon character as outlined in Chapter 2. It can, however, be argued that this led to an increasing mainstreaming of working-class activity and politics within the established Liberal Party, as opposed to the Marxist Social Democratic Federation (SDF), but nevertheless it acted as a significant force for what would later be termed consciousness-raising.

When it came to the question of 'welfare', there was a clear distinction within the labour movement between those who favoured a range of 'political' measures to bring about state welfare and those who were generally suspicious of state welfare and saw it as a 'capitalist tool' to subjugate the workers. Some within the SDF began to break from their generally held view that welfare reform should be a central element to their parliamentary programme. For example, John Burns argued that:

> palliatives are useless; these symptoms that we witness today are but the inevitable outcome of the disease that society has suffered since commercialisation held its sway. [...] The remedy is not to be found in [...] plausible transitory panaceas from the owning classes (Owen, 2008: 192)

However, Owen (2008:193) notes that he supported other 'palliatives' such as free school meals and the eight-hour day. For the most part, however, trades unionists believed that the modest proposals for pensions and other benefits of the late 19th century were wholly inadequate and that the main political parties would do little to improve the position of the working poor, let alone the unemployed and elderly. In Germany, as part of his plan to unify the former principalities into a powerful nation state, the Chancellor, Otto Bismarck, introduced a system of workplace insurances in one of the first moves towards state provision of welfare. Yet for some English trade unionists such a state-run system appeared to be paternalistic and a mechanism of control since under it:

> the people lose their backbone … the habit of leaning on a support grows stronger until in time there will be no individual strength left. We sincerely believe that is what the German Emperor is aiming at. When people look to the state and receive from it everything they get, they will become the strongest supporters of those from whom they obtain their privileges. But they may rest assured that they who pull the wires will take care for that in exchange for this the puppet shall not dance to a tune of its own calling. (*Cotton Factory Times*, 1890, quoted in Thane, 1984: 96)

The writers went on to argue that the 'workman's duty is to combine and see to it that he gets his full share of the produce of his labour' (1984: 97). Thus, welfare was seen as something that would depress wages and work against the long-term interests of the worker. Thane, drawing on Burgess (1978), noted that such pronouncements came from trades union leaders, yet the ordinary worker, who experienced low pay, poor housing and the threat of destitution in old age, were more than willing to 'place their faith in action by the state or local authority than in hypothetical long-term gains' (Thane, 1984: 97). When confronted with the daily reality, even theoretical opponents of welfare were moved to compromise and 'find some method of easing the suffering of our contemporaries' (Liverpool Trades Council, 1894, quoted in Thane, 1984: 98).

Undeniably, one of the movements that emanated from this was the demand for universal pensions – a key welfare reform. The national Committee of Organised Labour for Promoting Old Age Pensions was established in 1897, and drew support from both trades unionists and the progressive non-conformist Churches. The Committee on Old Age Pensions, who proposed modest reforms, saw these met with hostility, typical of which was the view of the Bradfield Board of (Poor Law) Guardians who argued that:

> The welfare of the nation is involved in everyone feeling that it is to his interest to avoid dependence from unearned public funds; and that therefore any system tending to make such dependence attractive, and even honourable is full of danger. (Bradfield Board of Guardians, 1899: 1)

Support also came from the Liberal Party, even those who were openly 'anti-socialist', perhaps a motive that fuelled the unions' antagonism to this type of provision. Pensions were finally established for all people over 70 by the Liberal government in 1908, yet they were set at a very low rate (five shillings a week) described by the Liverpool Trades Council as 'an insult and a mockery to the veterans of industry' (quoted in Thane, 1984: 108). Nevertheless, Saville (1957), writing 50 years later, argued that this was the decisive moment in the founding of a fledgling welfare state.

Key themes

This brief historical case study of the position of trades unions at the turn of the 20th century allows us to highlight some critical questions and developmental skills for contemporary welfare professionals. The ideological question raised here is 'reform' or 'transformation', that is, should they engage in the reform of a system that, as we read in the previous chapter, is 'exploitative' or should they seek its total transformation? Theorists and activists hotly debated this and perhaps it was best resolved by Rosa Luxemburg's early 20th-century aphorism that 'revolutionaries make the best reformers' (see Walters, 1970). The tendency to reform, however, was equally fuelled by what can best be understood as a compassion for the human condition and the need to ensure that in the short term something is done. In the words of a current West Midlands social worker, 'the people I work with need improved services and a better standard of living now. They cannot wait for a transformation of society sometime in the future'.

A second theme is that of unease about 'welfare'. The voices from the 19th century reveal much about dominant attitudes, yet they are not simply voices from the past. Were they to be put into contemporary language they would reflect many current views. A crucial point to consider, especially for welfare professionals, is that hostility to welfare in a general sense from the working class is best understood as hostility to *regulation*. Welfare comes with a price, and not just an economic one. It begins to be a regulatory factor on how people live their lives and we make links here with contemporary service-user movements, whose resistance to aspects of welfare professionalism is located within aspects of control and regulation.

A third theme is that welfare is part of an overall settlement between capital and labour, as Joseph Chamberlain, a Liberal, wryly observed in 1885, when launching a series of modest welfare proposals: 'I ask, what ransom will property pay for the security which it enjoys?' (quoted in Saville, 1957: 6). Welfare becomes a mechanism for social order and control and a force for maintaining existing social and economic relationships. It is one side of a broader 'welfare settlement' (Clarke, 1993a), which more latterly has come to embrace all the elements of civil society. Saville's view of the 1948 welfare settlement was that, welcome and rooted in struggle though it was, it still remained little more than a 'twentieth century version of self-help … the state now saves for the working class and translates the savings into social services' (Saville, 1957: 24). Saville's critique was that, despite the rhetoric of 'redistribution', the 1948 welfare state was anything but.

Radical welfare professionalism

At least in part, welfare came from a coalition of trades union and political activity resulting in the legislative reform of 1908, and the more significant and widely known reform of 1948, with the founding of the National Health Service, but trades unions have also taken on the role of defending these services or social gains. Within welfare professional groupings, however, the relative strength of trades union activity is uneven. The most highly unionised welfare profession is teaching, with the National Union of Teachers (NUT) pointing out its role in the 'struggle' for education and its historical disputes, notably the Burston School strike in Norfolk. After the school's teachers were sacked, almost certainly for their social and union activism, the villagers of Burston established an alternative school that functioned with trades unions' support until 1939 (see NUT, no date). Perhaps the most radical of the main teaching unions, the NUT has a membership of almost 290,000 teachers. The National Association of Schoolmasters and Union of Women Teachers (NASUWT) has a similar number of members and claims to be the largest union of 'teachers' – thus over half a million teachers are members of a trades union. UNISON has 400,000 members, including health and social care/work professionals and local authority employees, and is, thus, a substantial public sector union, and an amalgamation of several smaller unions. Nursing is represented by the Royal College of Nursing (RCN), which has strict rules about industrial action and, while not ruling it out, emphasises Florence Nightingale's dictum that 'Hospitals [and by inference nurses] should do the sick no harm' (Peate, 2008).

Social work is a more recent welfare *professional* grouping, which developed as a national profession following the Seebohm report (Seebohm, 1968). In the 1970s there was an influential radical social work movement, which saw trades union membership and action as a means for improving and defending conditions of service as well as defending public services per se. This culminated in a successful strike in 1978–79, which cost almost a quarter of a million working days (Joyce et al, 1988: 1). Further strike action by residential social workers in 1983 was eventually unsuccessful (Joyce et al, 1988: 147). Joyce and colleagues acknowledge that taking industrial action for social workers is not an easy option for a number of reasons, one of which is that they work with vulnerable people and have a sense of compassion and 'public service' – yet at the heart of the radical social work movement was the view that social workers are first and foremost 'workers' since 'social workers themselves suffer from economic exploitation – though far less severely than [other groups]' (Bailey and Brake, 1975: 9). It should be noted here that in the 1970s the term 'social worker' was used more widely, since it is now a title protected by law and refers only to those who are professionally qualified and registered with the regulatory body – a more accurate comment now would replace social worker with 'social care worker', many of whom earn the minimum wage (£5.93 an hour in October 2010) and in 2009 the average wage for the sector was little more than £6.50 an hour (UNISON, 2009).

Yet within the current context of welfare provision, the role of trades unions has become weakened by successive legislation (see Chapter 9) and, perhaps just as significantly, how the courts have interpreted that legislation. Increasingly, for example, the courts seem to be taking into account 'public disruption', notably in the rejection of ballots for strike action by rail unions and British Airways crew; both disputes were focused upon aspects of long-term public safely against short-term economic gain (Teather and Milmo, 2010). Notably, against this 'decline' there has been the rise of management.

New Public Management and welfare governance

Newman (2001) describes governance as a concept that has come to occupy an important position in the social sciences, and Daly identifies three disciplinary roots for the concept, one of which is:

> the capacity and competence of governments and representative political institutions to control events within and beyond the nation state and governance as the process of state adaptation to changes in its environment. (2003: 116)

Newman (2001) highlights the strong ideological component, with reference to the ways in which institutions and individuals should be 'governed'. As Daly notes, 'governance practices create and reproduce the subjects needed for governance to operate effectively' (2003: 118), and, therefore, there is a strong normative content in governance, as the concept and practices entail a 'set of prescriptions for the organisation of society' (2003: 120). For the purposes of this section and chapter we are interested in what Clarke (2004a: 120) describes as the 'shifting conditions and location of what might be called statework', and the universalisation of management, or, more specifically, New Public Management (NPM), as the solution to the problem of improving public services (Cutler and Waine, 1997).

NPM is a reflection of a number of different trends. Hood (1991) suggests that NPM consists of a number of different ideas, which are blended and mixed according to the specific public-sector circumstances under discussion. So, drawing upon earlier chapters, NPM represents a combination of 'technical' and 'consumerist' approaches to quality. NPM shares the consumerist objectives of increasing service responsiveness, but it is driven by a different underlying dynamic. Making services more responsive to consumers' needs and preferences is not carried out to secure greater market share, but to ensure public resources are used more *efficiently* and *effectively*. Put another way, this is the mechanism for achieving 'value for money'. In this respect the expertise is not necessarily that of the social welfare professional, but rather that of the 'manager'. There is less emphasis placed upon consumer rights than on service obligations to ensure that public funds are used to maximum benefit. Decision-making power is retained by service providers whose motivation to involve the public is driven by their need to increase efficiency by ensuring that services reflect patients' needs more precisely. Rather than serving to empower users or enabling them to exercise their rights as consumers, public participation is a means to increase organisational learning. The 'public interest' is in effect defined by practitioners and managerial professionals who mediate the views expressed by the public (McLaughlin et al, 2002).

The government has developed a number of levers in an attempt to drive up standards in public services (see Cabinet Office, 1999). The introduction of Comprehensive Spending Reviews established what was described as a new approach to improving service delivery, including:

- a coordinated set of objectives covering all public spending;
- Public Service Agreements, establishing targets for improving services over a three-year period;
- a cabinet committee to monitor progress on a regular basis with relevant secretaries of state;
- a New Public Service Productivity Panel, including public- and private-sector representation; and
- annual reports to summarise progress for parliament and the public.

Public Service Agreements (PSAs) set out in detail what return can be expected on any investment. The introduction of three-year spending plans for departments alongside resource budgeting was designed to provide clearer links between the inputs and outcomes of services and to increase the incentives for assets to be managed effectively. To ensure accountability, a system of inspection and performance management was developed and principles for performance management and inspection identified. Taken together a far greater emphasis was placed on a variant of 'professional' management, which included the introduction of explicit measures of performance, a focus on outputs and results, and an ever greater role played by 'private-sector styles' of management practice – essentially, a 'marriage' of 'administrative reform' with 'business-type managerialism'. It is argued that the impact of this marriage on those engaged in, and in receipt of, statework has been significant.

What about the workers?

For the workers themselves, Mooney and Law (2007) highlight how successive policy measures have led to workers undertaking additional responsibilities. New Labour's 'value for money agenda' demands 'more and more' from public-sector workers as they struggle to meet the bewildering host of targets and strategies that have been deployed since 1997 (Fairbrother and Poynter, 2001: 319). Sennett (2006) describes the 'spectre of uselessness' that can now be found among welfare workers as work becomes routine and degrading – a common feature is deskilling and the loss of autonomy. Clarke (2004b) describes the formation of a competition–evaluation nexus of regulation that lies at the heart of NPM and provides a mechanism for ensuring this investment continues. For instance, appraisal monitors a worker's 'personal development' and ensures that priorities and performance are aligned with the targets and priorities for the organisation as a whole. It is through this mechanism that the PSAs' priorities are 'cascaded' through the system and that control at a distance can be achieved. As a further education lecturer commented:

> in the late 1990s I was expected to recite by heart the college's 'mission statement' and this was a feature of 'appraisal'. Resistance to this appeared about as futile as knowing the mission statement! (West Midlands lecturer in further education)

The result is the development of a 'performance orientation' for the individual and the organisation, where an emphasis is placed on normative standards and competition. As a social worker presently working in the child sector commented: 'we are now a three star Authority – what we are now told is that we should say, "we are working towards four stars"'. Awards for worker 'excellence' are also commonplace within local authorities and other areas of the public sector, and are evidence of this competitive trend, where satisfaction is derived from doing better than others and there is a concern to prove one's own competence (Adcroft and Willis, 2005: 386).

A backdrop to this potent disciplinary measure for a number of workers is the fear of redundancy. In the New Labour era (1997–2010) this was justified as part of a commitment to develop a modern and professional public-sector workforce and to ensure value for money for the taxpayer. In other words, it was another 'welfare settlement', where increased public spending would be matched by increased 'efficiency' to placate the hostility of so-called 'Middle England'. Considering the scale and scope of the changes being proposed, it is worth noting the limited amount of attention that has been given to the impact of these 'efficiency savings' on the workers involved in delivering services and/or the degree to which the premise that enhanced provision can be provided when resources are being cut has so dramatically been challenged. In the 2010 general election campaign, where cuts in public expenditure were espoused in one form or another by all major parties, there was a consensus that significant sums could come from efficiency savings, and in the Labour Party's pre-election budget Alistair Darling proposed £11bn in 'efficiency savings'. Efficiency savings for welfare professionals usually translate into greater amounts of work to complete for no additional pay, and/or reduced services for their service users as they increasingly target the most vulnerable.

While performance measurement may be useful in giving some indication of the progress (however it is defined) that has been made, it is less useful in explaining what organisations and individuals should do differently (Meyer, 1994: 101). It is at this point that public-sector workers through their emotional, intellectual and physical labour are meant to make it all work. Social welfare professionals, by definition, are the ones given the task of implementing the government's social policy initiatives. It is here that a tension develops. If the welfare reforms are to be implemented, public-sector workers need to have positive vehicles of production and organisation. The very complexity and scale of work to be undertaken in order to meet this new welfare agenda requires public-sector workers to be involved in the day-to-day implementation of the very process that nevertheless appears to operate against their own interests (Curtis, 1996), the contradiction being that contemporary organisations seek to develop individual workers, while creating an environment that simultaneously seeks to diminish workers. This is something that a number of those working in public services are coming to recognise and, therefore, it would appear that although these organisational reforms have sought to depoliticise welfare, they have in fact inadvertently politicised the whole question of the nature and management of welfare in a number of ways.

Daly argues that those who both manage and deliver welfare are required to become subjects who are self-reliant and 'active in their own self-government' (2003: 121) – in other words, workers are required (in theory at least) to exhibit greater 'autonomy' and 'self-reliance', an example being that often management is consigned to the process of ticking off objectives that have been met and setting deadlines for those that have not, and thus quality is further reduced to a 'technical' exercise. Clarke (2004b: 120) suggests that on a wider level the processes involved include:

- statework being 'expelled' from the institutions of the state. Forms of privatisation and contracting out have shifted organisations, labour processes and jobs from the state to the private and voluntary sectors;
- the continuing universalisation of 'management' as the solution to the problem of improving public services;
- a tendency to shift what were occupational/professional identities to ones that are organisation-centred, where the organisation seeks to become the point of identification, loyalty and commitment;
- the treatment of externally oriented professionalism as suspect and as a 'special interest' that distracts from the 'organisation as common purpose'.

It has been argued that these changes are part of an attempt not only to improve quality and choice (see Chapter 3), but to align the operation of services with more accurate 'assumptions concerning human motivation and behaviour' (Le Grand 1997: 153–4), that is, that they are an appeal to the self-interested knave rather than the public-spirited knight. However, rather than being seen as an attempt to match organisational design to an essential (self-interested) human nature, we argue that these organisational changes have sought to shape and mould their workforces into a normative model of how workers (and recipients of services) should behave (Hunt and Wickham, 1993; Barry et al, 1996). So, welfare regimes do not just become a response to particular economic and social problems, but play a key role in shaping the nature of the welfare professional and service users

(Daly, 2003: 118). This means that the significance of 'disputes' in welfare is given extra weight, since attempts to reframe 'welfare' also represent attempts to reframe the relationship between the political arena and the administration of social and economic affairs.

More recently within the social care sector there have been a number of isolated episodes of industrial action and strikes. In the period 2004–05 there were over eight separate instances of strike action (Price and Simpson, 2007) – the majority of which were to defend services, including a strike in Liverpool which lasted for over four months. Mooney and McCafferty (2005) draw attention to a strike of over 5,000 nursery staff in Glasgow in 2004, which includes this view from a nursery worker:

> Lots of people think that all we do all day is change nappies, sing nursery rhymes and paint pictures of cows or hills or the like. They don't see the physical and emotional demands that go with the job, or the extra-unpaid work we often do, often with kids from very poor and disadvantaged backgrounds. And what they don't see either is that we are providing an education service, and an important service that helps to shape a child's future. (Susan, 24, a nursery nurse in Glasgow with four years' experience, quoted in Mooney and McCafferty, 2005: 225)

What emerges is that there is a history of union action within the welfare sector, both to enhance conditions of employment and increasingly to defend services for vulnerable people. What is missing is that these disputes are often not widely reported in either the national or social work media and are seen as 'local' when in fact they frequently reflect 'national' issues. For example in relation to personalised budgets, UNISON (2010) reported that 'social work professionals said that the introduction of personal budgets has led to vital local services being shut down, and qualified social workers being replaced with cheaper staff'.

Conclusion

We began the chapter with a focus upon the trades union and organised labour movement at the turn of the 20th century and briefly discussed their, at times, ambivalent role in relation to state welfare. We then moved to discuss some of the themes that emerged, both in relation to a theoretical position towards welfare or wages, as well as the view that even though welfare may have been a 'ransom' paid by capital, it still came as a result of a collective struggle. This fed into a short account of radical welfare professionalism and trades unionism, which was then set against the background of 'New Public Management', ending the chapter with a return to a discussion about how this impacts upon the workforce, notably as a mechanism of control and regulation, and a focus upon 21st-century trades union disputes. It draws to a close this section on 'working in society' and we suggest that understanding (and, for that matter, becoming involved in) collective action and the role of organised labour is a crucial tool for understanding policy for social welfare professionals. This is a theme that we will return to in the final chapters of the book, but prior to that final discussion, we are going to focus upon the skills and knowledge needed to explore the wider social context.

REFLECTIVE EXERCISES

- ➔ With reference to an organisation that you are familiar with, ask and answer the following questions. Who gets to define the problems and priorities? Does everyone make a contribution to setting priorities? Who has the most status and why? Whose terms tend to get used: for example, do you talk about patients, clients, services users, students, consumers and so on? Who decides what resources are needed and how they are allocated? Are questions regarding the use of resources mutually agreed, determined in accordance with varying professional contributions or dictated by one professional group/partner? Finally, who would be missed the most if they did not turn up the next day and who would be missed the least?
- ➔ We have used the term 'welfare professional' throughout this chapter. Most of the people reading the book are likely to be either qualified welfare professionals or students working towards a professional qualification. So, how far do you see yourself as a 'worker'?
- ➔ Would you engage in a trade dispute (for example, a 'work to rule' or a strike)? Whatever you have answered, think about why you have reached this view and the factors that have determined your thinking.

Part Three
Setting people and society in context

CHAPTER 7

Economic theories

In this chapter we explore how recent welfare policies aimed at individuals have promoted a particular form of economic organisation and priorities. We contrast the freedom to choose, adapt and be flexible, to a freedom that is 'transformative' and includes the possibility of redefining the conditions of existence and the parameters of one's own actions (Piven and Cloward, 1977; Schram, 1995; Howard, 2000; Lavalette and Mooney, 2000; Zizek, 2001; Annetts et al, 2009). An examination of these alternatives needs to be a part of any attempt to provide a critical analysis and response to contemporary forms of welfare. In addition to outlining some macroeconomic theories and the implications these have for social welfare, we highlight examples in contemporary social welfare of how a process of 'empowerment' (essentially a positive force) has been compromised by a neo-liberal economic agenda. Other case examples will be used to enable welfare professionals to make explicit links between areas of welfare work and economic imperatives.

Case study: Meaningful work? The case of Remploy

In November 2007, Remploy, an organisation in the UK that had as part of its remit the goal of providing secure employment for thousands of people with 'disabilities', proposed the closure of 28 of its 83 factories. Established under the 1944 Disabled Persons (Employment) Act by the Minister of Labour, Ernest Bevin, Remploy has employed thousands of people with 'disabilities' in the manufacture of a range of goods, including furniture, car parts, wheelchairs, nurses' uniforms, and chemical and biological warfare suits for the Ministry of Defence. Following reports published by the National Audit Office (2005) and PricewaterhouseCoopers and Stephen Duckworth (2006), Remploy was instructed to 'modernise and restructure'. Its new emphasis was to be in securing job placements, rather than subsidising factories; this would provide better 'value for money' and be more in line with government policy on integrating disabled people into their communities. Support for the modernisation programme, including the factory closures, came from the Employers' Forum on Disability (2007) and, notably, six leading disability charities who, in a letter to a national newspaper, argued that although the Remploy factories had been useful in the past, 'disabled people are far more likely to have fulfilling lives, and to reach their potential, by working in an inclusive environment which the rest of us take for granted' (Leonard Cheshire et al, 2007). In this respect, the factory closures were cast as an attempt to find 'meaningful work' in the open marketplace, secure independence and move beyond the 'yoke of paternalism'. In contrast, the unions representing the members of those employed at the factories not only questioned the evidence drawn upon in the various reviews, but in a series of campaigns and protests against the closures, argued that far from representing an opportunity for its members, the factory closures represented a push towards a future of low-paid and low-skilled work or no work at all (Transport and General Workers Union, 2008; GMB, 2009; Taylor, 2009).

Why is it that the closure of Remploy's factories, which once offered secure employment to thousands of individuals, is viewed as an 'opportunity', while those who opposed the closures are cast as being unable to recognise or assume the agency and independence of people with 'disabilities'? At the same time, why is it that the collective agency and action of the Remploy employees in their trades unions is deemed 'old-fashioned' and considered to be acting against the 'real' interests of people with 'disabilities'? To answer these questions, we argue that we need to first take a step back and examine the argument that political priorities are driven by economic choices.

'It's the economy, stupid' (Bill Clinton, presidential campaign slogan, 1992)

One of the most important stated aims of contemporary governments is to achieve high economic growth. The logic behind this is that increases in economic growth will lead to increases in income, which in turn will lead to increased living standards. This sounds simple enough, but the question is how this is to be achieved. This chapter introduces some of the major economic theories and tools that are drawn on and used in attempts to secure the goal of economic growth. Thus, the aim of this chapter is to:

- develop an awareness of the economic context within which social welfare policies and practice operate;
- consider the political choices that can be made with regard to the economy and the implications of these choices; and
- consider the relationship between the economy and specific social policies.

The relationship between the state and the economy is unclear and contested, yet for many social welfare professionals, there is an instinctive grasp that many of the difficulties they face in the provision of services are located in the availability or otherwise of 'resources' and that these depend upon fiscal policies – commonly referred to as 'public expenditure'. It is the theories behind this 'intuitive' understanding that we aim to introduce, since we believe that this is an essential tool for understanding social welfare and for understanding the limits upon professional practice.

So what is the economy?

The economy can be described simply as the system of production, distribution and consumption of resources. Economics is a wide-ranging subject, and economists make a distinction between the 'actual economy' and the so-called 'economic imaginaries'. The actual existing economy has been described by Jessop as the:

> chaotic sum of all economic activities ... the totality of economic activities is so unstructured and complex that it cannot be an object of calculation, management or governance or guidance. (2004: 162)

This is the sum of the production, distribution and consumption of goods and services, that is, that which is made, bought, sold, speculated upon or even provided as a service, be that a service provided voluntarily or as part of a welfare economy – hence the view that it is beyond easy calculation. Economic imaginaries refer to a range of theories, or schools of economic thought, which help make sense of and shape the actual economy. As Jessop writes, they are:

> subsets of economic relations (economic systems or subsystems) that have been discursively and perhaps organizationally and institutionally fixed as objects of intervention ... [which] must have some significant, albeit necessary partial, correspondence to real material interdependencies in the actual existing economy and/or relations between economic and extra economic activities. (2004: 162)

As such these theories are 'real' since they inform institutions and practices, having widespread impact on people's lives and social welfare. There are a number of different economic imaginaries (theories or schools of economics), and many of them disagree on what should be the focus of study, how the economy should be studied and what measures should be taken to 'manage' the economy. In this chapter, we focus upon macroeconomics, with particular reference to its impact of social welfare.

Samuelson and Nordhaus (1989) highlight how the study and operation of economics was an attempt to answer the following questions:

- What goods and services should be produced and made available with scarce resources?
- How should we combine the basic resources that are available, including labour, to produce the goods and services that we want?
- Who should receive the goods and services that have been produced and what system should be used to distribute the resources?

A common misconception of economics is that it is a study of the market. The market may be a central concern of mainstream economics and there are different theories of how the market does and should operate, but it is worthwhile noting that it is only one system that is available for organising the production, distribution and consumption of resources. An alternative lies in the variety of forms of collectivism, or command planning, where: 'economic decisions are taken collectively by planning committees and implemented through the direction of collectively owned resources, either centrally or at a local level' (Beardshaw et al, 2001: 9).

The UK, as with most economies, is best described as operating as a mixed economy. This is where some decisions are taken by the market mechanism and some decisions are taken collectively. The question is which decisions, if any, should be left to the market and which decisions, if any, should be left to some form of collective? In answering this we adopt a political economy approach, recognising that the answer reflects particular political perspectives, and cannot be provided by economic theory alone (Glyn, 2006).

Making sense of the economy

Macroeconomics focuses upon economic growth, unemployment, inflation, the balance of payments (the difference between 'imports' and 'exports') and to a greater or lesser degree the distribution of income and wealth. As we explore these, albeit briefly, to provide a knowledge base for the social welfare professional, we also argue that as these reflect political viewpoints, they should be met with the refrain 'Who benefits?'. We begin with what amounts to a brief glossary of these frequently heard terms.

Economic growth

This refers to an increase in the overall output of the economy, as measured by changes in national aggregate output. Economic growth is considered important by many across the political spectrum (although Greens add the caveat of 'sustainability') because if there are more goods and services available, there are more to share out. In attempts to achieve economic growth, efforts are made to maintain the level of demand in the economy. Put simply, to increase growth the options available include: cutting direct taxes (e.g. income tax) and/or indirect taxes (e.g. VAT); cutting interest rates; and/or increasing government expenditure. If the economy is growing too slowly then in an attempt to boost demand, spending can be encouraged by either cutting taxes or cutting interest rates. The idea behind these measures is that it will give people more money to spend and thereby boost the economy, assuming that people will now consume more with the increase in money available to them. An alternative approach is for the government to spend more (increase the level of government expenditure).

Unemployment

Unemployment is where individuals want to work but cannot find paid employment. If the economy is growing, then the argument is that there will be jobs created to satisfy this demand. Conversely, if growth slows, or the economy goes into recession, then people may have to lose their jobs as companies reduce output. As such, levels of (un)employment are closely linked to the level of economic growth. In times of economic growth (boom), unemployment will be lower. In periods of recession (bust), there will be higher levels of unemployment. As economic growth is considered to be cyclical (goes up and down in cycles over a period of time), levels of unemployment also tend to follow this cycle. This is what is called cyclical unemployment where unemployment is caused by a downturn in the trade cycle. There are other measures that can be used to reduce unemployment – for example, workfare policies that effectively provide benefits in return for what amounts to very low-paid work, or merely the reduction of benefit rates aimed at the belief that some people choose not to work.

Inflation

Put simply, inflation is the rise in the general level of prices. There are a number of explanations available for inflation, but two theories tend to predominate. Demand/pull inflation is when the level of demand grows too fast. As noted in the discussion on economic growth, if companies cannot keep up with the growth in demand for their products, prices may increase (inflation) and more imports are brought into the country. Cost/push inflation is when wages or prices rise too fast. If the economy is growing quickly, and there is low unemployment, employers may have to offer higher wages to attract people. This can lead to an increase in prices (inflation) as the firm's costs increase – what is described as a wage–price spiral. As inflation increases, there may understandably be calls for an increase in wages in order to keep up with the cost of living. This in turn can increase costs and so on. To avoid this type of inflation, once again, deflationary policies can be employed in order to slow the economy down and ensure that economic growth does not rise too fast. However, if the economy slows down too much, unemployment can increase significantly. At the same time, the government may seek to limit the ability of employees to make claims for higher wages, by reducing the scope and power of trades unions.

Balance of payments

The balance of payments is like a nation's accounts, showing its transactions with the rest of the world. A number of economic transactions can lead to finances flowing into or out of the country, namely:

- exports and imports of goods such as oil, agricultural products, other raw materials, machinery and transport equipment, computers, white goods and clothing;
- exports and imports of services such as international transport, travel, financial and business services;

- income flows such as dividends and interest earned by non-residents on investments in the UK and by UK residents investing abroad; and
- financial flows, such as investment in shares, debt, securities and loans.

As with a number of economic indicators, policymakers and economists have very different opinions as to the merit, and implications, of operating a trade surplus. Efforts are directed towards achieving a balance of trade or what can be described as an 'external balance', where the flow of money into and out of the country is balanced over a period of time (normally a set period of years).

Distribution of income and wealth

While frequently not a feature of economic textbooks, we include it here since it is important to consider the impact of economic policies on the distribution of income and wealth within a country. As we noted in Chapter 5, the gap between rich and poor is a social problem in its own right (Orton and Rowlingson, 2007b; Wilkinson and Pickett, 2009). Inequality remains high in the UK (see Chapter 5).

Economic choices

All of these targets may appear desirable, but attempts to achieve one of these targets may take place at the expense of one of the others. For example, unemployment and inflation in particular tend to move in opposite directions. This is because in attempts to increase economic growth, increase incomes and improve living standards, inflation may also increase, as businesses may not be able to increase output quickly enough to meet this increase in demand, with the result that prices may rise. Added to this, with an unmet demand there may be an increase in the level of imports, thus changing the balance between exports and imports. It may also be that the nature of economic growth leads to an increase in the inequality in income and wealth across the country. So by attempting to hit two targets, you end up missing three.

This, then, begs the question as to which one of these economic targets is to be the priority or, more accurately, what 'trade-offs' can be achieved between the different targets. This can be cast in discussions of what is an acceptable level of economic growth, unemployment, inflation, balance of trade and inequalities. As noted throughout this book, as this is a political decision, it is best considered in the context of who benefits. To put it bluntly, if you are currently unemployed, your view as to what are 'acceptable' levels may differ sharply from that of the director of a hedge fund.

Case study: The national debt

The government deficit (as opposed to a trade deficit/surplus) is the difference between the money the government takes in (through a variety of taxes) and what the government spends for a particular year. The government debt can be described as accumulated deficits. So if a government carries a deficit from one year into the next, the total size of the debt will be increased. In reality, a number of countries exist with large deficits, but for a variety of reasons, governments may, if not seek to achieve a balance of payments, then at least attempt to maintain a reasonable limit on either the surplus or deficit.

The numbers when looking at national debts can be staggering. In the financial year 2009/10, the UK recorded general government net borrowing of £159.8bn. At the end of March 2010, the UK's general government debt was £1,000.4bn. However, it is instructive to put these figures into historical context (O'Hara, 2010). Figure 7.1 shows national debt as a percentage of the UK's Gross Domestic Product (GDP – a measure of the national economy's performance).

Figure 7.1: UK public debt as a percentage of Gross Domestic Product

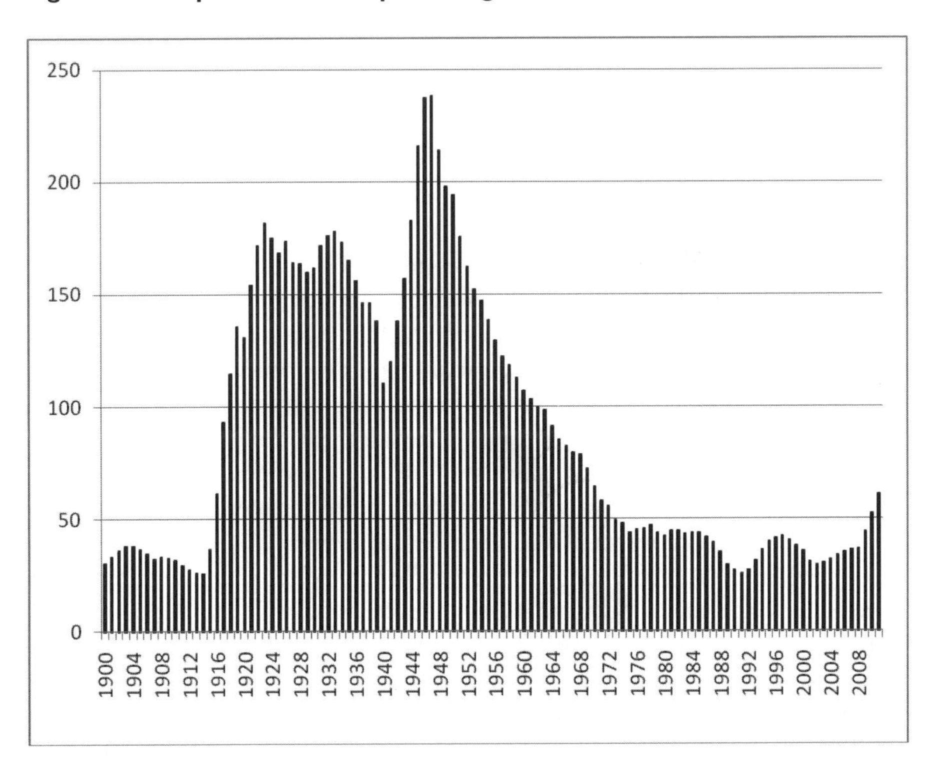

At the beginning of the 20th century, the national debt was approximately 30% of GDP. The middle of the graph shows a very sharp increase where national debt initially peaks to 150% during the First World War, and then peaks again, reaching over 200% of GDP, at the end of the Second World War (and the creation of the 'welfare state'). For the next 40 years national debt as a percentage of GDP declined to a low of 25% by the 1990s. Since then, the national debt as a percentage of GDP has begun to increase again, and although it has undoubtedly risen sharply in recent years, particularly in light of the most recent worldwide financial crisis of 2008, in historical terms it is far from unprecedented. It is notable to compare the different responses of governments to the question of the national debt, for example, compare and contrast the response of the Labour government of 1945 to that of the coalition government of 2010.

This is not to say that questions regarding the national debt can be ignored, but rather that there are competing claims as to the nature and scale of the problem and the range of possible policy solutions available. In attempts to reduce a national deficit/debt, a government can either attempt to stimulate economic growth, increase its income (raise taxes), reduce spending (cut or reduce the rate of increase in spending), or borrow to pay its bills. This can be in the form of borrowing from overseas governments or banks, or by attempting to attract what is described as inward investment into the country. Of course, the loans will need to be paid back at some point, or, at the very least, the interest on the loans will have to be paid. This can be expensive and difficult to sustain, so it may be desirable to avoid deficits in the balance of payments over the long term.

There is no doubt that a significant increase in public expenditure in 2008/09 played a large part in contributing to the scale of the government deficit for that year and its accumulated debt. The coalition government in 2010 argued that unless public spending and borrowing was addressed, the national debt would become insurmountable and Britain would risk losing credibility on the money markets. It is interesting to consider what accounts for this increase, however. Table 7.1 shows that although spending increased across most departments and government as a whole, it was the Treasury's increase in spending that is most notable.

The extraordinary 48,672% increase in Treasury spending (the equivalent of spending on the Department of Health) reflects the government's attempt to 'bail' out the banks, which cost £109.5bn. Putting the merit or otherwise of such actions aside for the moment, it does beg the question of why, if it is this area of public spending that is in large part responsible for such a significant increase in the deficit and the overall debt, other areas of public spending, most notably social welfare, are subject to the cuts that have been announced. Put another way, there are political choices to be made in response to these economic issues. In essence it tends to come down to the question of whether people should be subject to the demands of the economy or whether the economy should be subject to the demands of people. To explore and help make sense of these issues, we now turn to an outline of some macroeconomic theories. As we discuss different theories, we are not engaging in a discussion about the extent to which they are successful, but rather focusing upon their impact upon social welfare.

Table 7.1: UK government public expenditure, including inflation, 2007/08–2008/09 and percentage change

DEPARTMENT	2007/08, £bn	2008/09, £bn	% change
UK GOVT TOTAL EXPENDITURE	582.676	620.685	4
Debt interest payments	22.5	24.1	4
Department for Work and Pensions (DWP)	125.3	135.7	6
Her Majesty's Treasury (HMT)	0.219	109.5	48,672
Department of Health (DH)	101.5	109.4	5
Department for Children, Schools and Families (DCSF)	60.6	63.18	2
Ministry of Defence (MoD)	42.4	44.6	3
Communities and Local Government (CLG)	34.3	36.8	5
HM Revenue and Customs (HMRC)	30.9	34.1	8
Department for Innovation, Universities and Skills (DIUS)	21.6	23.0	4
Department for Transport (DfT)	16.3	15.4	–8
Home Office (HO)	9.5	9.98	2

Source: UK government departments' annual reports.

(Neo-)classical theories

In the 18th and 19th centuries those who we now describe as the classical economists – for example, Smith (1976 [1776]) and Ricardo (1895 [1817]) – developed theories about the way markets and market economies work. Attempts to revisit these theories in contemporary society are described as neo-classical economics, the word 'neo' meaning 'new'. Central to classical economics is the notion of 'laissez faire', where free trade and markets are considered the only way to encourage economic growth. As noted earlier, it is a combination of individuals pursuing their own interests and the price mechanism that enables the invisible hand of the market to produce and distribute resources most efficiently. The state, therefore, should limit any attempts to intervene in the working of the free market. The assumption is if the economy was left to itself, then it would tend towards 'full employment equilibrium', where everyone who wants to work is able to. In times of unemployment, wages fall, which in turn leads to a demand for labour, resulting in 'full employment among those able to work' – according to the theory, only those who choose not to work at the wages offered will remain unemployed.

Classical economic theories have very real implications for economic and social policies. If the state is to have a role, it is to be limited to using 'supply-side policies' and helping to ensure a balanced budget. Classical economics suggests that the key to long-term stable economic growth is to use money supply policies to help control inflation and, most relevant to the topic of social welfare, to use supply-side policies to ensure free markets with no imperfections. The logic behind the use of supply-side measures is that supply creates its own demand, that is, the capacity of the economy to produce is increased, thereby creating increased demand – economic growth. Examples of supply-side policies include:

- improving education and training to make the workforce more 'occupationally mobile';
- reducing the level of benefits to increase the incentive for people to work;
- reducing taxation to encourage enterprise and encourage hard work;
- policies to increase the mobility of labour (scrapping rent controls, making house-buying easier and quicker); and
- reducing the power of trades unions so as to allow wages to be more flexible.

Classical economic thinking was the orthodoxy throughout most of the 19th and the beginning of the 20th century. However, the Great Depression of the 1930s led many to question the assumptions and practices of classical economics, including, most notably, an economist called John Maynard Keynes.

Keynesian economics

Keynesianism challenges the assumptions, theories and policies of classical economics. The theory needs to be understood in the context of the Great Depression of the 1930s. The main contention was the faith classical economists placed in the market on reaching full employment equilibrium. Keynes (1997 [1936]) argued that market economics had no automatic capacity to generate full employment and that economic policy is and should be inextricably linked to social policy.

If the market could not be relied on to reach full employment, then it was argued that the state would need to intervene. Keynes argues that the state should have a role in managing demand as well as supply in the economy, that is, should use demand management policies, through the use of a combination of budgetary and fiscal policies, commonly referred to as 'public expenditure'. Keynes' central insight was that changes in government income and spending are the most effective instrument of government economic policy. For Keynes, saving during a depression only made a community poorer; therefore, governments should spend in hard times and save in a boom. Keynes argued that the lack of demand for goods and rising unemployment could be countered by increased government expenditure to stimulate the economy.

With respect to the policies and tools that the state could employ, Keynesianism argues that in a recession, if the market is not willing or able to boost demand in the economy, then the state needs to play an active role in stimulating the economy, possibly by increasing government expenditure and thereby running at a deficit (running up a debt). Once the increased demand leads to a growing economy and the private sector spending again, the state can then reduce its expenditure, or at least pay off the deficit that had been accumulated in the recession.

A common misconception is to equate Keynesianism with socialism. This is understandable, as they are both critical of classical economic theories and see a greater role for the state. However, it is here that the major similarities end and it is notable that Keynesianism was an economic doctrine adopted by a range of political regimes following the Second World War.

Monetarism

Monetarism has some notable similarities to classical economics, and its most notable theorist is Milton Friedman (1962). Monetarism needs to be understood in the context of attempts to revisit classical economics to counter the post-1945 orthodoxy of Keynesian economics. In the 1960s and 1970s there was the phenomenon of 'stagflation' – the simultaneous existence of stagnation (minimal economic growth and rising unemployment) and inflation (increasing prices normally associated with a growing economy). One of the principal innovations of monetarists was the argument that if workers expected inflation to occur, then they would anticipate this and expect a correspondingly higher wage rise. Inflation was considered to be bad because of the uncertainty it created with regard to spending and levels of investment and the damage it could have on the competitiveness of companies trading internationally. This reflects classical theories, but what monetarists argued was that any increase in employment will be quickly erased as workers and companies anticipating inflation make claims for higher wages, which would not only add to inflation, but also lead to job cuts. Therefore, attempts by the state to boost the economy and reduce unemployment will only lead to increased unemployment and higher levels of inflation (stagflation) and be counterproductive.

The implications of this for social welfare is that, like classical economics, the role of the state is to be limited to the use of supply-side policies, as outlined earlier. The main role for the state is the control of inflation to attain stability. If Keynesianism, or at least a version of it, was the post-1945 orthodoxy, monetarism became the orthodoxy of the late 1970s and 1980s in the UK and the USA. However, purist monetarist policies were dropped and towards the end of the 1980s and arguably up until recent events there has been a return to a modern form of classical economic management. More recently, during the 2008 recession, the bailing out and in some instances nationalisation of banks and industry witnessed a selective return to some of the practices, if not the principles, associated with Keynesianism.

'Work' and 'welfare' as policy

Having set out three major economic theories (or economic imaginaries) we return to the theme of the chapter, that an understanding of economics is crucial to understanding the policies and practice of social welfare. 'Work' and supply-side approaches to labour markets have entered into the ascendancy within the academic and political discourse, becoming the cornerstone of New Labour policy (see Thompson, 1996; Peck, 2001; Zeitlin and Trubeck, 2003; Daguerre, 2007).

Within contemporary social policy, work, or more accurately, paid employment, is seen as the means by which economic, emotional and moral welfare is secured (Clarke, 2004b), the route out of poverty and the means to 'earn' citizenship (Lister, 2004). A wide range of social policies are now imbued with efforts to secure paid employment, including many of those more traditionally associated with 'social welfare' – for example, education, community development, social inclusion and even *Every Child Matters* (HM Treasury, 2003).

Jessop (1994, 1999, 2004) offers a substantial analysis of the shifts in UK policy throughout the 1990s, culminating in New Labour's policies during their first term (1997–2001). He argues that the policy adopted attempted to manage the supply side of labour to help ensure that the economy did not face what are described as the destabilising effects of (wage) inflation. The diagnoses of the problem included a combination of supply-side failings:

- successive failures to address welfare recipients/unemployed people becoming detached from labour markets;
- unemployed people having the wrong skills; and
- those not in paid work being unwilling to adapt to the demands/'realities' of the labour market.

This analysis of the problem links together what Bryson (2003) has described as economic, behavioural and institutional factors. Exponents have argued that the previously existing system of support was 'too passive', offering cash payments and expecting little in return. In response to this passivity, the government sought to devise a system that was more 'active', where benefit payments would become more conditional on undertaking activities geared to labour market (re-)entry. Prospective claimants would now be offered the clichéd refrain of 'a hand up, not a hand out'. Thus, behavioural outcomes (unemployed people lacking the motivation to seek work) were linked to institutional structures (the system failing to create the conditions for active engagement with the labour market). Consequently, welfare reform, through what is described as the development of a 'workfare' regime, is considered pivotal to successive governments' attempts to manage economic stability, that is, securing the aim of increasing the number of work-ready people 'actively' searching for paid employment.

Welfare incentives or coercion?

Attempts to 'make work pay' have played a pivotal role in contemporary attempts to provide individuals with incentives to enter paid employment. By providing 'incentives' to work, not only is a commitment to paid employment maintained, but, through in-work tax credit payments, the wage at which people should be willing to work is lowered (Grover and Stewart, 1999) and the number of people willing to work is increased. Policymakers have long struggled with the question of how to maintain financial incentives to work while ensuring that individuals and families are not living on unacceptably low incomes (even if the concern is not always born of altruistic motives). We can see this historically in the UK Reports of the Select Committee on the Poor Laws (1817) and the Royal Commission on the Poor Law (1834), which raised concerns that state-organised systems of poverty relief had the potential to provide a disincentive to work (Wilkinson, 2001). Providing tax credits for low-paid workers is to subsidise low-waged jobs and as such represents a shift away from Keynesian economics. Such 'workfare' regimes seek to achieve a lowering of wages through two mechanisms:

- Keeping wages down by increasing the supply of labour. This is done by providing employers with a greater pool of potential labour to choose from, that is, the more people available for work, the cheaper they should be to hire.
- Subsidising low-paid work through tax credits by maintaining a deflationary pressure on wages, a workfare regime encourages job growth by making wages at entry level as cheap as possible.

Grover (2006) suggests that by increasing the number of people competing for paid employment and directly subsidising wages, a workfare regime is able to restrain wage levels (see Chapter 5 for a historical example of the role social policies have played in achieving this downward pressure on wages). Although the introduction of the minimum wage under New Labour would appear to undermine this argument, the minimum wage can be seen as helping to achieve a fine balance between the aim of increasing the numbers of workers available for 'entry-level' employment and not allowing wages to fall too low, which in turn would undermine the sustainability of the 'tax credit' mechanism inherent in a workfare regime.

While any attempt to increase the incomes of those with few resources can appear laudable, one of the major criticisms of a subsidised workfare regime is that it has the potential to institutionalise low wages. Wages remain at a minimum level and, consequently, the limited number of higher-paid jobs makes 'moving on' all the more difficult. Most people, therefore, leaving out-of-work benefits face employment in low-paid, 'flexible' sectors of the economy where there are few long-term prospects for career or wage advancement. Given the reality that for many people 'entry-level employment' is the limit of their expectation, it is necessary to consider the sanctions that have been developed to help ensure that 'work pays'. It is also worth recalling from Chapter 6 that much of the work in social care and other allied welfare jobs, for example, teaching support staff and auxiliary nurses, is at this 'entry-level' wage – little more than the minimum wage at best (TUC, 2008).

Peck and Tickell (2002: 389) note that recent forms of social policymaking can be characterised as the 'aggressive re-regulation, disciplining and containment' of targeted populations. Deacon (1997, 2002) highlights that a moral authoritarian regime is based on the premise that if economic rationality is not enough to guarantee that people will enter or stay in paid work, then measures must be taken to provide 'encouragement'. Successive Conservative, Labour and coalition governments' welfare reform agendas have shared this strand of thinking, as Callinicos highlights in a critique of New Labour:

> Unemployment is in these circumstances a consequence of the dysfunctional behaviour of individuals who refuse to work, and this behaviour must in turn be caused either by their individual moral faults or by a more pervasive 'culture of poverty'. The kind of coercion implicit in the New Deal for the long-term unemployed, where government benefits are denied those refusing to take part, is therefore legitimate. (2001: 62)

The aim, therefore, of a workfare regime is to increase pressure on claimants to seek paid employment and, if required, to take part in 're-motivation' courses. Claimants, such as lone parents, disabled people and partners of unemployed people, are now required to attend work-focused interviews and can be sanctioned for non-attendance. Some proposals introduced by New Labour (for example, those concerning disabled people) have the potential to address exclusionary forces. Yet any 'support' mechanism that incorporates 'triggers' for sanctions and makes the receipt of benefits conditional establishes a principle and provides an infrastructure for even tougher sanctions-based approaches to be adopted (see DWP, 2010).

A benefit of 'work activation' within a workfare regime is that it has the potential to increase the size of the effective labour supply, since those who had previously been described as economically inactive (Grover, 2005; Grover and Piggott, 2005) are now expected to be at least preparing to be available for work. This type of welfare reform also helps to create and sustain an environment where welfare claimants are vilified by sections of the UK's media – in part both prompted by and taken advantage of by government ministers (Connor, 2007). They are seen as being 'socially less eligible' (Ginsburg, 1979; Jordan, 1998) than New Labour's preferred 'hard-working families' (Brown, 2000).

There is a need to advance the social rights of economically vulnerable and excluded individuals and groups and address the exclusionary forces faced by people with 'disabilities' (Thornton, 2005; Leonard Cheshire, 2008). However, this advancement has been reduced to a project of employability (Grover and

Piggott, 2005) and paid employment is the means by which economic, emotional and moral welfare is secured (Clarke, 2005). Returning to the case of Remploy, paid work in itself does not seem to be sufficient – a workplace that is subject to the 'discipline' of the market is also required. The benefits to the individuals entering the paid workplace are considered to be self-evident, yet the type of jobs offered to people with 'disabilities' are low-status, low-waged occupations with poor working conditions and few opportunities for advancement (Taylor, 2009). Keeping people in low-paid employment becomes part of a strategy to legitimate and enact a neo-liberal project of welfare reform, where attempts to reduce collective responses to risk are recast as opportunities for individuals to realise their life project (Jordan, 2004). Short-term contracts and the privatisation of welfare are recast as opportunities to exhibit freedom. This rhetoric of 'freedom' and 'choice' has played an important part in building up an acceptance or tolerance of a neo-liberal regime (Schram, 1995; Fairclough, 2000; Bourdieu and Wacquant, 2001; Clarke, 2005; Harvey, 2007). For those who are unwilling to exercise their 'freedom', rewards and sanctions are available to provide encouragement (Piggott and Grover, 2009; Schild, 2007). However, if the choices were really in people's (self-)interest, it raises the question of why any sanctions are deemed necessary to support them.

Conclusion

We began with the case study of Remploy and then moved into an explanation of frequently used economic terms, before examining the economic theories adopted, in one form or another, by post-war UK governments. We concluded with a focus upon specific aspects of policy after 1997 and examined aspects of workfare policies and the attendant incentives and sanctions necessary in 'disciplining' the workforce. The role of low-paid work is doubly significant for welfare professionals. First, many policies (for example, the Department of Health's *Valuing People* (2001), *Valuing People Now* (2009) and *Every Child Matters* (HM Treasury, 2003)) make explicit reference to employment, not to mention school-based curricula with an equally explicit emphasis upon skills and qualifications to ensure employment. Second, there is strong evidence (TUC, 2008) that the type of work being offered, and the attendant stress levels, increase the likelihood of both physical and mental ill health. Finally, many of the more menial tasks in the area of social welfare are carried out by this low-paid, flexible and often gendered workforce.

REFLECTIVE EXERCISE

- → To what extent do you reinforce the current trend towards work and a 'disciplined workforce', either in your personal or professional capacity? How far has this just become a 'taken-for-granted' part of a 'common-sense' approach?
- → Should the role of welfare be one that seeks to produce a certain type of 'worker' or should it be seen as a set of insurances provided by the state for individuals who need and have a right to draw upon it?

CHAPTER 8

Globalisation

Following on from economic theory, outlined in the previous chapter, we begin our exploration of globalisation with a discussion of global capital and how the pressures to maximise profit – from a whole range of economic activity – led to a global financial crisis, which was acknowledged in 2008. The impact of this upon social welfare is explored, and then we move on to consider other aspects of globalisation that impinge upon social welfare provision, notably migration and the development of the term 'the global is local'.

Globalisation as a theoretical construct, as opposed to the reality of the so-called credit crunch, is a contested concept, not so much in whether or not it actually exists, but more in terms of its form and political nature. Held et al (1999: 2) define globalisation as 'the widening, deepening and speeding up of worldwide interconnectedness in all aspects of contemporary life' and later write of globalisation in terms of its ability to 'transform social relations and transactions' (1999: 16). Deacon argues that, in general, within the social sciences the term is used to underscore the fact that 'social phenomena in one part of the world are more closely connected to social phenomena in other parts of the world' (2007: 8) – a definition that, at the very least, can be adopted by those on all sides of the debate! In relation to economic globalisation there are two main groupings.

Ohmae (1995) and Fukuyama (1992) see it as a positive development, both in relation to the expansion of markets, and also in relation to the development of a 'free' world, although recently Fukuyama (2006) has slightly revised his position. For these theorists and their supporters, the spread of global capital and the 'free economic market' cannot be separated from 'freedom' in general, following the essential elements of Hayek's philosophy. The credit crunch would be explained either by criminal activity (for example, the case of Bernie Madoff, who was sentenced to 150 years' imprisonment in June 2009 for a multi-billion dollar fraud over many years) or as part of capital's cyclical nature.

Others take issue with these so-called 'strong globalisation' theorists, arguing that globalisation is hardly a new phenomenon, as well as questioning the extent to which it supports 'freedom' (Hirst and Thompson, 1996). Callinicos (2003, 2005) argues that 'globalisation' is just a new term for capitalist development, and the nature of this has remained largely unchanged over the last 150 years, with capital continually seeking out new markets and cheaper labour to exploit. Both sets of theorists can find some common ground in the rise of technology, especially information and communications technology (Castells, 2001), which has most definitely changed the nature of the global economy (Yeates, 2008; Ritzer, 2010). It is to this topic and the credit crunch of 2008 that we now turn.

Case study: Global capital, the banks and the 'credit crunch'

'Government support for Britain's banks has reached a staggering £850bn and the eventual cost to taxpayers will not be known for years, the public spending watchdog says today.

The National Audit Office (NAO) revealed that £107m will be paid to City advisers called in to work on the rescue because the Treasury was too "stretched" to cope with the sudden financial crisis which broke in the autumn of last year.

The commitments include buying £76bn of shares in Royal Bank of Scotland and the Lloyds Banking Group; indemnifying the Bank of England against losses incurred in providing more than £200bn of liquidity support; guaranteeing up to £250bn of wholesale borrowing by banks to strengthen liquidity; providing £40bn of loans and other funding to Bradford & Bingley and the Financial Services Compensation Scheme; and insurance cover of over £280bn for bank assets.

In its report [National Audit Office, 2009], the NAO ruled that the "unprecedented" £850bn of support for the banks was 'justified' to head off the potential damage of one or more of them going bust, and preserving people's savings and confidence in the financial system.' (Grice, 2009)

To underline the connection with social welfare policy, *The Guardian* listed the public bodies with the highest amount of money in the Icelandic banks:

> **Kent County Council:** £50m (£15m with Glitnir Bank, £17m with Landsbanki and just over £18m in its UK subsidiary, Heritable)
>
> **Nottingham City Council:** £41.6m invested in Glitnir, Landsbanki and Heritable
>
> **Transport for London:** £40m deposit with Kaupthing Singer & Friedlander
>
> **Haringey London Borough Council:** £37m
>
> **Norfolk County Council:** £32.5m in three banks
>
> **Metropolitan Police Authority:** £30m. Its total budget is £3.5bn.
>
> **Dorset County Council:** £28.1m in temporary loans to Landsbanki and Heritable. (See http://www.guardian.co.uk/politics/2008/oct/10/localgovernment-iceland)

In May 2010, in response to the financial difficulties of this level of government support, which had all-party approval, the Coalition government announced £6.2bn of cuts in public expenditure, including the first round of cuts to local government finances (£1.164bn) as well as a number of schemes targeted at poorer children. These were the first of a series of cuts to public expenditure that the then new coalition government promised to deal with the budget deficit, much of which had been accrued through the decisions to 'bail out' the banks (see Chapter 7). This was undertaken against an uncertain global economic background, which had seen an earlier attempt to rescue the ailing economy of Greece with a £645bn 'rescue plan', and the euro currency subject to global speculation and a subsequent fall in the markets on 25 May.

The 'crisis' of 2008 is worth exploring briefly in the context of the globalisation of capital. The economic crisis of 2008 had been defined as 'a severe shortage of money or credit', with its origins being found in the relatively sharp increase in interest rates in the USA between 2004 and 2006 (from 1% to 5.35%). This in itself was not problematic, but default rates on sub-prime loans, that is, high risk loans to clients with poor or no credit histories, rose to record levels. The impact of these defaults was felt across the financial system as many of the mortgages had been packaged and sold on to other banks and investors. In other words, the banks had become major businesses, buying from and selling to each other in an attempt to create greater profits – failure in one part of the system led to a global crisis, which in turn led to the huge amount of government money being provided to effectively shore up the banks – businesses which were deemed too big to fail.

Marx argued that capitalism is driven to search for ever increasing gain. There are three ways to increase profit:

- expand the marketplace;
- increase the level of exploitation; and
- technological advances to make production cheaper.

As a result the raison d'être of capitalism is to expand across the globe, to improve technologically and to exploit workers to the maximum in order to increase profit. Yet capitalism will, periodically, reach a point where this is no longer possible and businesses cannot secure sufficient profit to cover their investments, thus the rate of profit falls. Unable to secure a profit, capital moves on, and, therefore, crisis can be seen as an inherent part of the capitalist system. When the rate of profit falls below a certain point, the result is a recession or depression in which certain sectors of the economy collapse. Each crisis does not herald the end of capitalism though. Although many will suffer as a result of these recurrent crises, for a number of businesses new opportunities are made available. This is because during such a crisis, the price of labour will also fall, which eventually makes possible the investment in new technologies and the growth of new sectors of the economy.

The predominance of a small number of large businesses means that their influence becomes entangled with a number of other businesses. If the large businesses go bust, the implications are felt far and wide, so they become 'too big to fail'. The market as a whole becomes disrupted, with previously profitable firms dragged into bankruptcy in what can soon turn into a 'cumulative collapse'. When this happens, businesses tend to turn to the state to 'bail them out', that is, protect them. More often than not, states are willing to oblige as they fear the fallout of the large businesses failing. A price may be some restrictions upon the 'freedom' of industries for this state aid. In relation to the banking crisis, the rhetoric of 'deregulation' has been replaced with that of the regulation in financial markets and institutions and this culminated in the outlining of new government policy in May 2010, which promised that 'legislation will reform the framework for financial services regulation to learn from the financial crisis' (BBC News, 2010).

Governmental fiscal policy has, therefore, been closely linked with supporting global capital, yet the global movement of capital has an equally significant impact upon welfare provision and the work social welfare professionals undertake, as reductions in public expenditure amply reveal. Yet for social welfare professionals it is also the impact of all aspects of global capital upon individuals and communities that they frequently have to deal with.

A long-standing feature of economic globalisation, for example, has been the relocation of businesses to a more profitable location. On the one hand, this has led to greater employment opportunities, notably in the developing industrial economies of India and China, where labour costs are significantly lower than in the developed welfare economies – for example, Europe. This is seen as an inevitable consequence of increased capital flows and investment (Deacon, 2007) and part of existing capitalist development (Callinicos, 2005), as outlined earlier in this discussion. Recent developments include 'outsourcing', the process by which aspects of a business are undertaken by another business at a more profitable rate, often exploiting workers in the developing nations (Manzoor, 2007). Typical examples in the UK involve the relocation of call centres. For example, in 2006 the closure of a substantial call centre in Perth (Scotland) led to the loss of 4,500 local jobs, at a saving of £50m to a company whose profits were recorded at £1.7bn (Ross and Brown, 2006). The theoretical debates, however, too easily conceal the human experiences that this generates. Rogers and Pilgrim (2009) suggest that in times of recession and increased poverty, there is a higher likelihood of those affected experiencing mental ill health. A campaigner against the closure of the Rover car manufacturing plant in Longbridge, Birmingham, commented:

> The area was devastated and still is. The workers were led to the slaughter. People have had their houses repossessed. There have been family break-ups, suicides and people have lost the inspiration to work. (Burgess, 2009)

Estimates of over 6,000 direct and 18,000 indirect job losses at the time of the closure proved accurate and the spatial effect on the local community was substantial (Chapain and Murie, 2008). Drawing upon their work, it is clear that the effects upon the locality manifested themselves in ways that placed an increased strain on localised social welfare services and professionals.

The race to the bottom and the impact on welfare policy

A feature of the global economy in relation to government expenditure has been what some commentators have termed 'the race to the bottom' (Mishra, 1999; Garrett and Mitchell, 2001). The argument is that states reduce their commitments to welfare expenditure to become more competitive and thereby retain (or secure) inward capital investment. The argument is extended to suggest that the market exercises a considerable level of international dominance, rendering nation states relatively powerless (Strange, 1996). In her wide-ranging literature review of the interplay between global capital and nation states, Mosley (2007: 111–16) identifies the continuing importance of the nation state and domestic institutions in mediating global pressures, often in highly resilient ways. She points to the different state variations in the organisation of 'capital' in the 'varieties of capitalism theses' and draws on evidence which suggests that domestic organisation still plays an important role as governments retain some 'room to move'. In his work, Esping-Andersen (1990, 1999) points out how the developed Western welfare economies organise differently, not just in response to global pressures, but, more tellingly, in the context of their own welfare histories and the politically achievable. Nonetheless, the thesis is important, since it reveals important aspects of some forms of fiscal policy advocated and, at times, adopted in the UK to reduce public expenditure to ensure investment and profitability. The importance here is often not so much in the policies themselves, but how sometimes these are promoted in a language that often resonates with welfare professionals' aims, yet where some of the outcomes are quite different (Simpson and Price, 2010).

Indeed, within the field of social work, early work by Dominelli and Hoogveldt (1996) argued that the advent of greater technological changes, alongside 'efficiencies', led to a reduction of relationship-based social work and the rise of the welfare technocrat. More recently, Dustin (2008) demonstrated that social work has been influenced by Taylorist employment practices and organised along assembly lines by utilising Ritzer's (1995) 'MacDonaldisation' thesis, which argues that a feature of globalisation is a particular form of work organisation that removes discretion and creativity with the aim of creating a completely uniform product. Her solution was that social work needed to rediscover the importance of relationships, a theme echoed later by Ferguson (2008) in his work, *Reclaiming Social Work*. The skill here for the welfare professional is to be able to move beyond the immediate and locate developments in their wider context, even being able to grasp the economic trends in order to understand how changes not just in funding, but also practice, can occur.

Global labour

A connected feature of the 'globalisation' debate is that of global labour and we will examine two aspects of it. The first is connected with the general movement of people or 'migration', and the second is related to the specific nature of the global movement of those seeking employment specifically within the social welfare sector.

General migration in the 21st century is frequently in response to crises caused by war and famine. In the final quarter of 2009, there were 4,765 applications for asylum to the UK (excluding dependants), which was a fall of 30% on the same period in 2008. Of the initial decisions, 77% were refusals. In the same quarter, 16,340 former asylum claimants or 'illegal migrants' were removed or voluntarily left the UK (Home Office, 2010). There is also a considerable amount of internal migration within the European Union, in accordance with its rules relating to the free movement of labour. Previous patterns of migration had located this within former colonies (for a thorough discussion of this within the UK context, see Gilroy, 1982; Sivanandan, 1982; Hall, 1992) or through the specific recruitment of guest workers, for example, Turkish *Gastarbieter* (guest workers) in post-war Germany (Castles and Kosack, 1980). Traditionally these patterns of migration were in response to a shortage of labour in the receiving country. It was (and in a different context still is) a source of potential and actual conflict, since migration creates competition for employment, notably among the lower paid, even though overall the receiving country obtains a net financial gain (Castles and Kosack 1980; Millar and Salt, 2006). It is interesting to note that global labour does not enjoy the same freedom of movement as global capital – indeed, quite the reverse appears to be the case.

Migration studies emphasise the so-called 'push/pull' factors in migration, that is, that within the country of origin there are factors that create the desire to leave (push) while the receiving countries have a need for labour (pull). After the Second World War, one of the first significant groups of migrant settlers to the UK (the so-called 'Windrush generation') were given clear incentives to move from the Caribbean to the UK to take up jobs, often in low-paid auxiliary welfare services (Gilroy, 1982). The demand for cheap labour led to inward migration. The subsequent existence of a clear community of people then becomes a later 'pull' factor as potential migrants seek out people of their own language and culture. 'Push' factors can include a poor local economy with few opportunities for either work or advancement, and, more recently, the effects of war and persecution (Zolberg et al, 1989).

Within the UK, inward migration has been a constant feature of policy, and different groups have been targeted for specific controls. Prior to the 1905 Aliens Act, there had been relatively free movement, though, as Sales (2007) notes, Jews and black people had been periodically expelled. Notably, there were substantial populations in the UK who had fled persecution and mass immigration from Ireland in the 1840s (Hickman and Walter, 1997). The 1905 Act sought primarily to control Jewish immigration and this remained in force for the next 40 years or so. A common feature of the language of immigration control is that migrants place undue demands upon welfare, take jobs from those already here and pose a threat to social stability – a theme emerging at the end of the 19th century and recurring ever since (Jones, 1977). Tensions were heightened in times of economic recession, when the potential conflicts in terms of jobs and other resources intensified (Holmes, 1988).

Although there was the much-celebrated arrival of the *Empire Windrush* in 1948, following the 1948 Nationality Act, which gave rights of entry to all citizens of the Empire and colonies, and which in the early 1950s was encouraged (Paul, 1997), the language of social unrest and the need to control numbers were never far beneath the surface, culminating in the 1962 Commonwealth Immigrants Act, which removed the theoretical equality between all 'British' citizens. Subsequent Acts in 1971, 1981 and 1988 not only made immigration more difficult, but also made deportation easier (Sales, 2007: 140–4). From the 1990s the focus shifted to asylum seekers and this has remained the core plank of policy ever since, with immigration made even more difficult through the policy of 'fortress Europe'.

At the same time as there was legislation to make immigration more difficult there was attendant legislation to outlaw discrimination, through a range of Race Relations Acts – beginning in the 1970s and more latterly including 'incitement to religious hatred' in 2007. A constant feature has been the dual language of control and 'integration' with what Sales (2007: 159) describes as a bipartisan approach, which has led to clear agreements in principle, if not detail, between the two main political parties.

Immigration controls, though, have led to increasing numbers of 'illegal migrants' both in the UK and Europe. People trafficking and smuggling has become a global trade, with high financial rewards for the traffickers and often a life of fear and exploitation for those trafficked. The deaths of 23 Chinese cockle-pickers in Morecambe Bay in 2004 proved a graphic example of the trade (Wingfield-Hayes, 2006) not to mention the exploitation of women and children in the 'sex industry', a feature across most of Europe including the UK (HumanTrafficking.org, 2010). Controls do not necessarily result in actual restrictions on numbers, but rather their consequences may lie in greater levels of human exploitation and potential misery.

The recruitment of social welfare professionals: the ethics of a global response

While there is a considerable literature devoted to all aspects of general migration and immigration policy, there is relatively less focus upon the specific aspect of the recruitment of social welfare professionals and auxiliary staff from overseas, either in the UK or wider EU/global context. One of the early areas to engage in the practice of overseas recruitment was that of nursing. While overseas recruitment has always been a feature of the National Health Service the percentage of internationally recruited nurses of all new admissions to the register of nurses remained fairly constant at around 10% until it doubled in 1996/97, reaching a figure of almost 55% in 2002 (Royal College of Nursing, 2002). While this provided a short-term (and in truth longer-term) fix to the shortage of nurses in the UK, it also led to accusations that the UK, like other developed economies, was taking vital health care professionals away from the greater needs of developing nations. As a result, in 2004 the Department of Health issued a code of practice for the recruitment of health care professionals (DH, 2004). There were seven core principles. Two of these clearly indicated the level of competence required to practise in the UK (principles four and five), while principles six and seven provided a framework to ensure that their employment and professional development rights were safeguarded. Of greater interest for this discussion are the first three principles of global recruitment.

The first principle argues that there is nothing new in international recruitment and that there is a 'long history of developing the knowledge and skills of healthcare staff coming to the UK at some time in their careers' with the rider that 'good practice and *value for money* should underpin all international recruitment activities' (DH, 2004: 7, emphasis added). The individual is, then, the subject of the guidance, which identifies not only the benefit to the individual nurse, but also to the country of origin – assuming the nurse returns – and that 'international healthcare professionals can bring a new and valuable dimension that enables the transfer of experience and the sharing of ideas' (DH, 2004: 7). Thus, the process is mutually beneficial. It is only the third core principle that addresses the 'ethics' of international recruitment. The overarching aim was to ensure that developing countries are not drained of resources unless there is 'an explicit country to country agreement' (DH, 2004: 7). The key principles are as follows:

- Skilled and experienced healthcare professionals are a valuable resource to any country. Active international recruitment must be undertaken in a way that seeks to prevent a drain on valuable human resources from developing countries.
- The Department of Health and the Department for International Development have identified developing countries that should not be targeted for international recruitment under any circumstances. This list can be accessed at the DH website (www.dh.gov.uk).
- Individual healthcare professionals from developing countries, who volunteer themselves by individual, personal application, may be considered for employment (DH, 2004: 7–8).

Good practice is then itemised (DH, 2004: 9–13) and there follows a section devoted to the clarification of the policy through 'frequently asked questions'. Willets and Martineau (2004), while acknowledging the full dissemination of the principles, questioned the extent to which they were being rigorously applied. Buchan and Seccombe (2006) identified that the Phillippines, Nigeria and South Africa were the countries most commonly recruited from and highlighted that the reasons for seeking employment in the UK were mainly personal (a desire to travel) and professional (career development), and the focus of their concern was that internationally recruited nurses were not discriminated against. Batata (2005) pointed out that pay structures (for example, low London weightings) and a range of other economic factors were to a significant degree important factors in failing to secure UK-trained nurses: thus, the 'crisis' was not primarily one of recruitment, but rather retention, with the added finding that pay rates for overseas recruits were lower than those for UK nurses. Aminuzammam, in a study of Bangladeshi health care professionals, noted that:

> Recently, however, an increasing number of expatriates have returned to their countries of origin, bringing with them the knowledge, information, networks, and capital they acquired abroad. It is argued that this 'brain-gain', if properly managed by supranational laws, may work to correct the losses produced by brain drain. (2007: 4–5)

Crucially it is the ageing populations in the high-income welfare economies that provide the greatest 'pull' factors, and although the UK has the ethical recruitment statement for the NHS, its implementation is patchy in that it does not apply to private hospitals and recruitment agencies. Aminuzammam (2007) argued that an important factor for the sending economy (in this case Bangladesh) was the level of remittances, that is, the money sent home by nurses working overseas. Representing a significant contribution to GDP, this unofficial flow of remittances helped 'resolve' foreign exchange constraints and improved the balance of payments (Quibria, 1988). In this context, international recruitment is not a straightforward matter, yet it does reflect global inequalities, wrought by global capitalism, in a country where the dominant industry is textiles and where the average wage of a textile worker was around $16 a month until a general strike in 2007 brought about an increase to $25 a month (£17.50) (Manzoor, 2007).

Social work has also sought to deal with its failure to retain staff through overseas recruitment, yet to date has not developed an 'ethical' policy. Berry (2004) argued that overseas recruitment was to be nothing more than a short-term measure, but by 2009 the UK was increasingly dependent upon overseas social workers and no recruitment policy as such was in place, yet the General Social Care Council (2008) produced a guide to overseas qualifications. In his analysis, Simpson (2009) points to the globalisation of knowledge as a key factor in the unwitting training of overseas social workers (and arguably, by extension, other welfare professionals). However important the existence of concordats may be (Wellbourne et al, 2007), the major factors lie in the globalisation of knowledge and the desire of people to utilise that to their greatest advantage (Simpson, 2009). The exact numbers of overseas social workers are not readily available, since the General Social Care Council records the numbers of those who have had their qualification approved, rather than those who are actually working. For the year 2008/09, 7,512 social workers had 'registered', with the highest number from the European Economic Area plus Switzerland (1681), but over 4,200 from countries where English is the first language. Within Europe the highest number came from Germany (*Community Care*, 2009a). Despite these levels of recruitment, vacancy rates remain high with an average of over 10%, rising to 18% in London and the West Midlands (*Community Care*, 2009b).

A final area in relation to the global movement of welfare professionals (or, to be more precise, auxiliary staff) is the recent trend within the UK and other Western economies to recruit unqualified staff from overseas. There are many agencies engaged in the recruitment of social care staff who are more likely to be recruited from low-waged economies in contrast to social workers. In 2006, 16% of the care assistant workforce and 19% of childminders and related occupations were recruited from overseas (Experian, 2007). The same report found that many care establishments were looking to Eastern European recruits to fill vacancies. Current salaries in the sector begin at the minimum wage (£5.93 an hour as of October 2010). Thus, low-paid wages are being offered to overseas workers in a repeat of the migration experiences of the 1950s – they remain a source of cheap labour to undertake vital, yet unappealing, jobs.

The global is local?

The interconnectedness of a globalised society is now beyond doubt, whatever perspective is adopted (Callinicos, 2005). Within much of the social welfare literature this has resulted in the coining of the phrase 'the global is local'. For example, the effects of the sub-prime mortgage crisis in the US were a key factor in the collapse of the banking system world-wide; the fast food chain MacDonald's is on every high street; and, for welfare professionals, the difficulties faced by diverse communities and asylum seekers are a feature of their daily work. The diversity of the service-user group, especially in large urban conurbations, is evidence indeed of the globalised world. Many of the new and existing migrant groups are among the poorest sections of the UK's population (Palmer et al, 2005) and they are far more likely to feature in social work caseloads (Chand, 2000). Migration and globalisation have created new forms of 'community'. Delanty (2003) identified eight forms of communities, one of which was 'cultural communities', a reference to multicultural societies whose 'dominant' (i.e. receiving) cultures, through migration, are also transformed. Another linked form is the cosmopolitan/global community, which differs from cultural communities in that it is explicitly linked to transnational communities and diasporas – for example Jewish groups, Irish groups and Muslim groups are typical examples in the UK. Local and national questions intersect, as global matters are played out on a local stage. The shrinking global world is readily exemplified by the experience of the family that is spread across three continents (India, Europe and North America) who all meet up each Sunday through the internet facility of 'skype'. The extent of global influence is exemplified in the West Midlands city that has an electoral ward where over 85 languages are spoken. In social welfare, it is reflected in the work undertaken by therapists in England with children who have experienced war and family death in other continents and have arrived here as asylum seekers (Kohli, 2006). There are countless other examples, all of which for welfare professionals present global issues through the lens of their day-to-day work in their own locality (Lyons et al, 2006).

Significantly, welfare professionals have a long history of developing a practice that meets the needs of people from other cultures, religions and language groups. Welfare professionals have sought to constantly reflect upon and reappraise their practice, whether this be in the form of Victorian Roman Catholic philanthropy aimed at the Irish migrants in Glasgow and Liverpool (Moore, 1988); more recent developments in the area of multicultural social work (Cheetham, 1982), anti-racist social work (Husband, 1986) or various different developments within anti-oppressive social work from its origins in the 1990s (Dominelli, 2002) to its more recent and sophisticated exposition (O'Laird, 2008); or the recent developments within health care and diversity (DH, 2009).

Conclusion

We began with a discussion about global capital and moved from this to explore some aspects of migration, featuring specifically the recruitment of welfare professionals from overseas and the ethical questions this may raise, to demonstrate the importance of understanding the global factors on welfare policy. These range from the impact upon fiscal policy and changes in methods of working, some of which are related to New Public Management, discussed in Chapter 6, to a brief reminder that for many welfare professionals the reality of globalisation is reflected in the communities in which they operate. Yet, as we suggested in our study of global capital and immigration policy, these matters are not subject to any inevitable outcome, but are shaped by the nature of the political choices made. It is to that question that we now turn.

REFLECTIVE EXERCISE

➔ These exercises are fairly obvious, but take time to think about how enmeshed you are in the global world: how interconnected you are with people who live overseas – this may be family members, or social networking 'friends'.

➔ How does your workplace or university/college class reflect 'globalisation' as we have discussed it here?

➔ Think about how people who migrate are seen as 'the other' and how this is reflected in your daily work/study settings.

CHAPTER 9

Political choices

Through reviewing many of the themes of earlier chapters, we argue that it is in the arena of political choice that welfare policies are actually created and sustained. The invitation is for social welfare professionals to develop their understanding of how and why particular policies and wider social and political orthodoxies are established and sustained. In this chapter we focus on questions regarding how wealth is created and how the negative social, political and economic consequences of wealth have been relatively neglected in social welfare – in sharp contrast to the degree of attention and energy that has been devoted to the problem of poverty. We attempt to redress this imbalance, and argue that poverty and wealth need to be seen as *political* issues.

Case study: *The Secret Millionaire*

Part of the 'big society' agenda is to foster a new culture of voluntarism, social action and philanthropy. The reality television show *The Secret Millionaire*, first broadcast in the UK in 2006, could be used as an exemplar for such an approach. In each episode a millionaire temporarily leaves behind their millionaire lifestyle, and takes on a secret identity to live in some of the UK's most deprived areas. For a week to 10 days the secret millionaires are living on a limited budget as they work and volunteer alongside members of the local community. Their task is to identify individuals and projects that they think deserve to benefit from a share of their own wealth. Unsuspecting members of the community are told the cameras are there to film a documentary. Each programme climaxes with the secret millionaires revealing their true identity and providing those who have been found deserving with cash donations to improve their lives and the lives of others.

Philanthropy has always been a feature of capitalism and proponents of the 'big society' are keen to highlight a long and generous history of philanthropy. Particularly notable is the life and work of Andrew Carnegie, a Scottish industrialist from humble beginnings, who managed to accumulate a personal fortune estimated at £225,000,000. He asserted that it was the duty of rich men to give away their wealth and, by the time of his death, Carnegie had given away huge sums of money, in the process establishing trust funds, academic and research institutes and building over 3,000 public libraries (380 in Britain). Yet, Carnegie was not without his critics. The Reverend Hugh Price Hughes, a preacher of the Methodist 'social Gospel', argued that Carnegie, or any other wealthy individual, should not be applauded for giving away money that was not theirs. Hughes explained that millionaires' fortunes were the 'unnatural product of artificial social regulations' and that 'they have no beneficent raison d'être ... millionaires at one end of the scale involve paupers at the other end, and even so excellent a man as Mr Carnegie is too dear at that price' (Hughes, 1891: 3). Hughes was referring to a society that denied workers trades union rights, yet imposed high protective tariffs to maintain prices, creating the conditions for individuals to accumulate vast fortunes at others' expense. An observation and criticism that still holds sway for contemporary philanthropists.

What is the problem?

Any attempt to identify what constitutes the 'common good' is contested, as is any attempt to establish how 'social problems' can be remedied. Implicit in such a 'subjectivist' outlook (Best, 2008) is what Bacchi (1999) describes as a 'What's the problem?' approach to policy analysis. The way that a problem is defined determines the proposed solutions (i.e. policies). Any definition carries a number of assumptions, not just assumptions about the topic concerned, but about the wider workings of society and questions of 'agency', which have been themes in this book. Furthermore, the chosen definitions betray a political and ideological element. What is considered a problem is, therefore, in large part a political act. By making poverty rather than wealth the social problem, the 'unnatural regulations' that create such a state of affairs are set to continue uninterrupted. In contrast, imagine a situation where:

> the habits, problems, secrets and unconscious motivations of the wealthy and powerful were daily scrutinized by a thousand systematic researchers, were hourly pried into, analyzed and cross-referenced, tabulated and published in a hundred inexpensive mass circulation journals. (Nicolaus, 1968, quoted in Wolfe, 1978: 209)

By asking the question of how wealth is created and discussing the consequences of these means and ends, not only do the political choices that inform such a project become clear, but sites for action become available that not only help resolve many of the contradictions of contemporary social welfare, but provide a potential means of transforming social relations. To this end, and following the sentiment expressed by Mary Wollstonecraft, it is argued that, 'It is justice, not charity that is wanting in the world' (2004 [1792]: 57).

Why are the rich getting richer?

We have responded to variations on the question of why the rich are getting richer throughout this book, but in this section we focus on the accumulation of wealth. Lansley (2008) compared the highest levels of wealth recorded in Britain in each decade from the 1850s to the 1970s and then compared these with the top five in the 2008 *Sunday Times Rich List*. This demonstrated that the wealth being acquired at the top in contemporary society is in excess of their immediate predecessors, and is beginning to exceed some of the great fortunes of the 19th century. These levels of wealth and associated disparities have not remained constant. The rich enjoyed rising fortunes from the second half of the 19th century, losing ground sharply from the 1930s and bouncing back in recent years. These changes in the fortunes of the wealthy correspond to the changes in the role of the state and specific policies. Over the course of British history, very different approaches to the accumulation of wealth can be identified. Each of these periods reflects not only different social, economic and technological circumstances, but different political choices, where the state has adopted different strategies and responses to questions of wealth and distribution (Daunton, 2007). In the late 19th century, monopolies could operate largely unchecked, the tax authorities were in their infancy, unions were few and regulations minimal. It was a society in the process of transition and the constraints on fortune-making were much weaker. The fact that the wealthy of today can enjoy shares of the national wealth that can surpass the richest Victorian and Edwardian industrialists and financiers is telling. Even in today's democracy and 'regulated' economy, the top few thousand individuals are able to win large shares of the country's economic wealth. How is this explained?

Choose your parents well

Much of the wealth of many rich people is due to inheritance and other forms of unearned income. Rowlingson and Connor (2011) outline how work undertaken by Atkinson (1971), Menchik (1979) and Wilhelm (1996) supports the argument that inheritance and a cycle of privilege are major sources of inequality. This is best expressed through the conclusion that the best way to become rich was not so much through individual effort and hard work, but to choose your parents wisely (Johnson and Reed, 1996). So while inherited wealth provides material advantages, at the other end of the economic scale, children born into low-income families have not only reduced 'life chances', but poorer outcomes as adults (Hobcraft, 1998; CASE and HM Treasury, 1999; Cabinet Office, 2009). Thus, 'brute luck' plays a major role in determining socio-economic life chances. Fiscal policies have traditionally been the mechanism through which the unearned, socially created aspects of wealth are redistributed. Inheritance tax would seem an obvious mechanism for reducing unearned wealth, but in October 2007, the Labour government reduced rather than increased inheritance tax – benefiting the top 5% of wealth-holders (Prabhakar et al, 2008) in a political reaction to the Conservative Party's proposals to raise the threshold to £1 million.

Taxation policies

Taxation is one of a number of sources of money available to government to finance expenditure. There are a number of reasons for collecting taxes – to finance the provision of government goods and services (public and merit goods);

to discourage the consumption of demerit goods (e.g. duties on tobacco and alcohol); to regulate the economy; and to provide 'fiscal welfare' and alter the distribution of income.

In addition to what may be construed as the political, social and economic issues of the day, there are a number of principles of taxation that are meant to be employed in order to maintain consent. These can be used to help decide if a tax is 'good' or effective:

- Certainty – a tax must be easy for taxpayers to understand and difficult to evade.
- Convenience – a tax must be easy for taxpayers to pay (e.g. Pay As You Earn [PAYE] income tax).
- Economy – a tax must be cheap to collect and should not act as a disincentive to effort by those being taxed or provide an incentive for those to avoid paying taxes.

Most notable for the purposes of this discussion are issues regarding the use of taxation policy to enable individuals to accumulate wealth and the impact this has on the fairness of the tax regime that has been put in place. Figures released by the Office for National Statistics (ONS) in 2006 showed that the burden of taxation was greatest upon the bottom 10%, and that this was primarily a result of indirect taxation. There are a number of different forms of taxation. These specific taxes can be classified in a number of ways.

A 'direct tax' is where the burden of the tax cannot be passed on by the taxpayer (e.g. income tax). Direct taxes are collected by the Inland Revenue. An indirect tax is a tax where some or all of the burden of the tax can be passed on by the taxpayer – for example, Value Added Tax (VAT) and excise duties are taxes on producers, but they pass on the burden to consumers by increasing the prices of their products. Indirect taxes are collected by the Customs and Excise Department. All taxes will be either direct or indirect. However, of more interest in this chapter is whether a tax is considered to be progressive or regressive.

Income tax is described as a progressive tax. A progressive tax is where the proportion paid in tax increases as the taxpayer's income rises. Income tax is an example of a progressive tax, as the rate increases as a person earns more. Rates of income tax in the UK have changed over the years. In 1974 the top rate of income tax (83%) applied to incomes over £20,000. There was also a 15% surcharge on 'unearned' income (investments and dividends), which could result in a 98% marginal rate of personal income tax for the wealthiest individuals (it is estimated that 750,000 people were liable to pay the top rate of income tax in 1974). Changes in the rate of income tax have been significant since the 1980s. There have been reductions in the rate of income tax (progressive taxation). In the first budget after the Conservative election victory in 1979, the top rate of income tax was reduced from 83% to 60% and then cut again in the 1988 budget to 40%. Similar cuts were seen in the basic rate where over time it has been cut from 33% to 30% in the 1980 budget, to 29% in 1986, 27% in 1987 and to 25% in 1988. In 2010, a new 50% tax rate for top earners was introduced. The new rate is levied on taxable incomes greater than £150,000 a year (falling on approximately 300,000 of the highest earners, out of the 29 million people who pay income tax in the UK). At the same time, those who earn more than £100,000 a year (approximately 600,000 individuals) will have their personal tax allowance eroded. However, these measures pale against those taken in the 1970s and, notably, a study by Grant Thornton concluded that Britain's 54 billionaires, with assets of £126bn between them, paid only £14m a year in income tax (quoted in Irvin, 2008: 13).

Tax can also be paid on a number of transactions. You may have to pay tax when you buy or sell things or give them away, for example, Capital Gains Tax (CGT) if you sell or give away assets, Stamp Duty when you buy property or shares, and Inheritance Tax on your estate when you die, including on some gifts made up to seven years beforehand. Combined changes in CGT (1998, 2000 and 2002) effectively increased the number of high-rate taxpayers allowed to pay as little as a 10% rate of tax on profits from the sale of assets. The introduction of taper relief reduced CGT liability for some basic-rate taxpayers to 5%. Ostensibly this was to encourage entrepreneurs; effectively, it meant that a number of wealthy individuals could make fortunes from buying and selling companies and only pay 10% on their profits. Notably, in 2007, Nicholas Ferguson, the head of SVG Capital, a British-based private equity and investment management firm, said that it was unfair that partners in private equity firms should pay less tax than their cleaners.

When you buy goods and services, there are various taxes you may have to pay. These include VAT, Fuel Duty, Excise Duty on alcohol and tobacco, and General Betting Duty. Taxes like VAT and the duties on fuel, alcohol, tobacco and betting are charged at flat rates and are added to the price you pay for the goods or services. This form of tax is described as regressive. A regressive tax is where the proportion of a taxpayer's income taken in tax falls as the taxpayer's income rises. In other words it is a tax that hits less well-off people harder than the better-off. An example of a regressive tax is the television licence. It is exactly the same amount for everyone, which makes it a much smaller proportion of a large income than a small one. Over the last 40 years, increased use has been made of indirect taxation (regressive taxation). The Conservative government replaced purchase tax with VAT in 1973, at a rate of 10% charged on a range of goods bought from a business. In the early 1980s the Conservatives scrapped what was described as a 'luxury rate' and created a new higher standard rate of 15%, raised to 17.5% in 1991 and 20% in 2011.

When combined, these changes in taxation policy and the shift in emphasis from progressive to regressive forms of taxation can in part explain some of the differences in incomes and wealth over the corresponding period. In short, an emphasis on regressive forms of taxation has meant that people with the lowest incomes pay a higher proportion of their incomes in taxes than those with the highest incomes.

Deregulation

During the 1980s, a policy of liberalisation was extended across the globe. This took a number of forms. State regulations on capital and trade were relaxed, and subsequently international capital mobility has grown as capital controls were reduced or eliminated virtually everywhere (see Chapter 8). Known as 'neo-liberalism', this approach contained policies and practices characterised by a range of measures that include:

> the deregulation of state control over the major industries, assaults on organized labour [sic], the reduction of corporate taxes, the shrinking and/or privatization of public services, the dismantling of welfare programs, the enhancement of international capital mobility, the intensification of interlocality and the criminalization of the urban poor. (Brenner and Theodore, 2002: 2–3)

Brenner and Theodore note that in the development of neo-liberal policies there have been moments of destruction coupled with moments of 'creation'. So, in relation to wages, assaults on trades unions and the spread of generalised economic insecurity was 'destructive', but then developed into the 'creation' of new forms of labour 'flexibility'. Many of these 'moments' related to wider forms of competition and international deregulation through trade liberalisation, that is, the removal of protectionist barriers to free trade. For welfare professionals, the most significant moments have been the so-called 'rolling back of the state', where Keynesian forms of demand management were abandoned in favour of monetarist programmes (see Chapter 8).

Specifically in relation to welfare, a number of measures have resulted from these direct political choices, many of which have been covered in greater depth in earlier chapters. Traditional mechanisms of welfare service provision have been abandoned, being replaced with supply-side programmes and the resurgence of 'civil society'. There has been a tendency to decentralise control, devolving welfare functions to lower levels of government, the 'social economy' and the family (again, strengthening the mechanisms of civil society); a further example has been the creation of public–private partnerships and 'networked' governance, which has effectively dismantled traditional forms of democratic control. For example, one of the first policy announcements of the Conservative–Liberal Democrat coalition in 2010 was that high-performing schools could apply for (and, by implication, receive) 'academy status' (Academies Act 2010). This meant that the head-teacher would have direct control over all funding. Aside from the obvious observation that this would privilege the better schools over 'failing schools', it would also privilege the middle classes by extension, as the better schools generally speaking reflect the surrounding socio-economic location (Evans, 2006). There have been a range of fiscal measures aimed at seeking 'value for money' and ensuring accountability, which have actually resulted in the creation of new 'authoritarian' state apparatuses and 'quangos' that have reduced the opportunities for public accountability and popular democratic control. These are well documented within the NHS, as exemplified by attempts to *Liberate the NHS* (DH, 2010).

Apparent devolved measures have been accompanied by increasing measures of national regulation and control. In education, the introduction of a national curriculum in 1988 by the Conservatives, which has been strengthened through greater regulation from 1997 under New Labour, established which subjects should be taught; the knowledge, skills and understanding that would be required; the targets for standards and attainment; and how children's progress should be assessed and reported.

While measures were put in place for regulating the welfare economy, elsewhere deregulation continued apace. In 1986, a number of changes were permitted by the government that radically changed the way the London Stock Exchange operated. 'Brokers' (investors) could now be employed directly by investment banks to provide a number of functions that had previously been kept distinct in order to prevent a conflict of interests. Pay levels increased significantly as the new firms sought to attract what were considered the best staff in what was now an extremely competitive environment. Twenty years after the deregulation of the London Stock Exchange in 1986, the value of traded shares had increased from £161bn to £2,496bn, an increase of 1,500%. For the same period, assets in the banking sector increased seven times to £5,500bn and the annual turnover of the equities market in the UK increased from £161bn in 1986 to £2.5 trillion in 2005.

Gabaiz and Landier (2006) noted a sixfold increase in Chief Executive Officers' pay between 1980 and 2003. In the UK a CEO was paid 25 times more than the average worker. Comparable figures show that in France the ratio was 15:1; in Sweden, 13:1; in Germany, 11:1; and in Japan, 10:1 (Ramsay, 2005). In the UK, as an incentive to improve company performance, many senior executives were offered share options in addition to their salaries. In the short term, however, one of the best ways to improve the value of shares is to 'downsize' the company, creating the impression to the stock market that the company is operating more efficiently and raising the share price. Workers may lose their jobs, but directors were able to receive huge bonuses (Lansley, 2006). Following the credit crunch, a Treasury Select Committee report (2009a) blamed bonuses for encouraging short-term risk-taking and for putting quick profits above more long-term goals. The Governor of the Bank of England, Mervyn King, argued that City bonuses were 'a form of compensation that rewarded gamblers if they won the gamble but there was no loss if you lost it' (*The Guardian*, 2009). The Treasury Select Committee (2009b: 3) agreed with him in their conclusion that: 'bonus-driven remuneration structures encouraged reckless and excessive risk-taking and that the design of bonus schemes was not aligned with the interests of shareholders and the long-term sustainability of the banks'.

De-unionisation

In sharp contrast to the ability of those at the top end of the economic scale to establish their own pay and conditions, the liberalisation of the economy has had dire consequences for the majority, and the ability of workers to protect their own interest in particular. At the other end of the economic scale, de-unionisation is also an important factor in explaining how wealth has been able to accumulate for a minority. Chapter 6 explored the role of the trades union movement, but in the 1980s and 1990s it faced several challenges, including high levels of unemployment, the continuing contraction of a number of traditionally unionised industries, the privatisation of most nationalised industries and the increasing use of private contractors in many public services. Notably, for the purposes of this chapter, a series of laws were enacted that, cumulatively combined, greatly restricted the degree and scope of trades union activity.

Case study: The anti-trades union legislation – a brief summary

The 1980 Employment Act abolished trades union recognition rights and restricted picket line numbers to only six and the 1982 Employment Act redefined what was to be understood by a 'trade dispute'. Political strikes were made illegal and action could only be taken against their immediate employer in relation to specific issues. The Act also allowed for employers to take out injunctions against unions and sue unions for damages – with the ultimate sanction being sequestration of the union's entire funds.

The 1984 Trade Union Act made it illegal to strike without a secret ballot, with further regulation as to how ballots were to be conducted. Subsequent to the Miners' Strike (1984–85), the 1986 Public Order Act introduced new criminal offences in relation to picketing. The 1988 Employment Act introduced the use of postal ballots for union executive elections or decisions on political funds, replacing workplace or branch meetings.

The 1990 Employment Act made secondary actions illegal and trades unions were held financially responsible for walkouts and unofficial action unless they publicly disowned a dispute. Employers could now dismiss key union members involved in unofficial action. Finally, the 1993 Trade Union Reform and Employment Rights Act allowed individuals to seek an injunction against any unlawful action. While not a comprehensive account of all the anti-union measures, this gives a clear indication of the ferocity of the attacks.

Successive Labour governments since 1997 did little to reverse these legislative changes with the exception of the 1999 Employment Relations Act, which offered the opportunity for increased union recognition. The Conservative–Liberal Democrat coalition is, if anything, likely to further tighten the legislation. Combined, this series of legislation has changed not only trades unions, but also relations across the social and economic landscape. With unions weakened, employers faced relatively little resistance to attempts to relocate or outsource production (see Chapter 8). As a consequence of 'the race to the bottom', national governments have competed for investment by promising to reduce the costs and, thereby, living standards and security of potential employees, something that seriously undermines trades union attempts to campaign for improved wages and working conditions (Bronfenbrenner, 1997, 2000).

Taken together, a policy of 'light-touch regulation' with regard to the wealthy and the increasingly stringent regulation of workers (and social security) have helped provide the conditions by which a huge and sustained source of revenue for those working in capital markets can be found. This model has proved to be attractive to successive governments as the wealth accumulated in these few hands became indicative and appeared to vindicate the liberalisation and deregulation of capital. Any challenge to this orthodoxy has been met with the claim that by providing greater incentives for people at the top, the wealth created would then 'trickle down' to those at the bottom. From this position it is argued that capital is best left in the hands of rich people, rather than the government (or spread more widely), as it is these individuals who would be more likely to save, invest and create wealth for the benefit of the population as a whole. This was an argument that was deployed in support of the Gladstonian Fiscal Constitution in the 19th century and resurfaced in the Reaganomics and Thatcherism of the 1980s.

However, the evidence on the changing distribution of income and wealth suggests that there has been a 'trickle-up' rather than a trickle-down in recent decades (Hills et al, 2009). Lansley (2006) and Irvin (2008) argue that many of those at the top have not created new wealth, but have merely grabbed existing wealth from others. The privatisations from the 1980s onwards transferred wealth from the state/nation as a whole to particular individuals within the country. The deregulation of markets and easier access to credit enabled 'corporate raiders' to acquire a company and then asset-strip it, which is far more profitable than investing in a new company. With reference to complex financial 'products' such as derivatives, Lansley (2006: 61) quotes one City worker who admitted, 'when I first went into the City, I could not believe that anyone would want to pay me so much for creating nothing'. A final example given by Lansley (2006) of wealth transfer rather than creation was the decision by many companies in the 1990s to take pension contribution holidays, which increased their short-term profits and pushed up their share prices to the advantage of the top executives and shareholders, but ultimately led to crisis for many final salary schemes – including many local authorities!

Inevitability or choice?

All of the above, most of which has occurred in the last 30 years, has been presented as an inevitable, necessary and even fair economic orthodoxy. Our position throughout has been that this is not so. It is that more could be done to counter the unearned wealth resulting from a growing and highly lucrative tax avoidance industry (Lansley, 2006), especially when the lengths of governmental campaigns targeted at 'benefit scroungers' are considered.

If the goal of society is wealth creation and universal welfare, then it might be more effective to raise taxes on higher earners and invest the resulting revenue in health, education, training, research and other areas. Counter-intuitively, such investment might actually increase productivity more than higher wages at the top. Studies are not conclusive, but there is evidence that countries with higher levels of inequality actually have lower levels of productivity (Corry and Glyn, 1994).

There is clearly a role for fiscal policy in reversing the trend towards a regressive tax regime. A comparison of high-tax Nordic countries and low-tax Anglo-American countries on 50 social and economic measures found that high-tax Nordic countries score better in 42 categories (Brooks and Hwong, 2006). In the UK, as far as income tax goes, the growing pressure on public finances led the government in March 2009 to introduce a new rate of 50% for earnings over £150,000. This has, however, already been heavily criticised as it could drive talent from the city, discourage entrepreneurs and result in less revenue through greater tax avoidance (Bowler, 2009). Tax avoidance is not illegal and it is the subject of many 'financial planning seminars'. However, its effects upon social solidarity and developing a fair society are never discussed. Equally, movement to other countries, often raised as a likely outcome, is not borne out by the evidence and, were the logic sound, an influx from Sweden and France (countries with high marginal rates of taxation) should be taking place. Isles (2003), however, found that 86% of FTSE 250 CEOs came from the UK and that most businesses did not recruit from overseas. Even the claim that premier league footballers will attempt to avoid the new tax rate and consider a move to a league with a more favourable tax regime (*The Sunday Times*, 2009) does not seem to have dampened the reception of the higher tax rate by the public, with 57% of those questioned supporting the 50% tax on income for those earning over £150,000 (Populus, 2009).

A policy pledge from the Conservative–Liberal Democrat coalition is that no local authority CEO can earn more than 20 times the salary of the lowest paid. If applied to the university sector this would have an immediate impact given that the average salaries of Vice Chancellors in Russell Group universities was over £308,000 a year (using the Cameron formula this would either raise the salaries of the lowest paid university staff by almost £2,500 a year, or result in a loss to Vice Chancellors of an average of £40,000 a year). The idea could have been more widely applied. Voluntary ratios limiting earnings differentials are already in operation in Japan and some European companies (Lansley, 2006). The government could be even bolder and propose a maximum wage (Ramsay, 2005). The advantage of having some kind of maximum wage or required ratio for earnings would be that original income would be set in a fair way rather than relying on tax to redistribute from rich to poor. Glyn (2006) argues that as he principle has been widely accepted in terms of the *minimum* wage it is difficult to reject a similar principle of a *maximum* wage.

Conclusion

The purpose of this chapter has been to highlight some of the political choices that have helped lead to wealth being accumulated by a small minority. These have allowed us to revisit some of the earlier themes in the book, which all coalesce to create a particular welfare landscape. The first indications from the Coalition government in 2010 were that cuts in a range of welfare services were inevitable. Little was said about raising taxation on the very richest. There appears to be very little evidence that policies that seek to 'create' more wealth for the few lead to an increased share of that wealth being made available to the majority. And yet, despite the economic convulsions witnessed across the globe, the notion that the presence of the 'super-rich' is good for Britain proves to be a resilient element of a broad political consensus (Lansley, 2008). However, we argue that the current set of 'unnatural products of artificial social regulations' for creating wealth are also dependent upon and help sustain poverty and inequalities. The virtues of flexible labour, extolled by successive governments, are in truth a low-wage and 'casualised' labour market in which the means by which pay and conditions can be protected have been cut to the bone. It is notable that the establishment of these 'artificial social regulations' is the outcome of specific political choices, or as a well-known critic of capitalism famously wrote: 'The executive of the modern state is but a committee for organising the affairs of the bourgeoisie' (Marx and Engels, 2003 [1848]: 3).

REFLECTIVE EXERCISE

- This is not really an exercise, but more a combination of 'action' and 'reflection'. Whatever your current sources of information on news and current affairs may be, try changing them for a fortnight. This works best when thinking about newspapers, as these tend to have more explicit editorial viewpoints. In addition to noting any differences they may have on reporting on a particular issue, also consider what issues received the greatest prominence and what narratives are used to frame and respond to these issues.

Part Four
Why study social policy?

CHAPTER 10

Engaging in policy-oriented practice

We begin this chapter with a discussion of the theoretical framework of agency and structure, highlighting the importance of the dialectic and the contradictions social welfare professionals face. We then move on to consider more explicitly what has been termed 'policy practice' and use this to demonstrate the practice legitimacy of such a project. We aim to promote what we call policy-oriented practice. We use case material to explore where the opportunities for such practice show themselves and offer insights into how professionals can develop this skill.

Not a case study: An analogy

> '"You know", he said, "sometimes it feels like this. There I am standing by the shore of a swiftly flowing river and I hear a cry of a drowning man. So I jump into the river, put my arms around him, pull him to shore and apply artificial respiration. Just when he begins to breathe, there is another cry for help. So back in the river again, reaching, pulling, applying, breathing and then another yell. I am so busy jumping in, pulling them to shore, applying artificial respiration, that I have no time to see who the hell is upstream pushing them in."' (Zola, 1972: 488)

Zola's well-known 'river analogy' reflects a common experience for those engaged in social welfare work: the actual work of dealing with the symptoms frequently means that the cause is obscured. So far, we have argued that the current social welfare landscape is the result of choices rather than an inevitable, natural or 'rational' outcome, and have sought to identify a number of analytical tools and skills for understanding aspects of social policy. It should by now be clear that alternatives have been and still are available, yet, in the words of one social worker of a few years' experience:

> 'It is just relentless. No sooner have you dealt with one case, there is another, and another and another. There is no time to stop and think. It is easy to say that we should work for change ... we all want that, but it's just impossible, isn't it ...?'

We will now devote the remainder of this book to an attempt to answer that question, by offering a combination of theoretical paradigms and possible practice actions.

Agency: a hope and an obstacle?

We have introduced the concept of agency in the first section, noting how service-user agency has had a significant impact upon practice, and have also explored aspects of collective agency, for example, through the trades union movement. Yet within the theoretical debates around agency, there is a dichotomy that is clear to many people engaged in social welfare. Those who engage in practice do so on an individual level – not just *as individuals*, but also *with individuals*, yet many of the causes of the difficulties they deal with are, as we have argued here, located within social *structures*. A polarised debate can result: on the one hand, individual forms of agency are criticised by exponents of a structural position (Corrigan and Leonard, 1978), since it is premised upon individual accountability; on the other, those who promote 'agency' frequently point to the deterministic nature of structural accounts as a denial and neglect of the potential for 'agents' to not only make choices, but also shape their circumstances. Lavin (2005) attempts to reconcile this by arguing that the individual will of liberalism and the abstract forces of structuralism are mutually constitutive, beginning with the concept that the 'agent' has to understand their position within wider social relations (Connor, 2011). This, we suggest, is of central importance for social welfare professionals – to avoid separating 'policy' and 'practice'.

Taylor-Gooby (2008) argues that the orthodox conception of agency in social policy embodies the idea that 'actions, activities, decisions and behaviours', represent a 'meaningful choice' (Deacon and Mann, 1999: 413). The main characteristics of agency are that the action is intentional and directed to a specific objective and that beliefs or desires can act as motives and explanations for action (Callinicos, 2004).

In social policy, one important paradigm was developed by Le Grand (1997) who argued that people acted out of public spiritedness (knights), self-interest (knaves) or were passive (pawns). Murray (1984) had earlier argued that agency could be appealed to by incentives and rewards, and more latterly others have suggested it should be encouraged through duty and obligation (Dwyer, 2000, 2004; Etzioni, 2000). When considering these types of agency, Callinicos (2004) argued that they represent a 'methodological individualism' in that they attempt to explain *social* phenomena through the motives and actions of *individuals*.

There has long been scepticism of, if not outright hostility to, the discussion of agency in the context of welfare (Ryan, 1976; Donnison, 1979; Townsend, 1979). 'Agency' in this tradition detracts from an analysis both of how the structures that create and sustain enduring social inequalities operate and how they can be transformed. Within the social welfare professions, many of the ethical exhortations are located within philosophical systems premised, at the onset at least, on the actions of individuals (Elster, 1989), and as such it has always been a feature of professional practice. Yet structure has always been present and runs through many codes of conduct and ethics alongside individual agency. With reference to social justice, the International Federation of Social Workers' (IFSW's) ethical principles include:

> Challenging unjust policies and practices – Social workers have a duty to bring to the attention of their employers, policy makers, politicians

> and the general public situations where resources are inadequate or where distribution of resources, policies and practices are oppressive, unfair or harmful. (IFSW, 2001: section 4.2.4)

Thus, the action may be 'individual', but the location is most definitely 'structural'.

Structure: the grounds for action?

A range of theories and approaches can be described as representing a structural approach to understanding society – indeed, many of the tools for understanding that we have introduced focus upon 'structure'. When used in relation to the idea of agency, the term structure suggests some form of enduring material relationship between individuals and communities (Musolf, 2003). In this respect, structures refer to supra-individual phenomena that need to be considered when examining the operation of society as a whole and attempting to explain the behaviour of individuals. Discussions of structure tend to be infused with connotations (Blau, 1975), most notably, that of determinism (Crothers, 1996: preface). People's (or actors') positions within wider social relations are emphasised, and used to explain people's attributes, attitudes and behaviour. As such this becomes an ill-defined device, but one taken as explaining, if not even determining, a complex social reality (Sewell, 1992: 2).

An example can be found in the work of Althusser (1969, 1971), where individuals are the supports of systems that 'reproduce themselves' – the important factors are the structures; the actual people are largely irrelevant. History is made by the social relations of production, political struggle and ideology, so people can be 'reduced' to their position in the social structure – for example, the relationship of the labourer and the capitalist as defined by their different relations to the means of production within a capitalist mode of production. Structures become the 'determining mechanisms' and make redundant the consideration of an orthodox conception of agency. For Althusser, individuals exist, but they should not provide the starting point for an analysis of society.

Welfare professionals, however, are often caught in this 'trap' between structure and agency. They know that structure is important in that it impacts upon people's lives and the resources made available to improve them – simply put, welfare professionals know only too well that structure has a large impact upon, for example, life expectancy. If you live in a poor area your life expectancy can be 20 years less than if you live in one of the wealthiest areas of the country (ONS, 2010b). By the same token, welfare professionals also know that 'agency' is important. The choices people make, however flawed and constrained by circumstances, are 'real' choices. We also saw in Chapter 1 that the place to begin is where the 'client is' (Mayer and Timms, 1970).

Beyond a simple dichotomy

A number of writers, most notably Bourdieu (1990), Giddens (1984) and Latour (2005), have moved beyond the dichotomy of structure and agency. The theories of agency these writers propose are considerably different, but they share an attempt to recognise the 'situated nature' of people's practice and give sufficient account to both structure and agency (Parker, 2000). For the welfare professional, such an approach reflects daily realities of practice. Elias (1978) was critical of accounts where people are conceived in the singular and where a rigid barrier is created between the person 'inside' and the world 'outside'. Elias noted how this person is always thought of as an 'adult', already fully equipped with the skills necessary for living, and he further suggested that in part this is because often sociology uses concepts that are not fully 'appropriate to the investigation of specifically social functional nexuses [relationships]' (Elias, 1978: 111). He argued that concepts and practices are needed that are better attuned to the study of networks of interdependent human beings. Elias criticised what he described as a 'process reduction' where there is a recurrent tendency to make 'senseless conceptual distinctions' between the individual and society' (1978: 113).

Elias argued that people are bonded together in a continuum of changes in time and space: each of us stands on the shoulders of others. People and their understanding of a situation and the goals that they pursue from their understanding are shaped over time and space within social structures. The consequences of people's actions are not felt at random, but according to the figuration in which they are enmeshed. The knowledge of the networks within which people live is virtually always imperfect and incomplete, but this in itself does not deny that intentionality and a degree of power and control can be exhibited by individuals. In this way, Elias attempts to reframe our understanding of power and subjectivity. Yet, by neglecting the existence and operation of social structures, whatever form these may take, the conditions of life continue, by and large, to be shaped by the powerful so that the adoption of situated practices can quickly descend to a subtle form of victim-blaming – something that social welfare professionals understand from their work experiences.

The dialectic

The basic elements in this dialectical system are opposing ideas, called thesis and antithesis. The struggle between the thesis and antithesis, driven by a contradiction, inevitably leads to a resolution *or* synthesis of both. However, this is not the end of the process, because the synthesis will have its own contradictions, which then leads to the establishment of a new thesis, which will then stand in an antagonistic relationship to a new antithesis, and the process of historical development continues.

The dialectic is not intended to complicate reality; rather, it is intended as a means to understand a world that is often presented as fragmented and chaotic.

There is a distinction drawn between the surface appearance of things and their underlying reality. So, we are only able to understand events and phenomena in the context of the web of relationships that bind them together into a single interconnected whole. This totality is not harmonious: 'Contradiction is at the root of all movement and life, and it is only insofar as it contains a contradiction that anything moves and has impulse and activity' (Hegel, 1969: 67). A major insight of the dialectic is that conflict and struggle are not a secondary aspect or by-product of reality that can be resolved either through policies or calls for harmony and partnership, but constitute the very nature of social reality.

The dialectic for Hegel was concerned with ideas. Marx took the concept and argued that it could also be applied to the material nature of society. In relation to agency, Marx was critical of the theoretical and political implications of a liberal form of individualism: 'It leads every man to see in other men, not the realization, but rather the limitation of his own liberty' (Marx, 1963 [1843]: 25). However, Marx was equally sceptical of what can be described as 'structural' accounts, where attributing power to structures can be considered a form of superstition.

Marx argues that we need to penetrate beneath the abstract categories of political economy and social life generally, to the human reality underlying them; and then in turn to exhibit the meaning of these categories in terms of *human* activity. Marx conveys first of all how structural forces provide the very possibilities of agency (Lavin, 2005: 442–3). In short, everyone is both the product of conditions and has the potential to change those conditions. Marx locates his theory firmly in an analysis of capitalism. Most people have to sell their labour to acquire the means to exist, something that is seen as the natural state of affairs. Yet, this labour is controlled and exploited by another, resulting in the experience of alienation – it is only through action that people who sell their labour can become 'free'. Marx argues that to achieve this we must:

> recognise that material conditions condition us. However much we seek to change those conditions, they provide us with our origins … no individual can choose the class or historical period in which they are born. It is these conditions, the social relations that we come to inhabit, that both constrain and provide the opportunities available to an individual … transformation … is not possible without the community (Marx and Engels, 2004 [1845]: 83).

For Marx, agency – or action – is ultimately only possible in 'community', that is, 'agency' is an act of individual and collective will. He further suggests that there is a desire to 'conceal' the reality of such social relations in stories of heroism and achievement, and also in determining what is 'feckless' behaviour. Thus, this is a form of agency that recognises that the social order (eg liberal capitalism) not only produces subjects with desires and abilities to act, but also the resources (ie ideology) through which we experience and interpret events – the dialectical force (or, more simply, the paradox) is that we are also constrained by those same orders (Lavin, 2005).

Service-user movements are an example of 'collective agency', which have, at times, been constrained by existing social relationships, but, at other times, arguably when they can be more readily recast to suit specific ends, they have used resources inherent within 'structure' to achieve their aims. As Callinicos (2004) suggests, agents (people) are both potentially constrained and enabled by the social relations they find themselves in. This is because structures are recast as relational and capable of conferring power on and between agents (Archer, 1995). In essence what we are emphasising is that a distinction between agency and structure, while understandable, is in a sense a 'false dichotomy' (Connor, 2009). They are separate entities, but, and this is crucial, *agency* cannot be understood outside of *structure*, in the same way that *structures* cannot be understood without reference to a notion of *agency*.

When these ideas are applied to social welfare, we would argue that collective forms of social agency – more simply put, social welfare professionals working collectively and not just individually – offer the best opportunity to impact upon welfare policies and bring about some transformational change. This demands identifying aspects of contradiction in existing structures and using them as a background to action. Thus the question is not whether one exhibits agency, but at what level and to what end. Social welfare needs to ensure that the opportunities available to its agents (here we mean service users and welfare professionals), at a regional, national and global level, are not *limited* to the potential role they can play in attempts to secure the participation of the population in 'delegated' governance structures – for example, in the duty and capacity of communities to play a vital role in 'civil society', so vital to a neo-liberal project. It is people's social existence that determines people's consciousness. This is not to suggest that there is no room for 'agency' or that behaviour is determined. Although the origins and ability to control social forces may appear outside the control of any one individual, far from being forever above and beyond our control, the circumstances in which we find ourselves are the product of human labour and current social relationships.

A challenge for those in social welfare is to engage with these structures and take the opportunities available to develop alternative social relations and forms of organisation. We need an understanding of agency that includes the capacity of individuals to redefine the parameters of their actions (Connor, 2010).

Social welfare professionals: towards a policy-oriented practice

Building from the theoretical discussion, we want to move forward into how social welfare professionals can begin to use their agency in relation to welfare policy. First, we will set out a background as to why using agency in this way has a long-standing legitimacy within social welfare *practice*. Earlier chapters have shown that from the early days of what was philanthropic provision, there has always been an attendant action to bring about changes to policy and the basis upon which society is formed ('structure'). These actions were at one and the same time both the outcomes of societal structures and relationships and yet the aim was to change these – so, drawing on our theoretical discussion, 'agency' is located within the very 'structure' it seeks to transform. Price and Simpson (2007) argued that social work in particular, but here we would extend this to social welfare work in general, has been characterised by a series of internal tensions and contradictions that shape not only people's professional working lives, but also the lives and experiences of those who use services. As such, social welfare professionals are in a contradictory position. Consider this statement from a social worker:

> Throughout my career I was always encouraged to develop a strong sense of ethics and values, to be as certain as I could be that service users were not 'oppressed' and that they were 'empowered'. Now, I have to complete plans for people to leave hospitals, when this is not always possible; on occasions when I have been away from the workplace service users have been moved against their wishes, by managers who are 'promoting' the virtues of choice and personalisation.

Or this statement from a young school teacher:

> It is against everything I was taught and actually believe in, but we teach to the test. I don't want to do this, but getting a GCSE pass in this subject can be so important for these kids' futures, I suppose you have to really … it's just not what I came into teaching to do, really.

In short, what the social worker and teacher are describing are situations where the language of their practice is shaped to fit with their inherent values, whereas the outcomes of those actions are not. A contradictory position that leaves them feeling potentially alienated from aspects of their practice and professional ethics.

Loney (1983) used the term 'in and against the state' to sum up this dialectical position and, even allowing for the relative demise of the state over the last 20 years, it still remains the main financier – if not provider – of welfare (Le Grand, 2007). Some 100 years earlier, a radical 19th-century churchman, engaged in social welfare work, stated that the Church should no longer be willing to 'be merely an ambulance to gather up the casualties of our social system, without being equally anxious to lessen the cause of those casualties' (Lidgett, quoted in Heaseman, 1962: 66). This statement accurately prefigures Zola's analogy, which we cited earlier.

Within the field of nursing, Hardingham also pointed to the need for a structural appraisal for action:

> the great problems of health care are structural and not the result of poor reasoning, the solutions cannot be created by increasing education, holding ethics seminars, or (alas) writing books. (2004: 130)

Yet, as she had already noted, the nature of the organisation and even perhaps the weight of professional ethics, as a contributory factor, had resulted in a degree of self-blame in that the nurse knew what they should have done, but felt responsible for not getting it done. Radical social workers of the 1970s recognised their dialectical position and posited a programme of radical action, which was premised upon social work's structural position as the 'handmaiden of the bourgeoisie' (Corrigan and Leonard, 1978). Within the anti-oppressive practice (AOP) of the 1990s, there was an initial acknowledgement at least of the need for structural change, although much of the anti-oppressive agenda became reduced to a series of professional competences, whose radical 'edge' was lost in a reduction to personal 'agency', often articulated through some aspects of 'reflective practice' (Fook, 2002). Webb (1991) had anticipated this dilution of action, and argued that AOP would be the means by which the laissez-faire agenda would be perfected. Nevertheless, the exhortation within AOP to engage in a practice that is 'anti-oppressive' remains, as does the exhortation for nurses to promote the 'health and wellbeing of those in your care … and the wider community' (NMC, 2008) – perhaps not a 'radical' statement, but one that, when analysed, cannot merely stop at the individual, and, therefore, encourages the professional to see health care as part of wider structures.

While the nursing codes of practice may be rather diluted in relation to acknowledging that people act within structures, the IFSW code for social work and social care is clear about what it considers the duties of a social worker to be in relation to social justice; in challenging negative discrimination and recognising diversity; distributing resources equitably; challenging unjust policies and practices; and working in solidarity with those who are excluded from society to move towards an inclusive society (IFSW, 2001). Tellingly the code begins by acknowledging that social workers face 'conflicting interests' and that 'resources in society are limited' – in other words the social welfare professional is beset by competing demands and interests. In short they work in the contradictions of society. Having set out a range of, arguably, 'traditional' justifications for engaging in a practice that is not merely individual-oriented, we now turn to a development that seeks explicitly to engage with policy as a paradigm for practice.

Craig (2002) argued that a commitment to social justice should be at the heart of social welfare work, as demonstrated by a commitment to a progressive approach to social welfare through state involvement directed at reducing social problems and promoting a redistributive policy agenda. Weiss-Gal and Gal (2007: 4) argued that social justice is generally perceived to include, among other things, a vision of a society in which all people have access to social resources, basic social goods and equal social rights and in which unacceptable inequalities in income, wealth and opportunities are reduced. Within the UK context, a most notable contribution is the 'New Manifesto of Social Work' (Jones et al, 2004), which began by arguing that people entered social welfare work as an 'ethical profession', but it is one in which there is a 'widening gap between promise and reality that breeds … anger and frustration' (Jones et al, 2004: 3).

We would suggest that frustration is widespread among many social welfare professional groups, and that this should be channelled into action. This is no easy matter, since the weight of organisations that bears down upon individuals may be demoralising, but it also serves to focus energy upon organisational function, rather than any wider social objective. Furthermore, the nature of training on qualifying programmes frequently emphasises competences in practice that are built around predetermined 'practice standards', which at best pay lip service to the question of active engagement with policy. An example is the social work national occupational standards, which contain over 21 professional competences that in the main are directed at the traditional area of 'individual' practice. Dustin (2008) saw this as an attempt to 'MacDonaldise' social work, following Ritzer (1996) and his MacDonaldisation thesis. Earlier, Harris (2003: 3) had written about 'scripted conversations' with contemporary social workers being devoid of meaning, and then developed a trenchant critique of modern social work in England, demonstrating how it had been shaped into the values and language of a business, while Price and Simpson (2007) argued that without a clear understanding of structure, social work would be reduced to yet another consumer-oriented service industry. What has been created, however, despite these critiques, is a certain type of professional hegemony, that is, a set of dominant ideas, which privileges a certain type of 'agency' and also a certain type of social work. Yet, there remains the imperative to demonstrate 'social work values', an example of the dialectic in relation to 'appearance' and 'reality'.

The question then remains: how do social workers move towards what Jones et al (2004) and more recently Ferguson (2008) have termed a new 'engaged' practice? Arguably a starting point is to acknowledge the nature of social policy and how this shapes the lives of all those who are engaged in it (as deliverers and recipients of services), and to that end, we argue, the previous chapters should have provided a range of tools for understanding policy and exploring the nature of policy in contemporary society – indeed, we would argue, in any past, present or future welfare configurations. Yet, however useful this is as a way of understanding, we want to argue that this has to be manifested in some form of action, and for this to have an impact, it needs to move beyond the individual and be located in a wider movement of people working towards a similar goal: in short the form of agency that recognises structure and works within it collectively. Jansson argued that welfare professionals should engage in what he termed 'policy practice', defined as: 'efforts to change policies in legislative, agency and community settings whether by establishing new policies, improving existing ones or defeating the policy initiatives of other people' (2003: 10).

It allows professionals to broaden the scope of their 'practice' by legitimately incorporating an engagement with policy at different levels of policy development.

It is also a strategy that promotes resistance to policy change as a legitimate response. This is an important point to grasp, since part of the current hegemony is that professionals need to respond 'flexibly' to change and to understand that this is part of the 'uncertain' world in which we live. In relation to staff in higher education, Taylor (1999: 157) set out a paradigm for academics to 'self-manage' change. What is interesting is that the language is a mixture of business, seeing change as 'opportunities', and psychological – that change brings about loss, and that the emotional attachment to things that are threatened by change needs to be 'grieved' so that people can 'move on'. This should be channelled into 'doubt', which will allow for the changing practices to be improved. Despite advocating collective responses with colleagues, this is directed not at resisting change, but rather at managing the process. Thus, the very mechanisms of change are appropriated by an individualistic, pseudo-psychological agenda that supports the neo-liberal notion of agency and denies 'structure'. Resistance may, in the end, prove to be of limited value – though this is not necessarily so – but this, like any other form of action, should be part of a 'collective agency' that confronts 'structure'.

Reviewing the debates

This chapter has sought to review and contribute to debates that have attempted to construct agency. We have set out some traditional models of 'agency' and 'structure' before developing the position of Elias. We then explored the question of the dialectic as providing what have been termed 'situated' accounts of agency that could be seen as representing a midpoint between two polarised positions, and which could be an attractive proposition to those working within social welfare. These accounts, and importantly the Marxian dialectic, recognise that people (notably in collaboration with each other) are capable of making history, that is, changing the nature of society, or, perhaps more explicitly for this book, that people can change policies. The importance of the dialectic, or what Callinicos (2004: 2) terms analytical dualism, is that it maintains the interconnectedness of structure *and* agency.

We then moved forward to explore the extent to which utilising such a concept of agency is legitimate for social welfare professionals. We argued that this has always been a feature of practice, but to a large extent has been sidelined through a focus upon narrower professional competences as welfare work increasingly takes on the form and language of business. Drawing upon experiences of welfare professionals in different sectors, we argued that there is a growing frustration and feeling that things are 'not right' and that against this background engaging in policy practice has legitimacy.

Anderson (1980) suggested that the field for action was more important than debate, so we now move forward into the final chapters exploring the scope for action in more detail. We do add a note of caution in that, following the UK general election of 2010, there will be a move towards what Cameron describes as the 'big society', or, as we argued, the reinvention of civil society. Schild (2007) argued that attempts to recognise the agency of citizens can all too easily be appropriated and emptied of their progressive intent, and the need for a constant critical and dialectic engagement with policy is vital to avoid what Deacon and Mann (1999) argued could be a descent into a moral and punitive individualism. A further warning is that hegemonic structures are quite likely to appropriate progressive language and ideas (Scull, 1979) into forms of welfare that reduce agency to a decontextualised language of consumer choice and empowerment (Clarke, 2004a; Simpson and Price, 2010).

Conclusion

We suggest that social welfare professionals could be entering a crucial era of welfare change, and the dominance of a neo-liberal agenda. In this context, it is important to acknowledge that structures, in whatever form they take, are not to be seen as some 'nebulous force', but as ongoing material processes that can not only be resisted, but overturned. People collectively construct the structures of the world and that world is alterable through and by human agency. History abounds with examples of people opposing those with more power and resources, and despite this managing to succeed and change the social structures that affect their lives (Musolf, 2003). As we enter the concluding part of the book it is worth recalling an earlier comment when discussing 'virtue' in social welfare practice, that to work for change and to strive for a new form of engaged practice does not only rely upon having all the analytical tools ready, but will also take 'courage' (Ferguson, 2008: 137).

REFLECTIVE EXERCISES

- ➔ The chapter is concerned with providing a range of material focusing upon developing a policy-oriented practice. Consider your own field of work or training: how can you become more 'engaged'? If you already consider yourself to be engaged, how can you encourage others?

CHAPTER 11

Using skills to understand the policy stereotypes

In this chapter we aim to consolidate two main areas of the text. First, we want to establish the skills we have already introduced to the readers by examining the way that policy is often premised upon a set of stereotypes and myths. Second, we invite those engaged in social welfare to consider – again through the use of case vignettes – how they can become 'engaged' and help bring about policy changes. This will re-enter the realm of dilemmas and we will locate this within the dialectical process of social welfare work, returning to a radical formulation of being 'in and against' the state, setting the scene for our final chapter. Essentially, we argue that those involved in social welfare need to become more attuned to the use of language and imagery in the framing of policy and practice and to engage in activities to counter this.

Welfare queens

A recurrent theme in this book has been what Bacchi (1999) describes as a 'What's the problem?' approach to policy analysis, that is, rather than start from the assumption that social policies reflect an inevitable response to pre-existing givens, attention is paid to how a 'problem' is fabricated and how a particular response to a 'problem' is legitimated. The role of language and imagery in enabling, constraining, including and excluding a range of policy actors becomes a focus of analysis and understanding in its own right, and it is possible, therefore, to identify particular discourses and place these in the context of a hegemonic struggle over the 'meaning' and practice of welfare (van Dijk, 1993, 1998; Marston, 2000, 2004; Caldas-Coulthard and van Leeuwen, 2003; Fairclough, 2003; Jessop, 2004). All forms of authority attempt to propagate a belief in their legitimacy (Weber, 1964). This can in part explain the way that governments and institutions are increasingly employing a range of discursive strategies and practices in an attempt to legitimise and realise particular policy projects (Franklin, 2004). It is important to acknowledge that the development and implementation of policy are now 'communicative events', where policymakers dedicate significant resources to communicating policy meanings to various 'audiences' or 'readers' (Marston, 2004; Yanow, 1996). At a time when it has been alleged that the role of the state with respect to welfare is being diminished, governments are working hard to ensure that they are seen as the administrative and value centre of society (Chandler, 2007). A particularly illustrative example of this can be seen in the propagation of the notion of the 'welfare queen'.

In 1976, Ronald Reagan, when seeking the Republican Party's nomination for the US presidency, included within one of his speeches, a story of a woman in Chicago who was alleged to have secured $150,000 through welfare fraud. The story of the woman who was considered to have treated herself 'royally' at the expense of the taxpayers was to become a shorthand for a new menace to society – the welfare queen.

The reality did not match the rhetoric though. A woman who was widely regarded to be the inspiration for Reagan's cautionary tale had been charged with welfare fraud by an Illinois investigation. However, far from, as Reagan had claimed, securing $150,000 through the use of 80 aliases, 30 addresses, 12 false Social Security cards and the collection of veterans' benefits on four non-existing deceased husbands, the actual charge consisted of the woman in question using four aliases to receive $8,000.

Clearly, there was a kernel of truth in Reagan's story, but the dubious basis and exaggerated nature of Reagan's claims did not stop 'welfare queens' becoming a prominent issue throughout Reagan's presidential campaign, tenure and beyond. Reagan's tale is significant and relevant to this chapter for three reasons.

First, alongside Margaret Thatcher and the Conservative Party in the UK, Ronald Reagan and the Republican Party were seen as overseeing the ascendancy of neo-liberalism; a political and economic orthodoxy that still holds sway today. As noted in Chapter 8, neo-liberalism is a political and moral project, rather than just an economic imaginary. Neo-liberalism seeks to remake and regulate society through the discipline of the market and the fabrication of an 'empowered' and active citizenry (Gill, 1995; Brenner and Theodore, 2002; Harvey, 2007; Leitner, Peck, and Sheppard, 2007; Schild, 2007). Paid work is made *the* route out of poverty and the means by which citizenship is earned and bestowed. Characterised by efforts to promote permanent innovation and flexibility in relatively open economies, the 'work first' and workfare regimes envisaged by exponents of a neo-liberal project attempt to reconstitute a population that is flexible, adaptable, entrepreneurial and self-reliant (Jessop, 1999). Through a combination of legislative and institutional mechanisms, the role of a neo-liberal social policy, or what Daly (2003) describes as 'societal policy', is to empower an idealised 'citizen-consumer' to act responsibly, that is, independent of the state (Bryson, 2003; Lister, 2004; Clarke, 2005; Newman and Vidler, 2006; Daguerre, 2007). Thus, alongside concepts of choice, there is an apparatus of social control extending into the areas in which social welfare professionals work. It is argued that the imagery of the 'welfare queen', if not the specific label, has played a part in helping to legitimate such a project, and in part explains why such an imagery has extended well beyond the shores of the USA.

Second, part of this neo-liberal ascendancy is what Schram (1995) has described as a rewriting of social welfare history. Rather than the welfare system being seen as part of the solution to the problem of poverty, in a neo-liberal narrative, it is seen as the cause of the newly defined problem of welfare dependency. It is here that the story of welfare queens is significant. The welfare queen became the latest and arguably most successful version of attempts to label those in receipt of benefits as dependent and manipulating the system. In the US the racial connotations of the term are clearly evident (Gilens, 1999). In the UK, to date at least, the racial aspects of the term are more implicit, but still telling, as the behaviour and imagery associated with the 'welfare queen' has found residence with the wider discourse of scroungers, 'bogus' asylum seekers, teenage mums and the underclass as a whole (Welshman, 2006). What they all share is that they are not only seen as a symptom, but as a cause, of the nation's decline (Boris, 2007: 603).

Third, the tale of welfare queens illustrates the importance of the symbolic aspects of welfare. The lack of substance behind the allegations against welfare queens and the other cast of characters that have come to inform the discussion of welfare does not inhibit the influence such tales can have on the public's understandings of social welfare and the development of social policy. Edelman (1988) notes that compared with the difficulties of communicating accurate and realistic accounts of society, it is much easier to conjure up imagined threats, heroes and issues. It is argued that social welfare professionals have an important role to play in not only identifying and challenging the circulation of such imagined threats, but also in developing alternative narratives and networks for communicating an understanding of social welfare. Part of this would need to include attempts to unsettle the taken-for-granted suppositions and meanings of policy to identify particular threads to be followed that may present possibilities for reconstructing social action. The following case study presents a particularly challenging example of how stereotypes are used to make sense of events.

Case study: The disappearance of Shannon Matthews and the press

In February 2008, the story of a community galvanised into action by the news that a local girl had gone missing began to emerge. Stories of local firms and stores contributing to the costs of printing, councillors commandeering photocopiers in a dozen community centres and taxis being put on standby in order to give volunteers free lifts to the latest leaflet drop were cited as examples of a community coming together, and one story reported a poignant candlelit vigil:

> 'Children carried a banner showing the youngster's face and a hotline to ring with information.... The march ended with the crowd shouting in unison: "Shannon, we want you home".' (Taylor, 2008: 4)

Within weeks, as suspicion started to grow with regard to the role of Michael Donovan and Karen Matthews in the kidnap and false imprisonment of Karen's daughter Shannon, accounts of a community's spirit and resilience were quickly revised. Reports of the news of Shannon Matthew's discovery, apparently unharmed, described how the 'Estate' raised toasts with 'beer and cheap wine', and 'youths' strutted and swigged from bottles (Norfolk, 2008a: 9). While acknowledging the efforts that had been made in the search for Shannon Matthews, the focus was now 'the rubbish-strewn gardens, the smashed windows, the discarded broken toys' (Norfolk, 2008a: 9). Attention all shifted to the 'Complex family tree [that] held up police' (Gardham and Stokes, 2008: 5), as it was suggested that efforts to unravel and make sense of the 'myriad of family members' and relationships that made up the extended network of Shannon Matthews' family was one of the main reasons why police had taken as long as they had to find her. Norfolk (2008b: 13) noted that during the investigation 'a grim picture of dysfunction emerged. As a portrait of 21st-century life on one of Britain's most deprived council estates, it made even hardened detectives despair'. Set in contrast to 'middle-class parents who could speak articulately of their grief', once the arrests of Michael Donovan and Karen Matthews were confirmed, the accounts of life on the 'estate' became unequivocal, as the following list of headlines attest:

- 'How One Case Exposed the Grim Reality of Life for Thousands in the Poorest Communities' (Norfolk, 2008a: 4).
- 'Children Were Just a Way of Getting Money From State' (Stokes, 2008: 11).
- 'More Shannons in Benefits R Us Hell' (Gaunt, 2008: 27).
- 'Force Low-Life to Work for a Living' (Malone, 2008).
- 'Now Teach the Sinks to Swim' (Nelson, 2008).
- 'New Tough Line on Welfare Mothers' (Oliver, 2008: 1).
- 'Well, We Did Pay Matthews to Keep Having Children' (Sergeant, 2008: 16).
- 'Mr Brown: Stop Being Kind to Be Cruel' (*The Sunday Times*, 2008: 16).
- 'Just a Shameless Breeding Machine' (Maxwell, 2008: 11).
- 'I Do Feel Pity Karen ... but Only for Taxpayers' (Moore, 2008: 8).
- 'Shameless Layabouts' (Randall, 2008: 26).
- 'We will all Pay the Price for Broken Britain' (Duncan Smith, 2008: 29).

As noted above with respect to welfare queens, taken as a whole, these stories represent a variation of a theme: one where the story of Karen Matthews offers a glimpse into a culture of dependency and 'worklessness', where the virtues of self-help and self-reliance have been eroded by a 'generous' benefit system. Put simply, deprivation is synonymous with depravation. The most significant of these stories and articles was that by Iain Duncan Smith, who at that time headed the Centre for Social Justice, but who, following the election in 2010, became the minister charged with overhauling the benefit system.

These headlines are part of the process of influencing political opinion and political perceptions through the evocation of the 'other', even if the 'evidence' is spurious (Edelman, 1977). This is highly evident in discussions of welfare reform, where, as Edelman (1988) notes, there is a ready-made cast of 'victims' and 'villains'. In contemporary society this cast of characters has tended to be subsumed under the label of the 'underclass' and, drawing on material already covered in Chapter 2, we can see the imagery of the 'deserving' and 'undeserving' poor, about whom there is a lengthy discourse (see, for example, Webb and Webb, 1927; Beier, 1985; Hindle, 2004; Lister, 2004), culminating in the discourse of 'scrounger mania' (Cook, 2006) and 'chavs' (Connor, 2007).

By focusing on the flawed personality of benefit recipients (e.g. Karen Matthews) (Sotirovic, 2003), these media representations clearly locate the origins of 'social problems' at the level of the individual and/or the social security system itself (Murray, 1994; 2001). The media representations of Karen Matthews, and of the mother of 'Baby P' or the frequent descriptions of 'feral young people', are all examples of 'mythopoesis' (van Leeuwen and Wodak, 1999). This is where there is a narrative with all the characteristics of a cautionary moral tale being used to give legitimacy to a particular perspective in maintaining a neo-liberal order (Fairclough, 2003; van Leeuwen, 2005, 2007).

Articles with headlines such as 'They Keep Having Babies – and We Have to Pick Up the Bills' (Moir, 2008), which detail life on the 'estate', now included descriptions of people regularly being seen 'walking to the shops in their pyjamas up to MID-DAY … even in the rain', bailiffs visiting as 'regular as the postmen' and 'lags openly showing off their electronic tags'. Not only were the efforts of the 'community' in the search for Shannon Matthews being erased, but a crime that many found difficult to comprehend was now being illuminated through reference to the familiar discourse of the 'underclass' (Welshman, 2006). The discourse presents the problems of society in terms of a moral malaise, in part created by a well-meaning, but ultimately destructive, intervention from the 'state'. This is perhaps exemplified in its invective by Jon Gaunt of *The Sun*:

> Karen Matthews isn't and doesn't represent the white working class. She's part of the chav class, the great unwashed. The clue is in the title 'working'. She and her ilk have no intention of ever working, they just want to leech off the sweat of the rest of us. It's time the Karens of this world were forced back into work. The liberal elite has created this underclass by excusing their slothfulness and by creating a benefit system that rewards them and discourages them from looking for work.… Let's get tough on these parasites. We need to have benefits time-limited and force people back into work. Let's allow the private sector to take over and give financial incentives to get the feral, the feckless and the freeloaders back into work. (2008: 7)

The power of this myth is that by providing a simple and familiar explanation, simple and familiar solutions are also made available. The longevity of the myth is assured, not only through its propagation by those with most to gain, but also by those simply looking to make sense of the world. Challenging myths becomes difficult as they are taken as common sense and there will always be some evidence to substantiate the case being made.

Confronting the myth: the challenge for welfare professionals

What emerges here is that there are significant efforts to influence and shape public opinion, particularly in relation to welfare – indeed, for dominant groups there is no enterprise of greater importance, and there is none that requires greater exertion on a continuous basis, since the battle is never finally won (Miliband,[1] 1973). Faced with this proposition, it is argued that those who work in social welfare have a role to play in showing how a prevailing discourse is communicated, reinforced and constructed, and that the myths that continue to be communicated with respect to the existence and causes of an 'underclass' need to be challenged. What is not being suggested is that the actions of Karen Matthews be defended. Rather, what is being questioned is the equivalence that has been drawn between the actions of Karen Matthews and Michael Donovan and all those people in receipt of benefits. Echoing the words and strategies of Ronald Reagan in 1976, in an article for the *Mail on Sunday*, under the heading 'There are 5 Million People on Benefits in Britain', David Cameron posed and then proffered an answer to the question, 'How do we stop them turning into Karen Matthews?' (Cameron, 2008:1-3).

In response to such myth-making, we argue that those engaged in social welfare need to engage in examinations of how this classification and categorisation is realised in a range of texts and practices. This involves attending to the:

> tendencies towards creating and proliferating differences between objects, entities, groups of people, etc. and collapsing or 'subverting' differences by representing objects, entities, groups of people etc, as equivalent to each other. (Fairclough, 2003: 88)

This analysis can provide a number of insights into the processes that fabricate the changing subjects of welfare. For example, Clarke (2004a: 39) notes that one of the key projects and questionable achievements of New Right politics was to 'split the citizen identity into three differentiated figures: the tax-payer, the scrounger and the consumer'. Once established, a dichotomy between welfare recipients and 'hard-working taxpayers' is maintained (Clarke, 2004a). In the case of Karen Matthews, the language and imagery of the 'underclass' provided a majority of the media and public with what Wright Mills (1967) called a 'vocabulary of motive': ideas, concepts and linguistic devices that reduce social problems to questions of morality, to be resolved through more effective technical mechanisms for managing 'problem populations' (Rodger, 2003), becoming part of a social control mechanism (Connor and Huggins, 2010).

According to Edelman (1988), the construction of social problems in this manner is designed to divert attention from certain threatening 'ideological' minefields. Drawing on two traditional and dominant classifications of the poor, the undeserving and the residuum (Lister, 2004), Karen Matthews becomes the embodiment of an 'underclass' constructed as being full of cunning, knowing and morally flawed characters. In this way, the focus on an underclass also contributes to the maintenance of what Young (1999) describes as an 'exclusive society' where the marginalised are managed by ever more sophisticated strategies of social control. Jordan (1998: 190) goes further to argue that by establishing the underclass in such a manner 'the self-righteous and judgemental majority are mobilised against those they neither know nor understand'. The abhorrence that may be felt towards the actions of an individual is fed and encouraged to include the recipients of welfare as a whole. Thus, the contrast between law-abiding and hard-working citizens is reinforced, and the 'other' becomes 'the object of intensified surveillance, criminalisation and incarceration in the drive to extend civility, reduce anti-socialness and enhance community' (Clarke, 2005: 458).

Myths and narrative: the shaping of public discourse

The myths created and sustained by the media can be overestimated, as may the ability of the public to resist such moves – yet the prevalence of such discursive strategies forms part of what Hall (1987) argued was the framing of what is and is not possible, in short the skewing of knowledge. Thus, we are not cultural dupes, but rather what we claim to 'know' about the social world is increasingly mediated and dependent on frames that we inherit rather than make for ourselves. The absence of alternative images and narratives in the public realm, contradicting and challenging the negative portrayal of welfare and its recipients, is a silence that can easily be construed as agreement and illustrates the limited nature of public discourse (Lens, 2002), particularly with reference to welfare reform. The case of Karen Matthews may represent a particularly powerful example of this categorisation, but it represents one of many examples of such ideological work. We have, of course, already explored some aspects of this narrative in the shaping of both welfare and the welfare subject in Chapters 1 and 2. In subsequent chapters, we explored the nature of contemporary capitalism and how it is dependent upon, and promotes, a certain set of 'taken-for-granted' norms. A brief rereading of our first two chapters will provide historical examples of this, and we now move to argue that we live in times where similar policies and ideas are being rerun. Welfare professionals are not immune from this myth-making, and, indeed, many of the families known to social workers, health visitors and other health service professionals, teachers and community workers are readily categorised as belonging to this 'myth' and possessing those character traits attributed to Karen Matthews. The crucial point about the myth is not that it is a total fabrication, but rather that it is developed into an all-embracing set of stereotypical assumptions that are removed from any political and social context, which may offer an alternative account. Such depoliticisation leaves no other set of explanatory factors other than a lack of *personal* morality, resulting in poor choices, rendering those who make them 'undeserving' – a construct which has its origins deep in the history of British welfare.

Reforming welfare: the new 'undeserving poor'

With the formation of a Conservative–Liberal Democrat coalition government in 2010, Iain Duncan Smith became the Secretary of State for Work and Pensions, charged with the responsibility of 'sorting out' the welfare system. In May 2010 he argued that the welfare system in Britain was 'bust' and that people should be encouraged to work and pay tax, and that he would end the 'scandal' that welfare claimants would be no better off if they took a job on £15,000 a year (Chapman, 2010) – yet given the current level of median income, this figure is only marginally higher than the measure of relative poverty. The budget of 22 June 2010 saw around £11bn 'savings' in benefits, almost one third of the total predicted 'savings' in the Chancellor's so-called 'austerity budget'. Within days the Institute for Fiscal Studies released projections showing that the overall measures 'hit the poor the hardest' (Browne and Levell, 2010). Such measures that attack benefits (and indeed the attendant attacks upon the public sector in general) cannot be seen as purely fiscal measures, isolated from a more general discourse that renders the measures to reduce benefits into something that is justified in the context of regular press features about benefit scroungers with headlines like 'Red Card for Benefit Scrounger Who Refereed 40 Football Matches ... While Claiming he couldn't Walk' (Freeman, 2009).

There are other groups of people with whom social workers are routinely engaged who are also part of a continuing negative discourse and media stereotyping . One example was alluded to earlier: disabled people. The discourse makes a clear distinction between the 'deserving' (who are never mentioned) and the 'undeserving' – that is, those who may be able to work but do not and become another group of 'scroungers'. This group is a clear target of the 'welfare reform' agenda, with the announcement that from 2013 all people in receipt of Disability Living Allowance (DLA) will have to complete an annual assessment. Even then, it should be remembered that the actual amounts of DLA paid are lower than the minimum wage. The example of disability highlights a central point in the maintenance of the 'myth'. There is little doubt that there are some people (relatively few, we would suggest) who make fraudulent claims. However, the discourse is developed in such a way as to suggest that this is the overwhelming majority and therefore 'something needs to be done about it' and as a consequence a group of people is potentially unfairly stereotyped and 'othered' (Brah, 1996).

A more obvious example is that of those who are seeking asylum: a typical headline in the *Daily Mail* runs: 'Free Treatment on NHS for Thousands of Asylum Rejects' (Martin, 2010). The story begins:

> NHS treatment will be available for tens of thousands of failed asylum seekers to ensure their human rights are honoured, it was announced yesterday. At present, they are denied free treatment if an asylum bid has been turned down but they have not left the country. But a Government U-turn means failed applicants who are destitute or cannot return home 'through no fault of their own', will be entitled to free care.

Thus, a government initiative aimed at protecting human rights is witheringly described as a 'U-turn', the ground 'through no fault of their own' is placed in parentheses to clearly indicate that this is perhaps not the 'real' reason and then the continued subtext is that such people are a drain on a 'cash-strapped' NHS. The piece continued to claim that this could 'open the floodgates up to a million illegal immigrants'. Later in the piece, GPs are criticised for suggesting that it is not their remit to check the status of a patient.

This returns to the central question of the relationship between the welfare professional and the general provision of welfare. The GP has a relatively high status, but here the clear implication is that determining whether or not someone is eligible for a 'service' – in this instance health care – is not their role: 'The British Medical Association said all failed asylum seekers should be treated free – and that it was not their job to decide who is eligible for free care and who is not' (Martin, 2010). This can be contrasted with the position of social workers who have a role to determine the age of juvenile and unaccompanied asylum seekers. In 2008, there were some 3,425 applications for asylum from unaccompanied minors (30% were from Afghanistan) and of these, in 2,370 cases the age of the applicant was disputed. Crawley (2006) had found that social workers were routinely disqualifying unaccompanied asylum-seeking children from foster care and school places by assessing them to be older than they actually were.

The consequence of the age being 'disputed' is that the onus shifts on to the claimant to prove their age and until they can 'prove' they are under 18 the applicants are treated as adults. A court judgment, reported on in February 2010, ruled that social work assessments could be challenged in the courts. The immediate response was for more thorough (and thereby costly) assessments. The question should be asked, though, why social workers are agreeing to undertake such assessments in the first place. By completing this role they become complicit in a draconian system of asylum control that, until early 2010, allowed for the immediate expulsion of unaccompanied asylum seekers without the standard 72 hours' notice given to adults. In June 2010 the suggested number of future deportations was set at around 12 each month (Pemberton, 2010). While there may be a legal mandate upon social workers to engage in age assessments, Dowty and Brown (2010) found that in many instances the full range of information gathered by social workers was being passed to the UK Border Agency – the clear implication being that local authorities are acting beyond any legal remit in this area to the detriment of children and entering into what Jones and Novak (1999) argued was the 'disciplinary state'.

The challenge for welfare professionals

There is a lengthy history in social work of challenging discrimination and oppression (O'Laird, 2008), and this needs to be maintained in a new era of welfare retrenchment where those who are the most vulnerable are looking increasingly likely to bear the brunt of fiscal demands to reduce the budget deficit, demands which are increasingly being portrayed as 'inevitable' and 'necessary'. Earlier chapters have argued, and hopefully demonstrated, that such measures are neither, but even were this so, it is most certainly *not* inevitable for the deficit to be reduced with proposals for such fierce measures of welfare reduction, which also include substantial reductions in public sector employment.

Yet the challenge for welfare professionals is substantial. The scope for challenge is limited by the increasingly restrictive and proscriptive demands of managerialist practice. Weakened trades unions have resulted in a marginalised voice for welfare professionals and allied workers as well as the service users they could also represent should the alliance proposed by Beresford and Croft (2004) ever be realised. In this context we argue that those engaged in social welfare need to articulate and develop a form of political practice that, where necessary, integrates an analysis of poverty, wealth and inequalities with anti-oppressive and anti-discriminatory practice (Langan, 2002). As noted in Chapter 5, we are arguing that there are limits to the degree that social inequalities can be reduced or liberation achieved within capitalist social and economic relations. Second, and more immediately, any attempts to reduce inequalities in any form can and should be supported by and with others resisting economic exploitation.

We do, however, return to the theme of this chapter and that of many radical groups in welfare provision, that in the context of welfare and public sector reform, the demonisation of the poor is not just an attack on those in poverty, but the living and working conditions of the wider population as well. Following the example set by Baptist and Bricker-Jenkins:

> A fundamental supposition from which we act is that the poor are only the first and most visible targets of an assault on the economic human rights of the majority by those whose class interests are thus served. (2001: 154)

In some ways it has always been the case (see Pearson, 1975; Jones and Novak, 1993; and Chapter 5, this volume) but current discourse gives this a greater urgency. It is the poor who are increasingly being 'targeted' as the main recipients of welfare (Jones, 2001) and this is the case in even the most universal of welfare services, the NHS. Reductions in welfare expenditure have a negative impact upon public health and those who are the poorest are more likely to see their life expectancy reduced (Stuckler et al, 2010). Others argue that income inequalities are the greatest impediment to a more equal public health (Wilkinson and Pickett, 2009). In the arena of education, hasty proposals to establish 'free schools' have brought criticism from educationalists, in that they are likely to result in a two-tier educational system, promoting the interests of the affluent above those of the poor and reversing the original aim of academies by allowing any school that has been deemed to be 'outstanding' to acquire 'academy status' and stand outside local authority control.

Within social work, there are 'pilot schemes' to develop what amounts to social workers creating their own 'social enterprises', which in the first instance are receiving increased funding in the UK. Those involved, often young, enthusiastic and highly service user-focused, argue that there is an improvement in services – yet, as Cardy (2010) argues, the analysis of these developments has to be placed in the social and political context which created them. Such schemes, however positive in the first instance, are part of a shift towards civil society as identified earlier, dependent upon the individualisation of social need and of developing a series of 'individual' as opposed to 'collective' solutions. The creation of the Conservative–Liberal Democrat coalition in 2010 has hastened the demise of the state and the creation of, at best, 'civil society' and, at worst, an individualised 'do-it-yourself' approach to seeking 'welfare' solutions, which underscore continuing neo-liberal economic policy. Such a project for the mutualisation of the distribution of resources through 'public' services will achieve little, and those services remain vulnerable if there is not also an accompanying attempt to provide democratic and collective control over the production of goods and resources.

Conclusion

In this chapter we have demonstrated how particular discourses can be created and sustained, which then form the background for what is seen as commonplace and 'taken for granted' (Hall, 1987). We used the case of Karen Matthews as the main exemplar, primarily because it showed how the language can change from one of being 'sympathetic' to individuals and a community to one that was critical of an individual who committed an act of cruelty, but also how this was so easily and almost gleefully extended to encompass a whole class of people who somehow 'shared' the same characteristics, thereby shaping the way in which welfare is viewed. We then extended this to other groups who are equally subjected to such negative discourses (although we have not attempted to create a 'definitive list') before returning to the poor and the budget of June 2010.

Part of the difficulty and solution is that welfare professionals are subjected to the same circulation of the language and imagery of groups that are 'demonised': most notably, asylum seekers and the poor, especially the section of the poor termed 'the underclass'. It is also the case that many of those who are engaged in the provision of direct services, the large body of public-sector workers who are earning slightly more than the minimum wage and may well belong to what has been termed the 'working poor', are also likely to feel aggrieved by the images of people 'getting away with it' and thereby develop a sense that society is unjust.

By evoking feelings of being wronged, and then suggesting to the viewer why they are feeling this way and what should be done, the underclass, asylum seeker and/or benefit scrounger discourse, and the moral authoritarian position it represents, exploits people's insecurities and misdirects a desire for social justice. Just as advertising does not create needs, but shapes existing needs, the rhetoric and practices of contemporary policy increasingly seek to identify people's needs and shape them to a particular agenda. It is therefore vital that, at these points, those working in social welfare start to identify their role in not only interrupting such discourses, but also helping to articulate and circulate alternative frames for understanding and realising social justice.

As such, language and discourse needs to be considered in a dialectical relationship to material and social practices. A critical examination of the imagery and language used in the communication of policies can be seen as augmenting – not replacing – existing methodologies and practices (Jacobs and Manzi, 1996). By understanding the challenge on a number of levels, social welfare professionals can begin to reclaim an agenda of genuine social justice.

REFLECTIVE EXERCISE

➔ The rather lengthier conclusion effectively sets out the theoretical and skills base needed by welfare professionals to engage in challenging the stereotypes and narrative myths. The challenge of the reflective exercise lies in recognising that you (which really means all of us) are subject to the narrative explanations and are part of the myth-making process unless you (we) stand outside of it and actively confront it. Consider your own situation and practice experience and then reflect upon to what extent examples of categorisation, labelling and 'myth-making' are evident and how you can engage in the process of confronting them.

Note

[1] The author of this text, Ralph Miliband, is the father of Ed Miliband, the Leader of the Labour Party.

CHAPTER 12

Reclaiming a radical agenda

This concluding section will develop an approach that sets policy transformation as a legitimate practice objective, and will develop the position that having the skills and analytical tools to analyse and understand social policy is essential for social workers committed to a transformative practice. The aim will be to answer the essential question we pose at the beginning of the book – why study social policy?

At the time of writing, the current political and economic circumstances appear to give very little reason for optimism. Increasingly, despite appearances, questions of welfare are being taken out of people's control, as defined through a political process, and being put under the aegis of rational, managerial and market-based processes, supported by an ideological stance that sees this and welfare reduction as 'inevitable' and 'necessary'. Privileging the alleged 'good judgement' of supposed experts is part of an ideological fiction that operates to the detriment of those most likely to be on the receiving end of such decisions:

> Corporate class interests require a broad acceptance of a new social impact, one that involves a significant change in the function of government and the relationship between government and the people. (Baptist and Bricker-Jenkins, 2001: 149)

As a consequence, the notion of welfare entitlements ends. As noted in Chapter 11, this is an assault not only on the recipients of welfare and the poor, but on the majority of citizens. We have identified a number of tools for understanding and analysing policy and hope that through this we have provided one answer to the question 'Why study social policy?'. We would, however, argue that the ultimate purpose of this book and the analysis of policy is to identify and pursue courses of action that will lead to significant social change.

In this chapter we aim to identify what concrete actions can and should be taken by welfare professionals who want to shape the circumstances in which they operate. We argue that a range of actions is available; however, if social welfare needs to be seen in a political context, then it follows that responses also need to have a political aspect.

We have already suggested that much of early 21st-century welfare work is technocratic in nature, with the emphasis being on achieving competence in work-based tasks. This aspect of the role results in 'technicians', which we will contrast with activists. Each of these roles operates from different assumptions about how the world works and how one should operate in it, and in this discussion the focus is on the relationship between the welfare practitioner, the service user and wider society.

Technicians and activists: who are you or what do you want to be?

Traditionally, the technician has developed a significant range of skills, knowledge and experience that they believe will benefit the needs of society, which Mayntz (1976) described as a *normatively rational* position. The technician will thereby focus upon practical activity and search for the best solution from the alternatives available. A criticism levelled at the technician is that they may ignore or neglect the powerful forces that shape their practice. It is worth asking to what extent our practice gives the 'illusion' that we are making a difference:

> by concentrating on the practical projects, rather than the education for which they are the vehicles, we allow ourselves to operate on principles of amelioration rather than transformation. We are distracted by the symptoms of injustice and fail to reach the root causes, and in doing so give free reign to the status quo. (Ledwith, 2007: 8)

Ledwith also notes that running parallel to this is a process of anti-intellectualism that discourages the development of a critical practice. 'Common sense' is valued, while theory is treated with suspicion and deemed ideological and dogmatic. From such a position, objectivity is considered 'both possible and preferable', and any problems influencing practitioners and policymakers can be solved through the development of better data (Whitelaw and Williams, 1994: 521). Policies of what is taken to be a broadly 'benevolent' state are understood to be serving the wider good, and so the technician is keen to work within, alongside and for the state and its related agencies. Technicians, although attempting to preserve a professional-like independence and autonomy, do not appear to question the nature of the state they work for.

The activist, like the technician, also believes that resources and expertise accrued through the process of becoming a professional should be used to serve wider society. In contrast, however, the activist will question who defines how these needs are to be met and would argue that it is not possible for a social welfare worker to act in a neutral fashion. Often orthodox accounts of policy and the policymaking process present them in a 'technical' and rational way with the exhortation to welfare professionals to 'engage' in a 'new reality'. We are quite certain that technicians can and do apply their knowledge to 'make a difference', but to do so without questioning, in a depoliticised framework, can lead to a situation where they become part of an apparatus for control, often in conflict with their value base.

So, returning to the example of completing 'age assessments' for unaccompanied asylum-seeking minors outlined in Chapter 11, the technician will seek to identify more effective, sensitive and caring ways of doing this, but this will inevitably lead to a series of depoliticised actions. Johnston (quoted in Shaw, 2004: 26) argued that 'actionless thought' and 'thoughtless action' is to be avoided. So, even for the technician (and there are many caring professionals who adopt such a stance), there always has to be an element of 'reflective' (if not reflexive) practice, a staple of the education of social workers (for an example, see Fook, 2002), nurses (Johns, 2000) and teachers (Loughran, 2002).

Perhaps the greater criticism of the technician is the notion of 'neutrality'. We have argued throughout that 'welfare provision' is not a politically neutral act and that practice cannot be rendered 'apolitical' and 'neutral'. If policy and practice is political, then it is not a question of whether you should choose sides, but which side is to be taken. Harrison et al (1992: 2) suggest that, if this is the case, then 'it follows that we have no real choice over whether to use theory or not; our only choice is to be implicit or explicit'. Paradoxically, even those who stubbornly assert a 'value-free' practice are promoting a specific set of values:

> Inquirers are human, and cannot escape their humanness. That is, they cannot by an act of will set aside their own subjectivity, nor can they stand outside the arena of humanness created by the other persons involved. (Guba and Lincoln, 1989: 88)

In response, the activist engages in 'critical praxis' (Freire, 1972; Harvey, 1990; Olsen, 1994; Popay and Williams, 1994). Within the social care/social work tradition this has been reflected in recent calls for an 'engaged' practice (Jones et al, 2004; Ferguson, 2008), alongside more conventional ethical arguments, which argue for 'morally active' practitioners (Husband, 1995).

Towards an active and engaged practice: setting out the parameters

Skills for understanding: a recap

Throughout the book we have attempted to demonstrate the skills that are needed for welfare professionals to engage in a critical and engaged practice. We have covered a number of areas, which have incorporated providing explanations of political choices, economic understanding and globalisation at a macro-level. This built upon analyses of the more immediate sphere for welfare professionals: managerialism; the decline of trades unions; the inequalities experienced so often by service-user groups; and the background to this in relation to the organisation of services. We began, of course, by looking at the development of social welfare in the 19th century and how it has developed in the 20th century, raising questions about what we termed the nature of the welfare subject as well as the welfare professional. We posed several questions at the onset that are worth reiterating here as the final reflective exercise in considering the book as a whole:

- Who has created and advocated for the policies?
- What story is being told? More specifically, what social issues have been identified, what justifications are provided for examining these social issues and what solutions are recommended?
- How are individuals and groups represented within these policies and what relationships exist within and across these individuals and groups?
- What is our role as 'recipients' of the policies in identifying with, or questioning, what we see and hear?
- How have policies been developed, administered and implemented?
- Whose viewpoint is not heard and what alternatives are not available?

These questions should lead to forms of engagement and it is to that which we devote the final chapter.

Developing 'critical praxis': from technician to activist

We start from the premise that theory and practice cannot be readily separated, and nor should they be, and this leads to what is termed 'critical praxis' – that is, practice and action. By failing to be critical, or even by just being focused upon the immediate, social injustices are not only perpetuated, but escalate. The difficulties and contradictions highlighted throughout this book cannot be addressed merely by thinking differently, or reframing the situation. This may be a necessary first step, but on its own has limitations. We argue that a critical praxis also seeks to uncover 'masks' that:

> make it seem either that the problems are insoluble, or that they are personal, not social, problems; identifying and explaining some structural elements that have contributed both to the problems, and to the perceptions that people have that may perpetuate them; developing action plans to transform society in relevant ways, including changing structures, where necessary and possible; changing perceptions of guilt, responsibility, rights, choices, etc (i.e. *consciousness*), where that is useful and possible. (Olsen, 1994: 5, emphasis in original)

This does not require a turning away from the everyday and the immediate – far from it. As we have tried to show in the quotes and observations highlighted throughout the book, a close attention to the language and practices of everyday life is a starting point for the development of a critical praxis. Freire (1972) argues that through engagement in practical projects, participants encounter situations that lead them to question their everyday reality. When situated and related to a wider political picture and analysis, and developed in conjunction with people, practical projects provide the context and starting point for attempts at developing a critical consciousness. Critical praxis needs to be grounded in people's everyday lives where there is an attempt to develop an understanding of the contradictory experiences of individuals through an 'extraordinarily re-experiencing' of the 'ordinary' (Shor, 1992: 122). In the context of social welfare, we argue that this can and should be done in conjunction with the application and development of a theoretical understanding of the welfare state in capitalist society. Those engaged in social welfare need to engage in an analysis of power and the structures of oppression that shape our circumstances and practices. If social welfare is limited to addressing the symptoms rather than root causes of injustice, then our practice, no matter what claims we may make for it, is likely to be tokenistic at best (Ledwith, 2007). Instead, strategies need to be rooted in an understanding of the state and in place within a capitalist society. For many welfare professionals this language will already sound very familiar, in that a significant element of training (for example, on social work awards) focuses upon challenging oppression (Braye and Preston-Shoot, 1995). Within other aspects of qualifying training the impact of social inequality is also a feature, even if locked into 'outcomes' (for example, in education and health).

Promoting social justice: whose side are you on?

We suggest that if practice is going to claim a commitment to social justice, the claim has to be supported by a clear and consistent attempt to engage with the exploitation and oppression that people experience in their lives. Thus, the activist rejects the engineering function of the technician, preferring a model that seeks to enlighten (Patton, 1988, 1990; Weiss, 1988). Rist suggests that the practitioner should 'create contextual understandings about an issue' and 'build linkages that will exist over time' (1994: 547). What should be evident in this account of critical praxis is that it cannot, and nor should it, be based on 'rules and procedures' handed down by some external authority:

> What is to be done ought not to be determined from above by reformers be they prophetic or legislative, but by a long work of comings and goings, of exchanges, reflections, trials different analyses. (Foucault, 1980: 12–13)

In a similar vein, Husband (1995) argued for the creation of morally active practitioners who seek to challenge arbitrarily arrived at definitions of 'need' – though we would suggest that such 'arbitrary' definitions are located within specific policy choices – through a process of constant critical questioning and engagement. As such the activist has to take responsibility for their actions – to return to an earlier theme, they need to demonstrate their own 'agency'.

Earlier we wrote that inevitably this involves not being 'neutral', but, to put it bluntly, 'taking sides'. Edwards and Cromwell make this clear:

> We should take the side of compassion [and engagement] against indifference, greed and hatred. Second, we should seek to identify the

> real causes of human … suffering with as much honesty as we are capable – we cannot hope to base real solutions on dishonest analysis and reporting. (2009: 240)

This will have an appeal for many social welfare professionals, chiming with the very reasons they entered their chosen profession in the first place, yet as many have already discovered, there are no easy answers or formulas for such engagement. This poses a tremendous challenge, both for individuals and to the policy and practice of social welfare as a whole. As constraining as procedures, rules and higher authorities can be, they do provide us with some security and act as safeguards for those in receipt of social welfare. Indeed, they can also offer a starting point for a critical engagement in that often those who seek to apply a regulatory framework to the application of services are themselves bound in its contradictions. For example, Aspect (2009) has produced a very clear guide in relation to staff duties and rights. Directors of Adult Services and, to a lesser, but nonetheless significant, extent, Directors of Children's Services are both bound by the General Social Care Council's code of conduct – a code that would render some of the more recent 'cost-cutting' decisions problematic at least. By 2009, only one case against an employer had been successfully brought to a GSCC code of conduct hearing.

Procedures should not, and cannot, displace our capacity to take responsibility for our actions. The question still remains, though: what can welfare professionals do? We have already commented upon 'policy practice' in an earlier chapter as a potential form of professional practice engagement, and Olsen, in a health context, sets out some potential areas for engagement:

> Changes in rules, provision, policy or law which are acceptable to all concerned and which help community health to improve; changes in perception among community groups such as young people, drug users etc., that offer them: a more realistic assessment of their health related choices; an understanding of structural factors to their long term health and; an improved sense of rights and responsibilities about their health; and finally, improved in-depth understanding on the part of so-called 'experts' (e.g. doctors, managers) of the multi-faceted social and family locations from which their clients/customers/patients come. (1994: 6)

In a similar vein, Ledwith (2007: 12), with reference to community action, provides examples of how critical praxis should seek to:

- contribute to change for a peaceful, just and sustainable future;
- develop anti-discriminatory analyses that reach from local to global, identifying the ways in which personal stories are political;
- build practical local projects with people in the community;
- teach people to question their reality;

- form strategic alliances for collective action, local to global;
- remain true to its radical agenda, with social and environmental justice at its heart; and
- generate theory in action, practical theory based on experience that contributes to a unity of praxis.

As we noted earlier, this type of language can be emptied of its radical intent and appropriated by policies and practices that appear to do the very opposite of what is being claimed. What is most important to note is that critical praxis involves the 'unity of theory and practice' (Marx, 1963/1843). An inability or unwillingness to generate theory in action will, at best, lead to a dissipation of the energy expended in practice and, at worst, leave the structures of exploitation and discrimination intact.

Reinsborough and Canning (2010) identify a range of sites for action. Their work covers a range of social and environmental campaigns and social movements, but is equally applicable to issues in social welfare. Five points of intervention are identified where action can be taken to challenge and transform a system of production, reproduction and consumption. These five points of intervention and potential forms of action include:

- Point of production – where products and services are produced and organised (strikes, pickets, work to rule, takeovers).
- Point of destruction – where resources are extracted, and the negative consequences of policies and actions are located (journalism. research and awareness campaigns).
- Point of consumption – where products and services are purchased (boycotts, sit-ins, point of purchase demonstrations, 'brand-busting', advocacy).
- Point of decision – where the authorities and 'power holders' who are responsible and accountable for services and products are located and if appropriate can meet a campaign's demands (protests, lobbying, petitions, letter writing, 'naming and shaming').
- Point of assumption – challenging dominant and powerful underlying assumptions. Making alternative narratives available and reframing the debate (media monitoring, alternative and independent media, 'subvertisements', 'culture jamming', campaigns).

Throughout this book we have sought to highlight how a range of institutions, policies and practices help to create and perpetuate the social problems that those in social welfare seek to address. The first four points of intervention represent tangible and material sites of action that seek to disrupt and, where necessary, reconfigure those institutions, policies and practices. The point of assumption is less tangible and reflects attempts to challenge and offer alternatives to the myths and assumptions that sustain the status quo (see Chapter 11). It is argued that actions at the points of production, destruction, consumption and decision are most successful and sustainable when integrated with action at the point of assumption (see Reinsborough and Canning, 2010, for more details and examples).

Creating alliances

When working with others, activists need to be skilled in policy and practice and to have the ability to interact with others. An important part of the activist's task is to encourage the participants to be proactive, and to facilitate this, practice should be made transparent and accessible to the participants. We saw in earlier chapters how the collective agency of service-user groups has wrought changes to the delivery of services, yet the wholescale co-opting of service users may deny the very voice they need. It is interesting that Beresford's (2008) arguments that service users prefer services that are funded out of direct taxation are largely ignored in favour of the more politically acceptable 'civil society' approaches. Perhaps a clear case of those being consulted giving the 'wrong' answer.

Within the recent social work literature, Ferguson (2008) has argued for a reclaiming of the radical agenda, lost perhaps in the abandonment of class as a focus for analysis. He argues that social workers – and we would extend this to all social welfare professionals – need to engage in actively 'reclaiming' the agenda in key areas: the ethical; the relationship and process; the social; the structural; and the political. Interestingly, given the radical history, a critical element is that of the relationship in social welfare work, often destroyed by a target-driven managerialist approach. Again, the essential dialectic is apparent in that arguably the very structures that have at least helped create the environment in which relationship-based work withered, are now seeking to restore it. The activist, therefore, should seek to reclaim the centrality of the relationship since 'it is often through such relationship based work that the damage and internalised oppression which results from living in an oppressive and unequal society can be addressed and a sense of self-respect and self-worth be re-created' (Ferguson, 2008: 133–4). There is of course an important caveat, an echo from the 1970s and a valuable reminder that 'casework' should always be viewed within its context, echoing Bailey and Brake's claim that radicals should seek to 'eliminate casework that supports ruling class hegemony' (1975: 9).

We have already noted the importance of service-user movements and also the argument that welfare professionals need to form active alliances with wider groups (Beresford and Croft, 2004). Annetts et al (2009) provide a comprehensive account of the role of social movements in challenging some of the more significant aspects of inequality. They adopt a historical approach to demonstrate that changes nationally and internationally have emanated from aspects of organised struggle in a wide range of welfare fields. They argue that while networks and interaction are important, 'an emphasis upon the state apparatus is vital' (Annetts et al, 2009: 8). They argue that social movements have developed a culture of opposition to neo-liberalism and have mobilised others to defend the basic principles of social welfare.

Those actively engaged in policy and practice (or 'policy practice') have to be 'participants', in the real sense of the word, in the development of the service's aims, the direction of the service and the evaluation and interpretation of the work that is undertaken. Such an approach will bring those engaged in it face to face with the core theme of this book: policy.

Engaging in action

We share the view that 'there is no social policy without a social movement capable of imposing it' (Bourdieu and Wacquant, 2001: 56). Historically a range of labour and social movements has sought to 'civilise', through welfare reforms, the market economy. The key to the development of welfare policies is, therefore, the actions of people engaged in activities as part of wider movements to both resist and develop alternative policies. The crux of the argument we have sought to establish is that people do matter, and that as policy is a concern of everyone, it should not be dismissed as 'top-down' or, even worse, regarded as something that belongs to powerful governmental offices or multinational capital.

Lavalette and Ferguson (2007), in discussing the role of international social professionals, argue that there is a lengthy tradition of social activism among this group, and argue, after Attlee (1920), that social agitation is a legitimate professional role. To help achieve this level of professional engagement, there needs to be a critical understanding of welfare and also a commitment to action of one form or another. Arguably, this begins with a genuinely 'reflexive' practice, which is concerned with social welfare professionals questioning the assumptions that are made through the policy and practice process, particularly with respect to those assumptions related to the worker's own social position (Hoggett et al, 2006). Most important is the privileging of engagement with participants in the policy and practice process. This should not be an inwardly focused 'reflection', but rather needs to be part of attempts to develop a critical consciousness, which becomes a requisite for collective action. Pivotal to this process, as reflected throughout this book, is that personal issues become social and political problems.

Thus, consciousness remains partial if we focus our analysis on a personal/local level and fail to notice the ways in which these are social trends that are linked to structural injustices. Practice will address the symptoms and overlook the causes, so we argue that the essential nature of an engaged practice is a practice that will address both symptoms *and* causes. All areas of welfare provision, therefore, become an arena for action, and organisations (whether pre-existing or not) become a place through which forms of action can be initiated.

Recognition that policy and practice is political does not mean that actions are restricted to or even require an involvement with political parties or parliamentary and/or local authority institutions and processes. The state is an important site for analysis and action, and the lobbying of elected representatives can and should be an important part of an engaged social welfare practice. However, the state should not necessarily be taken as the beginning or end of political action. A quick survey of historical and contemporary examples of social and political actions, particularly with regard to social welfare, reveals the range of measures available to those who seek to shape the circumstances in which they live and work. For example: 'How would you feel if you discovered that the society in which you would really like to live was already here … like a seed beneath the snow?' (Ward, 2008: 23).

In the search for alternatives, you may be best served by looking between and within the gaps of the established institutions for those informal, 'self-organising networks of relationships that make a human community possible' (Ward, 2008: 23). To this end, an immediate site of action is for those engaged in social welfare to identify, engage with, protect and develop instances of cooperation, mutual aid and support. At a very practical level sharing experiences and stories can be a big step towards realising that your problems are not individual issues, but located in structures. This understanding can open up a number of possibilities for mutual support. However, if you want to move things beyond 'coping' at work or with your circumstances, the next step is to identify and develop this network. This can sound very formal, but it is often best developed through a range of social networking activities. You will quickly find that there is a lot of knowledge and skills to be learned from each other. It also means that, if the time comes to take collective action, you are ready. Collective action can include a whole range of activities, from going to speak to a manager about a work issue as a group, using a 'telephone tree' to mobilise support for a friend or full industrial action. One example of this is the practice of direct action casework. This is a term used to describe a range of tactics to pressure an institution to recognise the needs and accept the demands of an individual, family or small group. This may involve organising protests at housing offices, job centres, local authorities, landlords or an employer. Direct action casework does not involve 'harassing' individual workers. Far from it, one of the aims is to establish solidarity and cooperation with those who work in these institutions and to disrupt the workings of the institution. For some this may seem an unreasonable action, but it is a practice that: (a) seeks to reflect and echo the disruption that these institutions can have on individuals' lives; and (b) explicitly attempts to recognise the role of power in institutions. Individuals can often feel powerless when set against the workings and resources of an organisation. Direct action casework is about attempting to redress this imbalance of power (see London Coalition Against Poverty [www.lcap.org.uk/]; and Hills, 2008).

Broadening the base for action: from the local to the global

More formal examples of such practice can be found within and across the labour movement. Trades unions can be criticised and dismissed by those who point to their primary concern with pay and conditions. Not that this is a problem in itself, but when this primary concern is able to be accommodated within existing social relations, the challenge and transformative potential of the union movement is blunted. Yet Fairbrother (2005) points out that unions at a workplace level represent a fundamental challenge to the social relations of the capitalist state, in that they can provide one of the means whereby social relations can be defined as collective problems subject to collective concern.

Social welfare professionals, as we noted earlier, can often have conflicting views about industrial action. For example, for those involved in industrial disputes, there is no doubt that the question of whether one should strike or not soon becomes infused with concerns over the harm that the strike can have on the client group. This can be a concern whatever sector of industry one is involved with, but when it comes to the welfare sector, where people are working with some of the most vulnerable individuals in society, the idea of withdrawing that support can weigh heavily. The challenge to social welfare professionals is reconciling this with a state that provides welfare, at best, reluctantly and, at worst, as little more than a very basic 'safety net' (George and Wilding, 1993). The danger lies in the promotion of a narrow professional interest. For example, in their declared opposition to the cuts outlined in the June 2010 budget, described by most commentators as the most 'austere' in living memory, the British Association of Social Workers, under the heading 'Grave Concern About Spending Cuts', goes on to confine this to 'a stark warning that cuts which fail to protect social work services will put the lives of vulnerable children and adults at serious risk' (BASW, 2010).

While we would fully concur with this sentiment, campaigns against cuts should not be restricted to 'social work services' when cuts to a whole range of other vital services and financial supports for vulnerable people are being enacted. Indeed, as we noted earlier, there have been social work strikes and industrial action directed at the defence of services against managerialist practices. Annetts et al (2009) draw on a wide range of evidence of social movements in relation to welfare provision, and these organisations, active in many areas of the UK and beyond, can form the basis of a more engaged practice for social welfare professionals. For social workers and allied professionals the Social Work Action Network provides an alternative voice for action, which grew out of the Manifesto of Social Work (Jones et al, 2004). The starting point was the high levels of disaffection and dissatisfaction felt by many, summed up by the statement 'We didn't enter social work to do this', and the network has continued to expand, despite some employer opposition. It was the *experience* of work that formed the starting point, and the network has provided a forum where welfare professionals can move towards what Gramsci (2003) termed 'aggregation'. This is the enabling every small piece of action to be joined (aggregated) to actions by others who are engaged in the same actions, which often take place elsewhere and as such are often not 'connected'. In short it turns the small scale into a larger movement.

Others seek to combine these local matters with global campaigns. Ferguson (2008: 127) draws attention to global anti-capitalist movements in relation to neo-liberalism in general and the wars it generates. Central to these movements is the notion of the 'radicalised enlightenment'. We have drawn attention in earlier chapters to the limits of individual agency and also to the Althusserian concept of 'structure', arguing that it is vital to understand the concept of agency within a given structure. The Enlightenment, with a focus upon 'agency', nonetheless promised a form of 'universalism', but has largely failed to create a genuine universalism and an inclusionary capitalism (Ferguson, 2008: 119). Ferguson goes on to cite Oliver and Barnes as offering an alternative:

> it is a world in which all human beings, regardless of impairment, age, gender, social class or minority ethnic status can co-exist as equal members of the community, secure in the knowledge that their needs will be met. (1998: 102, cited in Ferguson, 2008: 119)

This is perhaps the rallying call for all social welfare professionals who aspire to put the genuine needs of their service users first, and broadens this beyond the narrow parameters of 'professional concern' to encompass the whole range of social needs and relationships. This cannot be achieved, for example, in the application of a rhetorically 'progressive policy' within a welfare system that is built around neo-liberal policy – there has to be wider, transformative engagement (see Burton and Kagan [2006] and Simpson and Price [2010] for a discussion of this in relation to *Valuing People* [DH, 2001]; and Ferguson [2007] and Houston [2010] for a similar critique of the personalisation agenda). Piven and Cloward (1977), however, note that orthodox organisational strategies (building committees and organisations, appointing leaderships etc) can be largely irrelevant or even formidable obstacles to the development and success of particular struggles, particularly when seen as the end rather than the means. Leaderships, they say, are frequently co-opted and bought out, or the organisations muted through compromises, rapprochements and co-option with the state and the management of institutions. For example, in the 'reform' of health services:

> professional associations have been more muted [in opposition to forms of privatisation] and the larger service-user organisations, having been co-opted into the polity, have taken a more pragmatic approach to the privatisation of policy. (Annetts et al, 2009: 126)

In a different context, many social welfare professionals have also found that their engagement in policy questions and development is essentially 'tokenistic' in that their attendance allows those leading the policy to claim 'consultation', but leaves them largely 'free' to ignore their concerns. An account from a professional engaged in a consultation about privatisation is instructive:

> Initially I was welcomed, and my contributions 'valued'. By the third meeting these very same contributions were 'unhelpful'. Getting involved has made me even more determined to engage in the fight against how these policies are being abused in their implementation.

Thus, engagement in itself may not bring about the immediate desired objective, but the process can be one that generates greater levels of engagement. With these cautionary notes in mind, we would still argue and support the principle that while on our own we are weak, when we choose to act together, we can achieve far more than the sum of our parts.

Conclusion

Social welfare professionals are, for the most part, people who entered a particular profession with a strong desire to make a difference, yet in the face of increasing welfare changes and attacks on their ideas of 'professionalism', they are often at a loss as to what should and can be done. This is no surprise when increasingly our agency is being reduced to one of consumerism and our general interests equated with perceived self-interest. Even when managing to overcome such obstacles, and even when convinced that the problems do exist, that those who are exploited and oppressed are not responsible for their circumstances and that the system in place is in fact the source of the misery and inequality, one can still be faced with the plaintiff cry of 'What do we do? Tell me the answer!'. It is at this point that critics of an 'alternative' world view and direction frequently feel that they have clinched the victory, that is, they suggest that despite all the problems cited, in the absence of a 'feasible' alternative, any criticisms add up to nothing more than a series of complaints that offer no way forward. It is at this point that any pessimism of the intellect needs to be met by the optimism of the will. As we have already noted, the existing structures enable as well as constrain. Despite all the criticisms that can and should be levelled against contemporary policymaking, a collective form of social welfare has and still can represent an opportunity to make a real difference to the lives of marginalised communities and society as a whole. However, echoing the concerns of welfare professionals over the last 150 years, we need to remain critical, to prevent social welfare practice from becoming a 'sticking plaster on the wounds of injustice'. Without such engagement, practice becomes little more than efforts to secure improved 'service delivery'. Once again, if this improved service delivery leads to improved circumstances for the community as a whole, then this is not problematic. Yet, when the ends are to ensure the closer discipline and regulation of marginal groups, it is incumbent on those in social welfare to not only question such 'improvements' in service delivery, but also to seek to identify and address the causes of inequalities and marginalisation. The challenge for the social welfare professional is not only to ensure that, all other things being equal, they do not neglect the essential daily tasks (Walker and Beaumont, 1981), but also that they engage in a wider critical and transformative practice. Without such action Ledwith (2007) suggests the status quo of exploitative relationships will remain.

While we have sought to highlight where there are already activists and agendas of resistance, these are not intended as a 'blueprint' for action, but rather to identify pre-existing groups with which some social welfare professionals may wish to engage. We are fully aware that the daily demands of working in the various social welfare sectors can in their very nature be stressful, isolating and demoralising – therefore, information to make connections with others is often seen as a liberating experience even if it starts at the 'I am not alone' level. That said, we have tried to offer and develop paradigms for action without being prescriptive, since significant social change needs to be done with those with most to gain from such changes, and social welfare professionals operate in a range of organisational welfare settings.

So, there are no definitive lists, just a range of possibilities that are available. The ones that you, the reader, choose to pursue will be in part a reflection of your own strengths, predispositions and positions, but also, and possibly most critically, a reading of what is required and possible in your specific circumstances. The challenge is to get better at weaving theory into practice (Schön, 1983), which makes for an improved rationale for action at any stage of the policy/practice process. Modest acts are always possible and can form a potent site of activity, both for addressing immediate needs and for developing the means and ends towards the future. We can say this with such certainty because every day is filled with the most prosaic activities that refuse to bow to the market or hierarchical forms of authority. These can not only inspire, but also provide the threads of a new social fabric. None of this should be construed as a call for a modest reformism, where the changes are seen as the ends rather than the means, but, rather, as a recognition that large changes tend to come about as a result of a number of small-scale qualitative changes.

Finally, along with many others whose work we have drawn on, we argue that the radical agenda must be reclaimed from those who seek to reduce radical action to an individualised and diluted rhetoric of 'empowerment' and 'self-help', which in most instances only ends up blaming the 'victim'. Concepts like participation, empowerment, social justice and equality are not just pleasant ideas, but come from a world view founded upon cooperation and genuine democracy, rather than competition and neo-liberal politics. Ferguson wrote that there was a need for social welfare professionals to have 'vision, confidence, organisation and courage' (2008: 136). We hope that this book has contributed to the vision and that the skills developed here will give people renewed confidence. The challenge, therefore, is to organise and have courage to ensure that the principles of fairness, equality and social justice are realised.

References

Adburgham, A. (1989) *Shops and Shopping 1800–1914*. London: Barrie and Jenkins.

Adcroft, A. and Willis, R. (2005) 'The (Un)Intended Outcome of Public Sector Measurement', *International Journal of Public Sector Management*. 18(5): 386–400.

Alcock, P. (2008) *Social Policy in Britain*, 3rd edn. Basingstoke: Palgrave Macmillan.

Althusser, L. (1969) *For Marx*. London: Verso.

Althusser, L. (1971) *Lenin and Philosophy and Other Essays*, translated by Ben Brewster. New York/London: Monthly Review Press.

Amin, S. (1998) *Spectres of Capitalism: A Critique of Current Intellectual Fashions*. New York: Monthly Review Press.

Aminuzammam, S.M. (2007) *Migration of Skilled Nurses from Bangladesh: An Exploratory Study*. Sussex: Development Research Centre on Migration, Globalisation and Poverty, University of Sussex. Available at: www.migrationdrc.org/publications/research_reports/Migration_of_Skilled_Nurses_from_Bangladesh.pdf [accessed 29 October 2010].

Anderson, P. (1980) *Arguments within English Marxism*. London: New Left Books.

Annetts, J., Law, A., McNeish, W. and Mooney, G. (2009) *Understanding Social Welfare Movements*. Bristol: The Policy Press.

Archer, M. (1995) *Realist Social Theory*. Cambridge: Cambridge University Press.

Arksey, H. and Glendinning, C. (2007) 'Choice in the Context of Informal Care-Giving', *Health and Social Care in the Community* 15(2): 165–75.

Arnstein, S.R. (1969) 'A Ladder of Citizen Participation', *Journal of the American Institute of Planners* 35(4): 216–24.

Aspect (2009) *What If? Social Care Professionals and the Duty of Care: A Practical Guide to Staff Duties and Rights*. Wakefield: Aspect.

Atkinson, A. (1971) 'The Distribution of Wealth and the Individual Lifecycle', *Oxford Economic Papers 23*. Oxford: Oxford University Press.

Attlee, C. (1920) *The Social Worker*. London: Heinemann.

Auyero, J. (1997) 'Wacquant in the Argentine Slums', *International Journal of Urban and Regional Research* 27(2): 508–11.

Bacchi, C. (1999) *Women, Policy and Politics*. London: Sage.

Bailey, R. and Brake, M. (1975) 'Social Work and the Welfare State', in R. Bailey and M. Brake (eds) *Radical Social Work*. London: Edward Arnold.

Bailey, R. and Brake, M. (1980) 'Contributions to a Radical Practice', in R. Bailey and M. Brake (eds) *Radical Social Work*. London: Edward Arnold.

Banks, S. and Gallagher, A. (2009) *Ethics in Professional Life: Virtues for Health and Social Care*. Basingstoke: Palgrave Macmillan.

Baptist, W. and Bricker-Jenkins, M. (2001) 'A View From the Bottom: Poor People and Their Allies Respond to Welfare Reform', *The Annals of the American Academy of Political and Social Science* 577: 144–56.

Barnes, M. and Prior, D. (1995) 'Spoilt for Choice: How Consumerism Can Disempower Service Users', *Public Money and Management* 15(3): 53–9.

Barnett, S.A. and Barnett, H. (1972 [1888]) *Practicable Socialism: Essays on Social Reform*. Freeport, NY: Books for Libraries Press.

Barry, A., Osbourne, T. and Rose, N. (1996) *Foucault and Political Reason: Liberalism, Neo-Liberalism and Rationalities of Government*. London: UCL Press.

Batata, A. (2005) 'International Nurse Recruitment and NHS Vacancies: A Cross-Sectional Analysis', *Globalization and Health* 1(7). Available at: www.globalizationandhealth.com/content/1/1/7 [accessed 14 May 2010].

BBC News (2009) 'Huge Job Cuts for Public Sector'. Available at: http://news.bbc.co.uk/1/hi/uk/8102121.stm [accessed 11 October 2010].

BBC News (2010) 'Queen's Speech: Bank Regulation Reform Revealed. 25 May, 2010'. Available at: http://news.bbc.co.uk/1/hi/business/10153578.stm [accessed 21 October 2010].

Beardshaw, J., Brewster, D., Cormack, P. and Ross, A. (2001) *Economics: A Student Guide*. Harlow: Pearson Education.

Beier, A.L. (1985) *Masterless Men: The Vagrancy Problem in England 1560–1640*. London: Methuen.

Beresford, P. (2008) 'Service Users: Individualised Involvement or Collective Action?', *A Life in the Day* 12(4): 13–15.

Beresford, P. and Croft, S. (2004) 'Service Users and Practitioners Reunited: The Key Component for Social Work Reform', *British Journal of Social Work* 34(1): 53–68.

Berry, L. (2004) 'Report from the General Social Care Council: Overseas Workers', unpublished paper delivered at the Overseas Social Workers International Symposium, Sheffield, 10 November.

Best, J. (2008) *Social Problems*. London: W.W. Norton & Company.

Beveridge, Sir W. (1942) *Report on Social Insurance and Allied Services*. Cmd 6404. London. HMSO.

Biestek, E.P. (1961) *The Casework Relationship*. London: Allen and Unwin.

Blau, P.M. (ed) (1975) *Approaches to the Study of Social Structure*. New York: The Free Press.

Blaug, R., Horner, L. and Lekhi, R. (2006) *Public Value, Politics and Public Management*. London: The Work Foundation.

Boris, E. (2007) 'On Cowboys and Welfare Queens: Independence, Dependence and Interdependence at Home and Abroad', *Journal of American Studies* 41(3): 599–621.

Bourdieu, P. (1990) *The Logic of Practice*. Stanford, CA: Stanford University Press.

Bourdieu, P. and Wacquant, L. (2001) 'New-Liberal Speak: Notes on the New Planetary Vulgate', *Radical Philosophy* 105: 2–5.

Bowler, T. (2009) *Countering Tax Avoidance in the UK: Which Way Forward?*. London: Institute of Fiscal Studies.

Box, S. (1983) *Power, Crime and Mystification*. London: Routledge.

Bradfield Board of Guardians (1899) *Untitled document*. Available at: www2.lse.ac.uk/library/collections/pamphlets/SocialPolicy/pensions.aspx [accessed 20 December 2010].

Brah, A. (1996) *Cartographies of Diaspora: Contesting Identities*. London: Routledge.
Brandon, D. with Brandon, A. and Brandon, T. (1995) *Advocacy: Power to People with Disabilities*. Birmingham: Venture Press.
Brannelly, T. and Davis, A. (2006) *Service Users' Experiences of Transition Through Mental Health Services*. Birmingham: IASS and Suresearch, University of Birmingham.
Braye, S. and Preston-Shoot, M. (1995) *Empowering Practice in Social Care*. Buckingham: Open University Press.
Brechin, A. and Swain, J. (1983) 'Professional/Client Relationships; Creating a Working Alliance with People with Learning Disabilities', *Disability, Handicap and Society* 3(3): 213–16.
Brenner, N. and Theodore, N. (eds) (2002) *Spaces of Neoliberalism: Urban Restructuring in North America and Western Europe*. Oxford: Blackwell Publishers.
British Association of Social Workers (2010) On-line Press Release. Available at: http://news.basw.co.uk/post/725086455/basw-expresses-grave-concerns-at-spending-cuts [accessed 3 October 2010].
Bronfenbrenner, K. (1997) 'The Effect of Plant Closings and the Threat of Plant Closings on Worker Rights to Organize', supplement to *Plant Closings and Workers' Rights: A Report to the Council of Ministers by the Secretariat of the Commission for Labor Cooperation*. Dallas, TX: Bernan Press.
Bronfenbrenner, K. (2000) 'The American Labor Movement and the Resurgence in Union Organizing', in P. Fairbrother and C. Yates (eds) *Trade Union Renewal and Organizing: A Comparative Study of Trade Union Movements in Five Countries*. London: Cassell.
Brooks, N. and Hwong, T. (2008) *The Social Benefits and Economic Costs of Taxation: A Comparison of High and Low Tax Countries*. Ottawa: Canadian Centre for Policy Alternatives.
Brown, G. (2000) 'Chancellor of the Exchequer's Speech to the Labour Party Conference', Brighton, 25 September.
Browne, J. and Levell, P. (2010) *The Distributional Effect of Tax and Benefit Reforms to be Introducd between June 2010 and April 2014: A Revised Assessment*. Available at: www.ifs.org.uk/bns/bn108.pdf.
Bryson, A. (2003) 'From Welfare to Workfare', in J. Millar (ed) *Understanding Social Security: Issues for Policy and Practice*. Bristol: Social Policy Association/ The Policy Press.
Bryson, L. (1992) *Welfare and the State: Who Benefits?* Basingstoke: Macmillan.
Buchan, J. and Seccombe, I. (2006) 'Worlds Apart? The UK and International Nurses'. Available at: http://www.rcn.org.uk/__data/assets/pdf_file/0007/78703/003049.pdf [accessed 29 October 2010].
Buckner, L. and Yeandle, S. (2007) 'Valuing Carers: Calculating the Value of Unpaid Care', Carers UK and University of Leeds. Available at: http://www.carersuk.org/Professionals/ResearchLibrary/Profileofcaring/1201108437/main_content/ValuingcarersFINAL.pdf.

Burgess, K. (1978) 'Working Class Response to Social Policy: The Case of the Lancashire Cotton Textile Districts 1880–1914', Paper to SSRC conference on social policy, May, University of Glasgow.

Burgess, K. (2009) 'Longbridge: A Ghost Town, Haunted by the Spectre of MG Rover'. Available at: www.timesonline.co.uk/tol/news/uk/article6830880.ece [accessed 25 October 2010].

Burton, M. and Kagan, C. (2006) 'Decoding Valuing People', *Disability and Society* 21(4): 229-313.

Byrne, D. (2005) *Social Exclusion*, 2nd edn. Buckingham: Open University Press.

Cabinet Office (1999) *Modernising Government*, Cm 4310. London: The Stationery Office.

Cabinet Office (2009) *Unleashing Aspiration: The Final Report of the Panel on Fair Access to the Professions*. London: HMSO.

Caldas-Coulthard, C.R. and van Leeuwen, T. (2003) 'Critical Social Semiotics: Introduction', *Social Semiotics* 13(1): 3–4.

Callinicos, A. (2001) *Against the Third Way: An Anti-Capitalist Critique*. Cambridge: Polity Press.

Callinicos, A. (2003) *The Anti-Capitalist Manifesto*. Cambridge: Polity Press.

Callinicos, A. (2004) *Making History: Agency, Structure, and Change in Social Theory*, 2nd edn. London: Brill.

Callinicos, A. (2005) 'Imperialism and Global Political Economy', *International Socialism* 2(108): 109–27.

Cameron, D. (2008) 'There are 5 million people on benefits in Britain, how do we stop them turning into Karen Matthews?', *The Mail on Sunday*, 7 December: 1-3.

Cardy, S. (2010) '"Care Matters" and the Privatization of Looked After Children's Services in England and Wales: Developing a Critique of Independent "Social Work Practices"', *Critical Social Policy* 30(3): 430-442.

Carpenter, M. (1968 [1851]) *Reformatory Schools: For the Children of the Perishing and Dangerous Classes and for Juvenile Offenders*. London: Woburn Press.

CASE and HM Treasury (1999) *Persistent Poverty and Lifetime Inequality: The Evidence, CASEpaper 5*. London: LSE.

Castells, M. (2001) *The Internet Galaxy: Reflections on the Internet, Business and Society*. Oxford: Oxford University Press.

Castles, S. and Kosack, G. (1980 [1973]) 'Immigrant Workers and Class Structure', in R. Bocock, P. Hamilton, K. Thompson and A. Waton (eds) *An Introduction to Sociology: A Reader*. Glasgow: Fontana Paperbacks in association with the Open University.

Chand, A. (2000) 'The Over-representation of Black Children in the Child Protection System: Possible Causes, Consequences and Solutions', *Child and Family Social Work*. 5: 67–77.

Chandler, D. (2007) *Semiotics: The Basics*. London: Routledge.

Chapain, C. and Murie, A. (2008) 'The Impact of Factory Closure on Local Communities and Economies: The Case of the MG Rover Longbridge Closure in Birmingham', *Policy Studies* 29(3): 305–17.

Chapman, J. (2010) 'Work or lose your benefits: Iain Duncan Smith heralds biggest shake-up of welfare state since the war'. Available at: www.dailymail.co.uk/news/article-1281721/Iain-Duncan-Smith-heralds-welfare-states-biggest-shake-war.html#ixzz18pi53na6 [accessed 2 June 2010].

Cheetham, J. (ed) (1982) *Social Work and Ethnicity*. London: George Allen and Unwin.

Child Poverty Action Group (2009) 'Child Poverty Tool Kit'. Available at: www.childpovertytoolkit.org.uk/ [accessed 21 October 2010].

Clark, C. (2006) 'Moral Character in Social Work', *British Journal of Social Work* 36: 75–89.

Clarke, J. (1988) 'Unit 13 "Social Work: The Personal and the Political"', in D211, *Social Problems and Social Welfare*. Milton Keynes: The Open University.

Clarke, J. (1993a) 'The Comfort of Strangers', in J. Clarke (ed) *A Crisis in Care: Challenges to Social Work*. London: Sage Publications.

Clarke, J. (ed) (1993b) *A Crisis in Care: Challenges to Social Work*. London: Sage.

Clarke, J. (2004a) 'Creating Citizen Consumers: The Trajectory of an Identity', paper presented at the Centre for the Study of Commercial Activity Annual Conference, London, Ontario, 5–9 May. Available at: www.open.ac.uk/socialsciences/citizenconsumers/index.html [accessed 31 January 2007].

Clarke, J. (2004b) *Changing Welfare, Changing States: New Directions in Social Policy*. London: Sage.

Clarke, J. (2005) 'New Labour's Citizens: Activated, Empowered, Responsibilized, Abandoned?', *Critical Social Policy*. 25(4): 447–63.

Community Care (2009a) 'The Number of Overseas Social Workers in the UK', 17 March. Available at: www.communitycare.co.uk/Articles/2009/03/17/111018/The-number-of-overseas-social-workers-in-the-UK.htm [accessed 29 October 2010].

Community Care (2009b) 'Vacancy Rates: The Figures in Full', 18 March. Available at: www.communitycare.co.uk/Articles/2009/04/18/111285/vacancy-rates-the-figures-in-full.htm [accessed 14 May 2010].

Connor, S. (2007) 'We're Onto You: A Critical Examination of the Department for Work and Pensions "Targeting Benefit Fraud" Campaign', *Critical Social Policy* 27(2): 231–52.

Connor, S. (2009) 'Structure and Agency: A Debate for Community Development?', Paper presented to the Community Development Journal, International Symposium 'Community Development in an Age of Uncertainty', London, 3–5 September.

Connor, S. (2010) 'Promoting "Employ Ability": The Changing Subject of Welfare Reform in the UK', *Critical Discourse Studies* 7(1): 41–53.

Connor, S. (2011) 'Structure and Agency: A Debate for Community Development?', *Community Development Journal* 46(2), doi: 10.1093/cdj/bsr006.

Connor, S. and Huggins, R. (2010) 'The Technology and the Artefacts of Social Control – Monitoring Criminal and Anti-Social Behaviour Through and in Media Cultures', in J. Chriss (ed) *Sociology of Crime, Law and Deviance, Volume 15, Social Control: Informal, Legal and Medical*. Cambridge, MA: Emerald.
Cook, D. (1989) *Rich Law, Poor Law: Different Responses to Tax and Social Security Fraud*. Milton Keynes: Open University Press.
Cook, D. (2006) *Criminal and Social Justice*. London: Sage.
Corrigan, P. and Leonard, P. (1978) *Social Work Practice Under Capitalism: A Marxist Approach*. London: Macmillan.
Corry, D. and Glyn, A. (1994) 'The Macro-economics of Equality, Stability and Growth', in A. Glyn and E. Miliband (eds) *Paying for Inequality: The Economic Costs of Social Justice*. London: IPPR.
Cote, S. and Healy, T. (2001) *The Well-being of Nations.: The Role of Human and Social Capital*. Paris: Organisation for Economic Co-operation and Development.
Craig, G. (2002) 'Poverty, Social Work and Social Justice', *British Journal of Social Work* 32: 669–82.
Crawley, H. (2006) *Child First, Migrant Second*. London: Immigration Law Practitioners' Association.
Crothers, C. (1996) *Social Structure*. London: Routledge.
Crouch, C. and Marquand, D. (1989) *The New Centralism: Britain Out of Step in Europe*. Oxford: Blackwell.
Curtis, D.A. (ed) (1996) *The Castoriadis Reader*. Oxford: Blackwell.
Cutler, T. and Waine, B. (1997) *Managing the Welfare State*. Oxford: Berg.
Daguerre, A. (2007) *Active Labour Market Policies and Welfare Reform: Europe and the US in Comparative Perspective*. Basingstoke: Palgrave, Macmillan.
Dahl, R.A. (1961) *Who Governs*. New Haven: Yale University Press.
Dalrymple, J. and Burke, B. (1995) *Anti-Oppressive Practice*. Buckingham: Open University Press.
Daly, M. (2003) 'Governance and Social Policy', *Journal of Social Policy* 32(1): 113–28.
Daunton, M. (2007) *Wealth and Welfare: An Economic and Social History 1851–1951*. Oxford: Oxford University Press.
Davis, A. and Ellis, K. (1995) 'Enforced Altruism in Community Care', in R. Hugman and D. Smith (eds) *Ethical Issues in Social Work*. London: Routledge.
Deacon, A. (ed) (1997) *From Welfare to Work: Lessons from America*. London: Institute of Economic Affairs.
Deacon, A. (2002) *Perspectives on Welfare*. Buckingham: Open University Press.
Deacon, A. and Mann, K. (1999) 'Agency, Modernity and Social Policy', *Journal of Social Policy*. 28(3): 413–35.
Deacon, B. (2007) *Global Social Policy and Governance*. London: Sage.
Delanty, G. (2003) *Community*. London: Routledge.
de Montigny, G.A.J. (1995) *Social Working: An Ethnography of Front-line Practice*. Toronto, ON: University of Toronto Press.

DH (2001) *Valuing People: A new strategy for learning disability for the 21st century.* Cm 5086. London: The Stationery Office.

DH (2004) *Code of Practice for the International Recruitment of Healthcare Professionals.* London: DH Publications.

DH (2009) *Valuing People Now: A New Three-Year Strategy for People with Learning Disabilities.* London: The Stationery Office.

DH (2010) *Equity and Excellence: Liberating the NHS,* Cm 7881. London. The Stationery Office.

Dobson, R. (2008) 'Number of Items Dispensed in Wales Rose by 5% After Prescriptions Became Free', *British Medical Journal.* 337: 1444.

Dominelli, L. (1988) *Anti-racist Social Work: A Challenge for White Practitioners and Educators.* Basingstoke: Palgrave MacMillan.

Dominelli, L. (2002) *Anti-oppressive Social Work Theory and Practice.* Basingstoke: Palgrave Macmillan.

Dominelli, L. and Hoogveltd, A. (1996) 'Globalisation and the Technocratization of Social Work', *Critical Social Policy* 16(2): 45–62.

Donabedian, A. (1980) *Explorations and Quality Assessment and Monitoring, Vol 1: The Definition of Quality and Approaches to its Assessment.* Ann Arbor, MI: Health Administration Press.

Donnison, D. (1979) 'Social Policy since Titmuss', *Journal of Social Policy* 8(2): 145–56.

Dorling, D. (2010) *Injustice: Why Social Inequality Still Persists.* Bristol: The Policy Press.

Dowty, T. and Brown, I. (2010). *Unaccompanied Children Seeking Asylum: Privacy, Consent and Data Protection.* London: ARCH. Available at: www.archrights.org.uk/docs/ARCH%20UASCreport%20100215FINAL.pdf [accessed March 2010].

Duffy, J. (2008) *Looking out from the Middle: User Involvement in Health and Social Care in Northern Ireland.* London: Social Care Institute for Excellence (SCIE).

Duncan, S. (2000) 'Challenging Rational Action Theory', Workshop Paper No 5. Prepared for Workshop One: *Frameworks for Understanding Policy Change and Culture.* Leeds: CAVA, University of Leeds.

Duncan Smith, I. (2008) 'We Will All Pay the Price for Broken Britain', *The Daily Telegraph,* 6 December: 29.

Dustin, D. (2008) *The McDonaldization of Social Work.* Aldershot: Ashgate Publishing.

DWP (Department for Work and Pensions) (2010) *Universal Credit: Welfare that Works.* Cm 7957. London: The Stationery Office.

Dwyer, P. (2000) *Welfare Rights and Responsibilities: Contesting Social Citizenship.* Bristol: The Policy Press.

Dwyer, P. (2004) *Understanding Social Citizenship: Themes and Perspectives for Policy and Practice.* Bristol: The Policy Press.

Edelman, M. (1977) *Political Language: Words That Succeed and Policies That Fail.* New York: Academic Press.

Edelman, M. (1988) *Constructing the Political Spectacle.* Chicago: University of Chicago Press.
Edwards, D. and Cromwell, D. (2009) *Newspeak in the 21st Century*. London: Pluto Press.
Elias, N. (1978) *What is Sociology?*, translated (from German) by S. Mennell and G. Morrissey. London: Hutchinson.
Elster, J. (1989) *Nuts and Bolts for the Social Sciences*. Cambridge: Cambridge University Press.
Employers' Forum on Disability (2007) 'Employer's Forum on Disability supports Remploy's factory closures'. Available at: www.efd.org.uk/media-30 [accessed 9 August 2009].
Englander, D. (1998) *Poverty and poor law reform in Britain: from Chadwick to Booth, 1834-1914*. London: Longman.
Esping-Andersen, G. (1990) *The Three Worlds of Welfare Capitalism*. Princeton, NJ: Princeton University Press.
Esping-Andersen, G. (1999) *Social Foundations of Postindustrial Economies*. New York: Oxford University Press.
Esping-Andersen, G. with Gallie, D. Hemerijck, A. and Myles, J. (2002) *Why We Need a New Welfare State*. Oxford: Oxford University Press.
Etzioni, A. (1971) *A Comparative Analysis of Complex Organisations*. New York, NY: The Free Press.
Etzioni, A. (1995) *The Spirit of Community: Rights, Responsibilities and the Communitarian Agenda*. London: Fontana.
Etzioni, A. (1998) *The Essential Communitarian Reader*. Lanham, MD: Rowman & Littlefield.
Etzioni, A. (2000) *The Third Way to a Good Society*. London: Demos.
Evans, G. (2006) *Educational Failure and Working Class White Children in Britain*. Basingstoke: Palgrave Macmillan.
Experian (2007) 'Overseas Workers in the UK Social Care, Children and Young People Sector: A Report for Skills for Care and Development'. Available at: www.skillsforcare.org.uk/publications/Showall.aspx [accessed 29 October, 2010].
Experts by Experience (undated) 'A Window in our Lives'. Available at: www.expertsbyexperience.org.uk/ [accessed 12 October 2010].
Fairbrother, P. (2005) Book review of G. Gall (ed) 'Union Organising: Campaigning for Trade Union Recognition'. *Capital and Class* 37: 257-63.
Fairbrother, P. and Poynter, G. (2001) 'State Restructuring: Managerialism, Marketisation and the Implications for Labour', *Competition and Change.* 5(3): 311–33.
Fairclough, N. (2000) *New Labour, New Language?*. London: Routledge.
Fairclough, N. (2003) *Analysing Discourse: Textual Analysis for Social Research*. London: Routledge.
Ferguson, I. and Lavalette, M. (2004) 'Beyond Power Discourse: Alienation and Social Work'. *British Journal of Social Work* 34(3): 297-312.

Ferguson, I. (2007) 'Increasing User Choice or Privatizing Risk? The Antinomies of Personalization', *British Journal of Social Work*. 37: 387–403.
Ferguson, I. (2008) *Reclaiming Social Work: Challenging Neo-liberalism and Promoting Social Justice*. London: Sage..
Field, F. (1997) *Reforming Welfare*. London: Social Market Foundation.
Finch, J. (2000) 'Interprofessional Education and Teamworking: A View From the Education Providers', *British Medical Journal* 321: 1138–40.
Finch, J. and Mason, J. (1993) *Negotiating Family Responsibilities*. London: Routledge.
Fine, B. and Leopold, E. (2001) *The World of Consumption*. London: Routledge.
Finkelstein, V. (1980) *Attitudes and Disabled People: Issues for Discussion*. New York: World Rehabilitation Fund.
Fitzgerald, M., Halmos, P., Munice, J. and Zeldin, D. (eds) (1977) *Welfare in Action*. London: Routledge, Kegan and Paul.
Fook, J. (2002) *Social Work: Critical Theory and Practice*. London: Sage.
Foucault, M. (1977) *Discipline and Punish*. Harmondsworth: Penguin.
Foucault, M. (1980) *Power/Knowledge*. Brighton: Harvester Press.
Franklin, B. (2004) *Packaging Politics: Political Communications in Britain's Media Democracy*, 2nd edn. London: Arnold.
Freeman, S. (2009) 'Red card for benefit scrounger who refereed 40 football matches... while claiming he couldn't walk'. Available at: www.dailymail.co.uk/news/article-1231374/Red-card-benefits-scrounging-referee-claimed-walk.html#ixzz18pjzxnVT.
Freire, P. (1972) *Pedagogy of the Oppressed*. Harmondsworth: Penguin.
Friedman, M. (1962) *Capitalism and Freedom*. Chicago: University of Chicago Press.
Fukuyama, F. (1992) *The End of History and the Last Man*. New York: Basic Books.
Fukuyama, F. (2006) 'After Neo-conservatism', *The New York Times*, 19 February. Available at: http://zfacts.com/metaPage/lib/Fukuyama-2006-After-Neoconservatism.pdf [accessed 24 October 2010].
Gabaiz, X. and Landier, A. (2006) 'Why Has CEO Pay Increased So Much?', MIT Department of Economics working paper, Number 6-13.
Galbraith, J.K. (1983) *The Voice of the Poor*. Cambridge, MA: Harvard University Press.
Galper, J. (1980) *Social Work Practice: A Radical Perspective*. London: Prentice Hall.
Gardham, D. and Stokes, P. (2008) 'Complex Family Tree Held Up Police', *The Daily Telegraph*, 17 March: 5.
Garrett, G. and Mitchell, D. (2001) 'Globalization, Government Spending and Taxation in the OECD', *European Journal of Political Research* 39: 145–77.
Garrett, P.-M. (2009) *Transforming Children's Services: Social Work, Neo-liberalism and the 'Modern World'*. Buckingham: Open University Press.
Gaunt, J. (2008) 'More Shannons in Benefits R Us Hell', *The Sun*, 5 December: 27.
George, V. and Wilding, P. (1993) *Welfare and Ideology*. London: Prentice Hall.
Giddens, A. (1984) *The Constitution of Society: Outline of the Theory of Structuration*. Cambridge: Polity Press.

Gill, S. (1995) 'Globalisation, Market Civilisation and Disciplinary Neoliberalism', *Millennium: Journal of International Studies* 24(3): 399–423.

Gilens, M. (1999) *Whay Americans Hate Welfare: Race, Media and the Politics of Anti-Poverty Policy.* Chicago: University of Chicago Press.

Gilroy, P. (1982) *The Empire Strikes Back – Race and Racism in '70s Britain.* London: Routledge/Centre for Contemporary Cultural Studies.

Ginsburg, N. (1979) *Class, Capital and Social Policy*. London: Macmillan.

Glennerster, H. (2009) *Understanding the Finance of Welfare: What Welfare Costs and How to Pay for It*, 2nd edn. Bristol: The Policy Press in association with the Social Policy Association.

Glyn, A. (2006) *Capitalism Unleashed: Finance, Globalization, and Welfare.* Oxford: Oxford University Press.

GMB (2009) 'GMB Remploy Workers'. Available at: www.gmbremployworkers.info/index.html [accessed 23 July 2009].

Gough, I. (1979) *The Political Economy of the Welfare State.* London: Macmillan.

Gramsci, A. (2003) *Prison Notebooks: Selections.* London: Lawrence & Wishart Ltd.

Grice, A. (2009) '£850bn: Official Cost of the Bank Bailout', *The Independent*, 4 December. Available at: www.independent.co.uk/news/uk/politics/163850bn-official-cost-of-the-bank-bailout-1833830.html www.independent.co.uk/news/uk/politics/163850bn-official-cost-of-the-bank-bailout-1833830.html [accessed 31 March 2011].

Griffiths, R. (1988) *Community Care: Agenda for Action. A Report to the Secretary of State for Social Services.* London: HMSO.

Grover, C. (2005) 'The National Childcare Strategy: The Social Regulation of Lone Mothers as a Gendered Reserve Army of Labour', *Capital and Class* 85: 63–85.

Grover, C. (2006) 'Welfare Reform, Accumulation and Social Exclusion in the United Kingdom', *Social Work and Society.* 4(1). Online journal: www.socwork.net/2006/1/articles/grover/metadata.

Grover, C. and Piggott, L. (2005) 'Disabled People: The Reserve Army of Labour and Welfare Reform', *Disability and Society* 7: 705–17.

Grover, C. and Stewart, J. (1999), '"Market Workfare": Social Security and Competitiveness in the 1990s', *Journal of Social Policy* 24(1): 73–96.

GSCC (General Social Care Council) (2005) *Specialist Standards and Requirements for Post-pualifying Social Work Education and Training: Social Work with Adults.* London: GSCC.

GSCC (2008) 'Country Assessment Guidance'. Available at: http://www.gscc.org.uk/The+Social+Care+Register/Apply+for+registration/Social+ Worker s+trained+and+qualified+outside+the+UK/Country+assessment+guidance/Country+assessment+guidance.htm [accessed 29 November 200].

Guba, E.G. and Lincoln, Y.S. (1989) *Fourth Generation Evaluation.* Newbury Park, CA: Sage.

Habermas, J. (2005) *Truth and Justification*, translated by B. Fultner. Cambridge, MA: MIT Press.

Hall, S. (1987) 'Gramsci and Us', in *Marxism Today*, June 1987. Available at: www.hegemonics.co.uk/docs/Gramsci-and-us.pdf [accessed 20 December 2010].

Hall, S. (1992) 'The West and the Rest: Discourse and Power', in S. Hall and B. Gieben (eds) *Formations of Modernity*. London: Sage Publications.

Halmos, P. (1965) *The Faith of the Counsellors: A Study in the Theory and Practice of Social Case Work and Psychotherapy*. London: Constable.

Ham, C. and Hill, M. (1984) *The Policy Process in the Modern Capitalist State*. Hemel Hempstead: Harverster Wheatsheaf.

Hardingham, L.B. (2004) 'Integrity and Moral Residue: Nurses as Participants in a Moral Community', *Nursing Philosophy* 5(2): 127–34.

Harris, B. (2004) *The Origins of the British Welfare State: Social Welfare in England and Wales 1800–1945*. Basingstoke: Palgrave Macmillan.

Harris, J. (2003) *The Social Work Business*. London: Routledge.

Harris, J. (2009) 'The Webbs and Beveridge: From Workhouse to Workfare', in The Fabian Society (ed) *From the Workhouse to Welfare: What Beatrice Webb's 1909 Minority Report Can Teach Us Today*. London: The Fabian Society.

Harrison, S., Hunter, D.J., Mamoch, T. and Pollitt, C. (1992) *Just Managing – Power and Culture in the National Health Service*. London: Macmillan.

Harvey, D. (2007) *A Brief History of Neoliberalism*. Oxford: Oxford University Press.

Harvey, L. (1990) *Critical Social Research*. London: Unwin Hyman.

Headrick, L.A., Wilcock, P.M. and Batalden, P.B. (1998) 'Interprofessional Working and Continuing Medical Education', *British Medical Journal* 316: 771–4.

Healey, P. (2006) *Collaborative Planning: Shaping Places in Fragmented Societies*, 2nd edn. London: Palgrave MacMillan.

Heaseman, K. (1962) *Evangelicals in Action: An Appraisal of their Social Work*. Letchworth: Garden City Press.

Hegel, G.W.F. (1969) *Science of Logic*. London: Allen and Unwin.

Held, D., McGrew, A., Goldblatt, D. and Perraton, J. (1999) *Global Transformations: Politics, Economics and Culture*. Cambridge: Polity Press.

Hickman, M. and Walter, B. (1997) *Discrimination and the Irish Community in Britain*. London: Centre for Racial Equality.

Higgins, J. (1981) *States of Welfare. Comparative Analysis in Social Policy*. Oxford: Basil Blackwell & Martin Robertson.

Hills, J. (2008) 'Making Class Politics Possible: Organizing Contract Cleaners in London', *International Journal of Urban and Regional Research*. 32(2): 305–23.

Hills, J., Sefton, T. and Stewart, K. (2009) *Towards a More Equal Society*. Bristol: The Policy Press.

Hilton, M. and Hirsch, P. (eds) (2000) *Practical Visionaries: Women, Education, and Social Progress, 1790–1930*. Harlow: Longman.

Hindle, S. (2004) 'Dependency, Shame and Belonging: Badging the Deserving Poor, c.1550–1750', *Cultural and Social History* 1(1): 6–35.

Hirst, M. (2001) 'Trends in Informal Care in Great Britain During the 1990s', *Health and Social Care in the Community* 9(6): 348–57.

Hirst, P. and Thompson, G. (1996) *Globalisation in Question: The International Economy and Possibilities of Governance.* Cambridge: Polity Press.

HM Treasury (2003) *Every Child Matters.* Cm 5860. London: HMSO.

Hobcraft, J. (1998) *Intergenerational and Life-course Transmission of Social Exclusion, CASEpaper 15.* London: LSE.

Hobsbawm, E. (1987) *The Age of Empire 1875–1914.* London: Weidenfeld & Nicholson.

Hobsbawm, E. (2007) *Revolutionaries: Revised and Updated Edition.* London. Abacus

Holmes, C. (1988) *John Bull's Island: Immigration and British Society.* Basingstoke: MacMillan.

Hoggett, P., Mayo, M. and Miller, C. (2006) 'Private passions, the public good and public service reform', *Social Policy and Administration* 40(7): 758-773.

Homans, G. (1961) *Social Behavior.* New York: Harcourt, Brace & World.

Home Office (2010) *Control of Immigration: Quarterly Statistical Summary, United Kingdom. October–December 2009.* Available at: http://rds.homeoffice.gov.uk/rds/pdfs10/immiq409.pdf.

Homfeldt, H.G and Sting, S. (2006) *Soziale Arbeit und Gesundheit.* München u. Basel: Ernst Reinhardt Verlag.

Hood, C. (1991) 'A Public Management for All Seasons', *Public Administration* 69: 3–19.

Horner, L. Lekhi, R. and Blaug, R. (2006) *Deliberative Democracy and the Role of Public Managers. Final Report of the Work Foundation's Public Value Consortium.* London: The Work Foundation.

Houston, S. (2010) 'Beyond Homo Economicus: Recognition, Self-Realization and Social Work', *British Journal of Social Work.* 40: 841–57.

Howard, M.W. (2000) *Self-management and the Crisis of Socialism: The Rose in the Fist of the Present.* Oxford: Roman and Littlefield.

Hreinsdóttir, E.E., Stefánsdóttir, G., Lewthwaite, A., Ledger, S. and Shufflebotham, L. (2006) 'Is My Story So Different From Yours? Comparing Life Stories, Experiences of Institutionalization and Self-Advocacy in England and Iceland', *British Journal of Learning Disabilities* 34(3): 157–66.

Hughes, H.P. (1891) 'Irresponsible Wealth', *Poverty Bay Herald*, p 3.

Hugman, B. (1977) *Act Natural.* London: Bedford Square Press.

Human Trafficking.org (2010) a web resource for combating human trafficking. Available at: http://www.humantrafficking.org/regions/europe_and_eurasia [accessed 29 October 2010].

Hunt, A. and Wickham, G. (1993) *Foucault and Law: Towards Sociology of Governance.* London: Pluto Press.

Hunter, D. (1980) *Coping with Uncertainty: Policy and Politics in the NHS.* Chichester: Research Studies Press.

Husband, C. (ed) (1986) *'Race' in Britain: Continuity and Change.* London. Routledge.

Husband, C. (1995) 'The Morally Active Practitioner and the Ethics of Anti-Racist Social Work', in Hugman, R. and Smith, D. (eds) *Ethical Issues in Social Work*. London: Routledge.

IFSW (International Federation of Social Workers) (2001) *Ethics in Social Work, Statement of Principles*. Available at: www.ifsw.org/p38000398.html [accessed 15 February 2011].

Irvin, G. (2008) *Super Rich: The Rise of Inequality in Britain and the United States*. Cambridge: Polity Press.

Isles, N. (2003) *Life at the Top: The Labour Market for FTSE-250 Chief Executives?* London: The Work Foundation.

Jacobs, K. and Manzi, T. (1996) 'Discourse and Policy Change: The Significance of Language for Housing Research', *Housing Studies* 11(4): 543-560.

Jannson, B.S. (2003) *Becoming an Effective Policy Advocate. From Policy Practice to Social Justice*, 4th edn. Pacific Grove, CA: Thomson, Brooks and Cole.

Jaziri, N.T. (1976) *Approaches to the Development of Health Indicators*. Paris: OECD.

Jessop, B. (1994) 'The Transition to Post-Fordism and the Schumpeterian Workfare State', in R. Burrows and B. Loader (eds) *Towards a Post-Fordist Welfare State?*. London: Routledge.

Jessop, B. (1999) 'The Changing Governance of Welfare: Recent Trends in its Primary Functions, Scale and Modes of Coordination', *Social Policy and Administration* 33(4): 348–59.

Jessop, B. (2004) 'Critical Semiotic Analysis and Cultural Political Economy', *Critical Discourse Studies* 1(2): 159–74.

Johns, C. (2000) *Becoming a Reflective Practitioner*. Oxford: Blackwell Science.

Johnson, P. and Reed, H. (1996) *Two Nations? The Inheritance of Poverty and Affluence*. London: IFS.

Jones, C. (1977) *Immigration and Social Policy in Britain*. London: Tavistock.

Jones, C. (2001) 'Voices from the Front Line: State Social Work and New Labour', *British Journal of Social Work* 31(4): 547–62.

Jones, C. and Novak, T. (1993) *Poverty, Welfare and the Disciplinary State*. London: Routledge.

Jones, C., Ferguson, I., Lavalette, M. and Penketh, L. (2004) 'Social Work and Social Justice: A Manifesto for a New Engaged Practice'. Available at: www.liv.ac.uk/sspsw/Manifesto.htm [accessed 31 January 2007].

Jordan, B. (1998) *The New Politics of Welfare: Social Justice in a Global Context*. London: Sage.

Jordan, B. (2004) *Sex, Money and Power: The Transformation of Collective Life*. Cambridge: Polity.

Jordan, B. (2006) *Social Policy for the Twenty-First Century: Big Issues, New Perspectives*. Cambridge: Polity Press.

Jordan, B. and Jordan, C. (2000) *Social Work and the Third Way: Tough Love as Social Policy*. London: Sage.

Joyce, P., Corrigan, P. and Hayes, M. (1988) *Striking Out: Trades Unionism in Social Work*. Basingstoke: Macmillan.

Judt, T (2010) *Ill Fares the Land*. London: Penguin Books.

Julkunen, I. (2005) 'Ingegrated Social Services in Europe – Approaches and Implementation: A Scoping Research Review', Paper commissioned by the Council of Europe.

Karlsson, M., Mayhew, L. and Rickayzen, B. (2006) 'Future Costs for Long-Term Care: Cost Projections for Long-term Care for Older People in the United Kingdom', *Health Policy* 75(2): 187–213.

Keynes, J.M. (1997 [1936]) *The General Theory of Employment, Interest, and Money*. Amherst, NY: Prometheus Books.

Klein, R. (2001) *The New Politics of the National Health Service*. London: Prentice Hall.

Kohli, R. (2006) 'The Sound of Silence: Listening to What Unaccompanied Children Say and Do Not Say', *British Journal of Social Work* 36: 707–21.

Laming, H. (2003) *The Victoria Climbé Inquiry*. London: The Stationery Office.

Langan, M. (1992) 'Introduction: Women and Social Work in the 1990s', in M. Langan and L. Day (eds) *Women, Oppression and Social Work*. London: Routledge.

Langan, M. (2002) *The Legacy of Radical Social Work*. London: Macmillan.

Lansley, S. (2006) *Rich Britain: The Rise and Rise of the New Super-wealthy*. London: Politico's.

Lansley, S. (2008) *Do the Super-Rich Matter?* Touchstone Pamphlet No 4. London: TUC.

Latour, B. (2005) *Reassembling the Social: An Introduction to Actor-Network-Theory*. Oxford: Oxford University Press.

Lavalette, M. and Ferguson, I. (2007) 'Democratic Language and Neo-Liberal Practice: The Problem with Civil Society', *International Social Work* 50(4): 447–59.

Lavalette, M. and Mooney, G. (2000) *Class Struggle and Social Welfare*. London: Routledge.

Lavin, C. (2005) 'Postliberal Agency in Marx's Brumaire. Rethinking Agency in Marx's Brumaire', *Rethinking Marxism* 17(3): 439–54.

Ledwith, M. (2007) 'Reclaiming the Radical Agenda: A Critical Approach to Community Development', *Concept* 17(2): 8–12.

Le Grand, J. (1990) 'Re-Thinking Welfare: A Case for Quasi-Markets', in B. Pimlott (ed) *The Alternative: Politics for a Change*. London: W.H. Allen and Virgin Books.

Le Grand, J. (1997) 'Knights, Knaves or Pawns? Human Behaviour and Social Policy', *Journal of Social Policy* 26(2): 149–69.

Le Grand, J. (2007) *The Other Invisible Hand: Delivering Public Services Through Choice and Competition*. Princeton, NJ: Princeton University Press.

Leibenstein, H. (1966) 'Allocative Efficiency vs. "X-Efficiency"', *The American Economic Review* 56(3): 392–415.

Leitner, H., Peck, J. and Sheppard, E.S. (2007) *Contesting Neoliberalism: Urban Frontiers*. London: Guilford Press.

Lens, V. (2002) 'Public Voices and Public Policy: Changing the Societal Discourse on "Welfare"', *Journal of Sociology and Social Welfare* 29(1): 137–54.

Cheshire, L. (2008) 'Disability Poverty in the UK'. Available at: www.lcdisability.org/?lid=6386 [accessed 15 August 2008].

Leonard Cheshire, Mencap, Mind, Radar, Scope and the Royal National Institute of Deaf People (2007) 'Letter to the Guardian', *The Guardian*, 19 May.

Levitas, R. (1996) 'The Concept of Social Exclusion and the New Durkheimian Hegemony', *Critical Social Policy* 16(1): 5–20.

Levitas, R. (1998) *The Inclusive Society?*. Basingstoke: Macmillan.

Lister, R. (2004) *Poverty*. Cambridge: Polity.

London Coalition Against Poverty, www.lcap.org.uk/

Loney, M. (1983) *Community against Government: The British Community Development Project 1968–1978: A Study of Government Incompetence*. Heinemann: London.

Loughran, J.J. (2002) 'Effective Reflective Practice: in search of meaning in learning about teaching', *Journal of Teacher Education* 53(1): 33-43.

Lyons, K., Manion, K. and Carlsen, M. (2006) *International Perspectives on Social Work: Global Conditions and Local Practice*. Basingstoke: Palgrave-Macmillan.

MacKay, R.R. (1998) 'Unemployment as Exclusion: Unemployment as Choice', in P. Lawless, R. Martin and S. Hardy (eds) *Unemployment and Social Exclusion*. London: Jessica Kingsley.

Malone, C. (2008) 'Force Low-life to Work for a Living', *The News of the World*, 7 December: 13.

Manzoor, R. (2007) '25,000 Textile Workers Protest against Poor Wages'. Available at: http://socialistworld.net/eng/2007/10/26bangla.html [accessed 29 October 2010].

Marshall, T.H. (1967) *Social Policy*, 2nd edn. London: Routledge and Kegan Paul.

Marston, G. (2000) 'Metaphor, Morality and Myth: A Critical Discourse Analysis of Public Housing Policy in Queensland', *Critical Social Policy* 20(3): 349–74.

Marston, G. (2004) *Social Policy and Discourse Analysis: Policy Change in Public Housing*. Aldershot: Ashgate.

Martin, D. (2010) 'Free Treatment on NHS for Thousands of Asylum Rejects', *Daily Mail*, 26 January. Available at: www.dailymail.co.uk/news/article-1200930/Failed-asylum-seekers-free-care-cash-strapped-NHS-protect-human-rights.html#ixzz0rrQktbJT [accessed 28 January 2011].

Martin-Crawford, L. (1999) 'Empowerment in Healthcare', *Participation and Empowerment: An International Journal*. 7(1): 15–24.

Marx, K. (1963 [1843]) *Karl Marx: Early Writings*, translated by T.B. Bottomore. London: McGraw Hill.

Marx, K. (2005) *Capital*. London: Penguin.

Marx, K. and Engels, F. (2003 [1848]) *The Communist Manifesto*. London: Bookmarks.

Marx, K. and Engels, F. (2004 [1845]) *The German Ideology*. London: Lawrence and Wishart.

Massey, A. and Pyper, R. (2005) *Public Management and Modernisation in Britain*. Basingstoke: Palgrave MacMillan.

Maxwell, M. (2008) 'Just a Shameless Breeding Machine', *The Sun*, December 10: 11.

Maxwell, R. (1983) 'Seeking Quality', *Lancet* 8(8314–15): 45–8.

Mayer, J.E. and Timms, N. (1970) *The Client Speaks: Working Class Impressions of Casework*. London: Routledge, Kegan and Paul.

Mayntz, R. (1976) 'Conceptual Models of Organizational Decision Making and Their Application to the Policy Process', in G. Hofstede and M.S. Kassem (eds) *European Contributions to Organization Theory*. Amsterdam: Van Gorcum.

Mayo, M. (1994) *Communities and Caring: The Mixed Economy of Welfare*. Basingstoke: Macmillan.

Mayo, M. and Craig, G. (1995) 'Community Participation and Empowerment: The Human Face of Structural Readjustment or Tools for Democratic Transformation?', in G. Craig and M. Mayo (eds) *Community Empowerment: A Reader in Participation and Development*. London: Zed Press.

McBeath, G. and Webb, S. (2002) 'Virtue Ethics and Social Work: Being Lucky, Realistic and Not Doing One's Duty', *British Journal of Social Work* 32: 1015–36.

McCourt, W. and Minogue, M. (eds) (2001) *The Internationalisation of Public Management: Reinventing the Third World State*. Cheltenham: Edward Elgar.

McLaughlin, K., Osborne, S.P. and Ferlie, E. (2002) *New Public Management: Current Trends and Future Prospects*. London: Routledge.

Meads, G. and Ashcroft, J. (2005) *The Case for Interprofessional Collaboration in Health and Social Care*. Oxford: Blackwell Publishing Ltd.

Meiksins Wood, E. (1990) 'The Uses and Abuses of Civil Society', in R. Miliband and L. Pantich (eds), *The Socialist Register 1990: The Retreat of the Intellectuals*. London: Merlin Press.

Menchik, P. (1979) 'Intergeneration Transmission of Inequality: An Empirical Study of Wealth Mobility', *Economica* 46: 349–62.

Merrick, R. (2010) 'Cameron's Plans for Tax Breaks', *Liverpool Echo*, 6 October. Available at: www.liverpoolecho.co.uk/liverpool-news/local-news/2010/10/06/david-cameron-revives-controversial-plans-for-tax-breaks-to-reward-marriage-100252-27410808 [accessed 12 June 2010].

Merton, R. (1957) *Social Theory and Social Structure*, revised and enlarged edition. New York: The Free Press.

Meyer, L. (1994) 'How the Right Measures Help Teams Excel', *Harvard Business Review*. 72(3): 99–122.

Milewa, T., Valentine, J. and Calnan, M. (1998) 'Managerialism and Active Citizenship in a Reformed Health Service: Power and Community in an Era of Decentralisation', *Social Science & Medicine*. 47(4): 507–17.

Miliband, R. (1973) *The State in Capitalist Society*. London: Quartet Books.

Millar, J. and Salt, J (2006) 'Foreign labour in the United Kingdom: Current Patterns and Trends; this Article Presents the Current Situation with Respect to Stocks and Flows of Foreign Labour in the UK', *Labour Market Trends*. 114 (10) 335-355.

Minns, H. (2000) 'Catherine Mcauley and the Education of Irish Roman Catholic Children in the Mid-Nineteenth Century', in M. Hilton and P. Hirsch (eds) *Practical Visionaries: Women, Education and Social Progress, 1790–1930*. Harlow: Longman, 52–66.

Mishra, R. (1977) *Society and Social Policy: Theoretical Perspectives on Welfare*. London: Macmillan.

Mishra, R. (1999) *Globalization and the Welfare State*. Cheltenham: Edward Elgar.

Misztal, B. (2000) *Informality: Social Theory and Contemporary Practice*. London: Routledge.

Moffatt, K. and Irving, A. (2002) '"Living for the Brethren": Idealism, Social Work's Lost Enlightenment Strain', *British Journal of Social Work* 32(4): 415–27.

Moir, J. (2008) 'They Keep Having Babies – and We Have to Pick Up the Bills', *The Daily Telegraph*, 16 April: 19.

Molyneux, J. (2001) 'Interprofessional Teamworking: What Makes Teams Work Well?', *Journal of Interprofessional Care* 15(1): 29–35.

Mooney, G. and Law, A. (eds) (2007) *New Labour/Hard Labour? Restructuring and Resistance in the Welfare Industry*. Bristol: Policy Press.

Mooney, G. and McCafferty, T. (2005) '"Only Looking After the Weans?" The Scottish Nursery Nurses' Strike, 2004', *Critical Social Policy* 25(2): 223–39.

Moore, J.R. (ed) (1988) *Religion in Victorian Britain: Volume III, Sources*. Manchester: Manchester University Press.

Moore, J. (2008) 'I Do Feel Pity Karen … but Only for Taxpayers', *The Sun*, 10 December: 8.

Morgan, G. (2006) *Images of Organization*, updated edn. London: Sage.

Morris, J. (1991) *Pride against Prejudice: Transforming Attitudes to Disability*. London: The Women's Press.

Mosley, L. (2007) 'The Political Economy of Globalization', in D. Held and A. McGrew (eds) *Globalization Theory: Approaches and Controversies*. Cambridge: Polity Press.

Muirhead, J.H. (1911) 'The City of Birmingham Aid Society', in J.H. Muirhead (ed) *Birmingham Institutions*. Birmingham: Cornish Brothers.

Munday, B. (2007) *Integrated Social Services in Europe*. Strasbourg: Council of Europe Publishing.

Murray, C. (1984) *Losing Ground*. New York: Basic Books.

Murray, C. (1990) *The Emerging British Underclass. Choice in Welfare Series, No 2*. London: Health and Welfare Unit, Institute of Economic Affairs.

Murray, C. (1994) *Losing Ground: American Social Policy, 1950–1980*, 10th anniversary edition. New York: Basic Books.

Murray, C. (2001) *The Underclass Plus Ten*. London: Civitas.

Musolf, G.R. (2003) 'Social Structure, Human Agency, and Social Policy', *The International Journal of Sociology and Social Policy* 23(6/7): 1–12.

National Audit Office (2005) 'Gaining and Retaining a Job: The Department for Work and Pensions' Support for Disabled People'. Available at: www.nao.org.uk/publications/0506/gaining_and_retaining_a_job.aspx [accessed 12 August 2008].

National Audit Office (2009) *Maintaining Financial Stability Across the United Kingdom's Banking System*. London: The Stationery Office.
National Union of Teachers (no date) *NUT history*. Available at: www.teachers.org.uk/node/8515 [accessed 15 February, 2011].
Nelson, F. (2008) 'Now Teach the Sinks to Swim', *The News of the World*, 7 December: 3.
Nelson, J.I. (1995) *Post-industrial Capitalism*. London: Sage.
Newman, J. (2001) *Modernising Governance: New Labour, Policy and Society*. London: Sage.
Newman, J. and Vidler, E. (2006) 'Discriminating Customers, Responsible Patients, Empowered Users: Consumerism and the Modernization of Health Care', *Journal of Social Policy* 35(2): 193–209.
Nirje, B. (1969) 'The Normalization Principle and Its Human Management Implications', reprinted in *The International Social Role Valorization Journal* 1(2). Available at: www.socialrolevalorization.com/articles/journal/1994/english/normalization-principles.pdf [accessed 24 September 2010].
NMC (Nursing and Midwifery Council) (2008) 'The Code Standards of Conduct, Performance and Ethics for Nurses and Midwives'. Available at: www.nmc-uk.org/Nurses-and-midwives/The-code/The-code-in-full/.
Norfolk, A. (2008a) 'How One Case Exposed the Grim Reality of Life for Thousands in the Poorest Communities', *The Times*, 5 December: 4–5.
Norfolk, A. (2008b) 'Neighbours Who Stood by Family Watch It Fall Apart', *The Times*, 8 April: 13.
Novak, T. (1988) *Poverty and the State: An Historical Sociology*. Milton Keynes: Open University Press.
Nozick, R. (1974) *Anarchy, State and Utopia*. Oxford: Blackwell.
O'Connor, J. (1981) 'The Meaning of Crisis', *International Journal of Urban and Regional Research* 5(3): 301–29.
O'Hara, G. (2010) 'How (Not) to Cut Government Spending and Reduce Public Sector Debt', *History and Policy: Connecting Historians, Policymakers and the Media*. Available at: www.historyandpolicy.org/papers/policy-paper-95.html
Ohmae, K. (1995) *The End of the Nation State: The Rise of Regional Economies*. London: Harper Collins.
O'Laird, S. (2008) *Anti-oppressive Social Work: A Guide for Developing Cultural Competence*. London: Sage.
Oliver, J. (2008) 'New Tough Line on Welfare Mothers', *The Sunday Times*, 7 December: 1.
Oliver, M. (1990) *The Politics of Disablement*. Basingstoke: Macmillan.
Oliver, M.J. (1999) 'Capitalism, Disability and Ideology: A Materialist Critique of the Normalization Principle', in R.J. Flynn and R.A. Lemay (eds) *A Quarter Century of Normalization and Social Role Valorization: Evolution and Impact*. Ottawa: University of Ottawa Press. Available at: www.independentliving.org/docs3/oliver99.pdf [accessed 12 October 2010].

Olsen, W. (1994) 'Research as Enabler: An Alternative Model of Research for Public Health', *Critical Public Health* 5(3): 5–14.

ONS (Office for National Statistics) (2002) *Social Capital: The Question Bank.* Available at: www.ons.gov.uk/about-statistics/user-guidance/sc-guide/the-question-bank/index.html [accessed 20 December 2010].

ONS (2009) *Wealth in Great Britain. Main Results from the Wealth and Assets Survey 2006/08.* Available at: www.statistics.gov.uk/downloads/theme_economy/wealth-assets-2006-2008/Wealth_in_GB_2006_2008.pdf [accessed 29 March 2011].

ONS (2010a) *Centre for the Measurement of Government Activity.* Available at: www.ons.gov.uk/about-statistics/ukcemga/publications-home/publications/index.html [accessed 5 February 2011].

ONS (2010b) *Wealth and Assets.* Available at: www.ons.gov.uk/search/index.html?newquery=wealth+and+assets [accessed 18 December 2010].

Orton, M. and Rowlingson, K. (2007a) 'A Problem of Riches: Towards a New Social Policy Research Agenda on the Distribution of Economic Resources', *Journal of Social Policy* 36(1): 59–78.

Orton, M. and Rowlingson, K. (2007b) *Public Attitudes to Inequality.* York: Joseph Rowntree Foundation.

Owen, J. (2008) 'Dissident Missionaries? "Re-Narrating the Political Strategy of the Social-Democratic Federation, 1884–1887"', *Labour History Review* 73 (2): 187–207.

Palmer, G., Carr, J. and Kenway, P. (2005) *Monitoring Poverty and Social Exclusion.* York: Joseph Rowntree Foundation. Available at: www.npi.org.uk/publications.htm

Parker, J. (2000) *Structuration.* Buckingham: Open University Press.

Parkinson, G. (1970) 'I Give Them Money', *New Society*, 5 February: 220–1.

Parsons, G. (1988) 'Victorian Roman Catholicism: Emancipation, Expansion and Achievement', in G. Parsons (ed) *Religion in Victorian Britain: Part I Traditions.* Manchester: Manchester University Press:146–83.

Parsons, T. (1959) 'Voting and the Equilibrium of the American Political System', in E. Burdick and A. Brodbeck (eds) *American Voting Behavior.* New York: Free Press.

Parsons, T. (1966) 'On the concept of political power', in R. Bendix and S. Lipset (eds) *Class, Status, and Power*, 2nd edn. New York: Free Press: 240–65.

Patton, M.Q. (1988) 'Paradigms and Pragmatism', in D. Fetterman (ed) *Qualitative Approaches to Evaluation in Education: The Silent Scientific Revolution.* New York: Praeger.

Patton, M.Q. (1990) *Qualitative Evaluation & Research Methods*, 2nd edn. Newbury Park, CA: Sage.

Paul, K. (1997) *Whitewashing Britain: Race and Citizenship in the Post-war Era.* Ithaca, NY: Cornell University Press.

Payne, M. (2005) *Modern Social Work Theory*, 3rd edn. Basingstoke: Palgrave MacMIllan.

Pearson, G. (1973) 'Social Work as the Privatized Solution of Public Ills', *British Journal of Social Work* 3(2): 209–27.

Pearson, G. (1975) *The Deviant Imagination: Psychiatry, Social Work and Social Change.* Basingstoke: Palgrave Macmillan.

Pearson, G. (1978) *Welfare on the Move: Unit 4, DE206.* Buckingham: Open University Press.

Peate, I. (2008) *British Journal of Healthcare Assistants* 2(3): 109.

Peck, J. (2001) *Workfare States.* New York: Guildford.

Peck, J. and Tickell, A. (2002) *Neoliberalizing Space.* Oxford: Blackwell Publishers.

Pemberton, C. (2010) 'Afghanistan centre for deported child asylum seekers condemned'. *Community Care.* 8 June 2010. Available at: www.communitycare.co.uk/Articles/2010/06/08/114671/afghanistan-centre-for-deported-child-asylum-seekers-condemned.htm [accessed 8 August 2010].

Perlman, H.H. (1970) 'Casework and the "Diminished Man"', *Social Casework* 51: 16–24.

Peters, T. and Waterman, R. (1982) *In Search of Excellence: Lessons From America's Best Run Companies.* New York: Harper and Row.

Pickard, L. (2008a) *Informal Care for Younger Adults in England: Current Provision and Issues in Future Supply, England 2005–2041*, Report to the Strategy Unit (Cabinet Office) and the Department of Health, PSSRU Discussion Paper 2513. London: Personal Social Services Research Unit.

Pickard, L. (2008b) *Informal Care for Older People Provided by their Adult Children: Projections of Supply and Demand to 2041 in England*, Report to the Strategy Unit (Cabinet Office) and the Department of Health, PSSRU Discussion Paper 2515. London: Personal Social Services Research Unit.

Pickard, L. (2008c) *Sources of Informal Care: Comparison of ELSA and GHS (PDF)*, PSSRU Discussion Paper 2598. London: Personal Social Services Research Unit.

Piggott, L. and Grover, C. (2009) 'Retrenching Incapacity Benefit: Employment Support Allowance and Paid Work', *Social Policy and Society* 8: 159–70.

Pinker, R. (1972) *Social Theory and Social Policy.* London: Heinemann.

Piven, F. and Cloward, R.A. (1977) *Poor People's Movements: Why They Succeed, How They Fail.* New York: Pantheon Books.

Pollitt, C. (1993) 'The Politics of Medical Quality: Auditing Doctors in the UK and the USA', *Health Services Management Research* 6(1): 113–17.

Popay, J. and Williams, G. (eds) (1994) *Researching the People's Health.* London: Routledge.

Populus (2009) 'Post Budget Poll', 22 April. Available at: www.populuslimited.com [accessed 24 April 2010].

Poulantzas, N. (1973) *Political Power and Social Classes*, translated by T. O'Hagan. London: NLB, Secker and Warburg.

Powell, M. (ed) (2007) *Understanding the Mixed Economy of Welfare.* Bristol: The Policy Press.

Prabhakar, R., Rowlingson, K. and White, S. (2008) *How to Defend Inheritance Tax.* London: Fabian Society.

Price, V. and Simpson, G. (2007) *Transforming Society? Sociology and Social Work*. Bristol: The Policy Press.

PricewaterhouseCoopers and Duckworth, S. (2006) 'A Strategic Direction for Remploy: Review of Future Business Options', commissioned by the Department for Work and Pensions. Available at: www.dwp.gov.uk/publications/dwp/2006/remploy [accessed 29 August].

Qureshi, H. and Walker, A. (1989) *The Caring Relationship: Elderly People and Their Families*. London: Macmillan.

Quibria, M.G. (1988) 'A note on international migration, non-traded goods and economic welfare in the source country', *Journal of Development Economics*. 28(3): 377–87.

Race, D., Boxall, K. and Carson, I. (2005) 'Towards a Dialogue for Practice: Reconciling Social Role Valorization and the Social Model of Disability', *Disability & Society* 20(5): 507–21.

Ramsay, M. (2005) 'A Modest Proposal: The Case for a Maximum Wage', *Contemporary Politics* 11(4): 201–15.

Randall, J. (2008) 'Shameless Layabouts', *The Daily Telegraph*, 12 December: 26.

Reidegeld, E. (2006) *Staatliche Sozialpolitik in Deutschland 1: Von den Ursprüngen bis zum Untergang des Kaiserreiches 1918*. Wiesbaden: VS Verlag für Sozialwissenschaft, GWV Fachverlag GmbH.

Reinsborough, P. and Canning, D. (2010) *Re-Imagining Change*. Oakland: PMPress

Ricardo, D. (1895 [1817]) *Principles of Political Economy and Taxation*, edited, with introductory essay, notes and appendices, by E.C.K. Gonner. London: Bell.

Rist, R.C. (1994) 'Influencing the Policy Process with Qualitative Research', in N.K. Denzin and Y.S. Lincoln (eds) *Handbook of Qualitative Research*. Thousand Oaks, CA: Sage.

Ritzer, G. (1995) *The McDonaldization of Society: An Investigation into the Changing Character of Contemporary Social Life*. New York: Pine Forge Press.

Ritzer, G. (2010) *Globalization: A Basic Text*. Chichester: Wiley-Blackwell.

Roche, M. (1992) *Rethinking Citizenship*. Cambridge: Polity.

Rodger, J.J. (2003) 'Social Solidarity, Welfare and Post-Emotionalism', *Journal of Social Policy* 32(3): 403–21.

Rogers, A. and Pilgrim, D. (2009) *A Sociology of Mental Health and Illness*, 4th edn, Buckingham: Open University Press.

Rolph, S., Atkinson, D., Nind, M. and Welshman, J. (eds) (2005) *Witnesses to Change: Families, Learning Difficulties and History*. Kidderminster: BILD Publications.

Ross, S. and Brown, C. (2006) 'Scottish Staff Stunned by Norwich Union Job Cuts', *The Scotsman Business*, 15 September. Available at: http://business.scotsman.com/jobexporting/Scottish-staff-stunned-by-Norwich.2810577.jp [accessed 31 January 2009].

Rowlingson, K. and Connor, S. (2011, forthcoming) 'The "Deserving" Rich? Inequality, Morality and Social Policy', *Journal of Social Policy* 40(4).

Royal College of Nursing (2002) *International Recruitment of Nurses: United Kingdom Case Study*. London: Royal College of Nursing.

Ryan, J. and Thomas, F. (1987) *The Politics of Mental Handicap*. London: Free Association Books.

Ryan, W. (1976) *Blaming the Victim*. New York: Vintage Books.

Sales, R. (2007) *Understanding Immigration and Refugee Policy: Contradictions and Continuities*. Bristol: The Policy Press.

Samuelson, P.A. and Nordhaus, W.D. (1989) *Economics*, 13th edn. New York/ London: McGraw-Hill.

Sapsford, R. (1993) 'Understanding People: The Growth of an Expertise', in J. Clarke (ed) *A Crisis in Care: Challenges to Social Work*. London: Sage Publications: 23-43.

Saville, J. (1957) 'The Welfare State: An Historical Approach', *The New Reasoner*. 3(Winter): 5–25.

Schild, V. (2007) 'Empowering Consumer-Citizens or Governing Poor Female Subjects?', *Journal of Consumer Culture* 7(2): 179–203.

Schön, D.A. (1983) *The Reflective Practitioner*. New York: Basic Books.

Schram, S.E. (1995) *Words of Welfare. The Poverty of Social Science and the Social Science of Poverty*. Minneapolis: University of Minneapolis Press.

Scull, A.T. (1979) *Museums of Madness: The Social Organization of Insanity in Ninetenenth Century England*. New York: St. Martins Press.

Scull, A.T. (1983) *Decarceration: Community Treatment and the Individual – A Radical View*. New York, NY: Rutgers University Press.

Seebohm, F. (Chair) (1968) *Report of the Committee on Local Authority and Allied Personal Services*, Cmnd 3703. London: HMSO.

Seldon, A. (1977) *Charge!* London: Temple Smith.

Sennett, R. (2006) *The Culture of the New Capitalism*. Newhaven/London: Yale University Press.

Sergeant, H. (2008) 'Well, We Did Pay Matthews to Keep Having Children', *The Sunday Times*, 7 December: 16.

Sewell, W.H., Jr (1992) 'A Theory of Structure: Duality, Agency and Transformation', *American Journal of Sociology* 98(1): 1–29.

Shaw, M. (2004) *Community Work: Policy, Politics and Practice*. Hull: Universities of Hull and Edinburgh.

Shor, I. (1992) *Empowering Education: Critical Teaching for Social Change*. London/ Chicago, IL: University of Chicago Press.

Silver, H. (1994) 'Social Exclusion and Social Solidarity: Three Paradigms', *International Labour Review* 133: 531–78.

Simpson, G. (2009) 'Global and Local Issues in the Training of "Overseas" Social Workers', *Social Work Education* 28(6): 655–67.

Simpson, G. and Price, V. (2010) 'From Inclusion to Exclusion: Some Unintended Consequences of "Valuing People"', *British Journal of Learning Disabilities*. 38(3): 180–7.

Sivanandan, A. (1982) *A Different Hunger: Writings on Black Resistance*. London: Pluto Press.

Smiles, S. (1997 [1851]) *Self Help: With Illustrations of Conduct and Perseverance.* London: Health and Welfare Unit, Institute of Economic Affairs.
Smith, A. (1976 [1776]) *An Inquiry Into the Nature and Causes of the Wealth of Nations.* München: Idion-Verlag.
Sotirovic, M. (2003) 'How Individuals Explain Social Problems: The Influences of Media Use', *Journal of Communication* 53: 122–37.
Spicker, P. (1987) 'Poverty and Depressed Estates: A Critique of *Utopia on Trial*', *Housing Studies* 2(4): 283–92.
Stedman-Jones, G. (1981) 'The Threat of Outcast London', in M. Fitzgerald, G. McClelland and J. Pawson (eds) *Crime and Society: Readings in History and Theory.* London: Routledge, Kegan and Paul.
Stedman-Jones, G. (1984) *Outcast London: A Study in the Relationship between Social Classes in Victorian Society.* Harmondsworth: Penguin.
Stokes, P. (2008) 'Children Were Just a Way of Getting; Money From State', *The Daily Telegraph*, 5 December: 11.
Strange, S. (1996) *The Retreat of the State: The Diffusion of Power in the World Economy (Cambridge Studies in International Relations).* Cambridge: Cambridge University Press.
Stuckler, D., Basu, S. and McKee, M. (2010) 'Budget Crises, Health and Social Welfare Programmes', *British Medical Journal* 340: 3311.
Suresearch (2010) www.suresearch.org.uk/ [accessed 20 December 2010]
Sweeney, A., Beresford, P., Rose, D., Faulkner, A. and Nettle, M. (2009) *This is Survivor Research.* Ross on Wye: PCCS Books.
Taylor, A. (2008) 'Night Marchers Want Shannon Home Again', *The Sun*, 27 February: 4.
Taylor, A. (2009) 'Remploy's Bad Timing', *Community Care* 29. January: 6–7.
Taylor, M. (2003) *Public Policy in the Community.* Basingstoke: Palgrave.
Taylor, P.G. (1999) 'Making Sense of Academic Life', *Higher Education* 40(4): 489–91.
Taylor-Gooby, P. (2008) 'Assumptive Worlds and Images of Agency: Academic Social Policy in the Twenty-first Century?', *Social Policy and Society* 7(3): 269–80.
Teather, D and Milmo, D (2010) 'Year of industrial unrest looms as union anger reaches boiling point', *The Observer*, 11 July.
Thane, P. (1984) 'The Working Class and State "Welfare" in Britain, 1880–1914', *Historical Journal* 27(4): 877–900.
The Guardian (2009) 'Switzerland Life Tempts High-end Taxpayers after Darling's Budget'. Available at: /www.guardian.co.uk/uk/2009/apr/24/income-tax-rise [accessed 24 April 2009].
The Guardian (2010) 'Iceland Bank Failure: Which Councils Are Affected? List of Local Authorities That Have Invested Money in Icelandic Banks'. Available at: http://www.guardian.co.uk/politics/2008/oct/10/localgovernment-iceland [accessed 21 October 2010].
The Sun (2008) 'Baby P's Chiefs Ascot Jolly', 16 November. Available at: www.thesun.co.uk/sol/homepage/news/1927180/Baby-P-chiefs-Ascot-jolly.html

The Sunday Times (2008) 'Mr Brown: Stop Being Kind to Be Cruel, Editorial', 7 December: 16.

The Sunday Times (2009) 'Football Stars Plan to Dodge 50p Tax Rate', 31 May. Available at: www.timesonline.co.uk/tol/sport/article6395778.ece

Thompson, E.P. (1963) *The Making of the English Working Class*. London: Victor Gollancz.

Thompson, M., Ellis, R. and Wildavsky, A. (1990) *Cultural Theory* Boulder, CO: Westview Press.

Thompson, N. (1996) 'Supply Side Socialism: The Political Economy of New Labour', *New Left Review* 216: 37–54.

Thompson, N. (1997) *Anti-discriminatory Practice*, 2nd edn. Basingstoke: Macmillan.

Thornton, P. (2005) 'Disabled People, Employment and Social Justice', *Social Policy and Society* 4(1): 65–73.

Titmuss, R. (1970a) *The Gift Relationship: From Human Blood to Social Policy*. London: Allen & Unwin.

Titmuss, R.M. (1970b) *Essay on the Welfare State*. London: Allen and Unwin.

Titmuss, R.M. (1974) *Social Policy*. London: Allen and Unwin.

Touraine, A. (1985) 'An Introduction to the Study of Social Movements', *Social Research* 52(4): 749– 87.

Townsend, P. (1979) *Poverty in the United Kingdom*. London: Allen Lane.

Transport and General Workers Union (2008) 'Remploy Campaign Fighting Back to Keep Remploy Factories Open'. Available at: www.tgwu.org.uk/Templates/Campaign.asp?Action=Display&NodeID=93587 [accessed 17 July 2008].

Treasury Select Committee (2009a) *Banking Crisis: Dealing with the Failure of the UK Banks*. London: TSO. Available at: www.publications.parliament.uk/pa/cm200809/cmselect/cmtreasy/416/416.pdf

Treasury Select Committee (2009b) *Banking Crisis: Reforming Corporate Governance and Pay in the City*. London: TSO. Available at: www.publications.parliament.uk/pa/cm200809/cmselect/cmtreasy/519/519.pdf

TUC (2008) *Hard Work, Hidden Lives: The Full Report of the Commission on Vulnerable Employment*. London: TUC, Commission on Vulnerable Employment.

UNISON (2009) 'NJC Payclaim 2010-2011'. Available at: www.unison.org.uk/file/B4778b.pdf [accessed 20 December 2010].

UNISON (2010) *Social Workers Raise Concerns about Personal Budgets in Social Care*. Available at: www.unison.org.uk/asppresspack/pressrelease_view.asp?id=1864

van Dijk, T.A. (1993) 'Principles of Critical Discourse Analysis', *Discourse & Society* 4(2): 249–83.

van Dijk, T.A. (1998) *Ideology: A Multidisciplinary Approach*. London: Sage.

van Leeuwen, T. (2005) *Introducing Social Semiotics*. London: Routledge.

van Leeuwen, T. (2007) 'Legitimacy in Discourse and Communication', *Discourse and Communication* 1(1): 91–112.

van Leeuwen, T. and Wodak, R. (1999) 'Legitimizing Immigration Control: A Discourse Historical Analysis', *Discourse Studies* 1(1): 83–118.

Vincent, A.W. (1984) 'The Poor Law Reports of 1909 and the Social Theory of the Charitable Organisation Society', in D. Gladstone (ed) *Before Beveridge: Welfare Before the Welfare State*. London: Institute of Economic Affairs.

Walker, M. and Beaumont, B. (1981) *Probation Work: Critical Theory and Socialist Practice*, Oxford: Blackwell.

Walters, M.-A. (ed) (1970) *Rosa Luxemburg Speaks*. New York. Pathfinder Press.

Ward, C. (2008) *Anarchy in Action*. London: Freedom Press.

Webb, A. (1991) 'Coordination: A Problem in Public Sector Management', *Policy and Politics* 19(4): 229–41.

Webb, S. and Webb, B. (1909) *The Break-Up of the Poor Law; Being Parts 1-2 of the Minority Report of the Poor Law Commission, with Introduction*. London: Longmans. Available at: www.archive.org/details/breakupofpoorlaw01webbuoft

Webb, S. and Webb, B. (1927) *English Poor Law History. Part I: The Old Poor Law*. London: Longmans.

Weber, M. (1964) *The Theory of Social and Economic Organisation*. New York: The Free Press.

Weber, M. (1979) *Economy and Society: An Outline of Interpretive Sociology*, edited by G. Roth and Cl. Wittich, translated (from German) by E. Fischoff. London: University of California Press.

Weiss, C.H. (1988) 'Evaluations for Decisions – Is Anybody There, Does Anybody Care?', *Evaluation Practice* (9)1: 34–41.

Weiss-Gal, I. and Gal, J. (2007) 'Social Workers' Attitudes to Social Welfare Policy', *International Journal of Social Welfare* 16(4): 349–57.

Wellbourne, P., Harrison, G. and Ford, D. (2007) 'Social Work in the UK and the Global Labour Market: Recruitment, Practice and Ethical Considerations', *International Social Work* 50(1): 27–40.

Welshman, J. (2006) *Underclass: A History of the Excluded, 1880–2000*. London: Hambledon Continuum.

Whelan, R. (ed) (1998) *Octavia Hill and the Social Housing Debate: Essays and Letters by Octavia Hill*. London: The Institute of Economic Affairs.

Whelan, R. (2001) *Helping the Poor: Friendly Visiting, Dole Charities and Dole Queues*. London: Civitas.

Whitelaw, A. and Williams, J. (1994) 'Relating Health Education Research to Health Policy', *Health Education Research* 9(4): 519–26.

Wilhelm, M. (1996) 'Bequest Behaviour and the Effect of Heirs' Earnings: Testing the Altruistic Model of Bequests', *American Economic Review* 86: 874–92.

Wilkinson, F. (2001) 'The Theory and Practice of Wage Subsidisation: Some Historical Reflections', *Radical Statistics* 77: 8–31.

Wilkinson, R. and Pickett, K. (2009) *The Spirit Level*. London: Allen Lane.

Willets, A. and Martineau, T. (2004) 'Ethical International Recruitment of Health Professionals: Will Codes of Practice Protect Developing Country Health Systems?'. Available at: www.medact.org/content/health/documents/brain_drain/Martineau%20codesofpracticereport.pdf [accessed 29 October 2010].

Williams, F. (2004) *Rethinking Families*. London: ESRC CAVA Research Group, Calouste Gulbenkian Foundation.

Williamson, D. (2008) 'England Cashes in on Free Prescriptions', *Western Mail*,16 April. Available at: www.walesonline.co.uk/news/wales-news/2008/04/16/england-cashes-in-on-free-prescriptions-91466-20770168/ [accessed 9 October 2010].

Wilson, E. (1977) *Women and the Welfare State*. London: Tavistock.

Wilson, D. and Game, C. (2006) *Local Government in the United Kingdom*. Basingstoke: MacMillan.

Wingfield-Hayes, R. (2006) 'Bitter Regret of Victim's Widow', BBC News, 24 March. Available at: http://news.bbc.co.uk/1/hi/world/asia-pacific/4823950.stm [accessed 29 October 2010].

Wolfe, A. (1978) *The Seamy Side of Democracy. Repression in America*, 2nd edn. New York: Longman.

Wolfensberger, W. (1992) *A Brief Introduction to Social Role Valorization as a High Order Concept for Structuring Human Services*, 2nd edn. Syracuse, NY. Training Institute for Human Service Planning, Leadership and Change Agency, Syracuse University.

Wolfensberger, W. (1999) 'Response to Professor M. Oliver', in R.J. Flynn and R.A. Lemay (eds) *A Quarter Century of Normalization and Social Role Valorization: Evolution and Impact*. Ottawa: University of Ottawa Press: 175–181.

Wollstonecraft, M. (2004 [1792]) *The Collected Letters of Mary Wollstonecraft*, edited by Janet Tood. London: Penguin.

Woolcock, M. (2001) 'The Place of Social Capital in Understanding Social and Economic Outcomes', *ISUMA Canadian Journal of Policy Research* 2(1): 11–17.

Wright Mills, C. (1967) *Power, Politics and People. The Collective Essays of C. Wright Mills*, edited by I.H. Horowitz. New York: Oxford University Press.

Yanow, D. (1996) *How Does a Policy Mean? Interpreting Policy and Organisational Actions*. Washington: George University Press.

Yeates, N. (ed) (2008) *Understanding Global Social Policy*. Bristol: The Policy Press.

Young, J. (1999) *The Exclusive Society: Social Exclusion, Crime and Difference in Late Modernity*. London: Sage.

Younghusband, E (1981) *Newest Profession: Short History of Social Work*. London. Community/Care/IPC Business Press.

Zeitlin, J. and Trubeck, D. (eds) (2003) *Governing Work and Welfare in a New Economy: European and American Experiments*. Oxford: Oxford University Press.

Zizek, S. (2001) *On Belief*. London: Routledge.

Zola, I.K. (1972) 'Medicine as an Institution of Social Control', *Sociological Review* 20: 487–504.

Zolberg, A.R., Suhrke, A. and Aguayo, S. (1989) *Escape From Violence: Conflict and the Refugee Crisis in the Developing World*. Oxford: Oxford University Press.

Index

Note: The following abbreviations have been used – *f* = figure; *t* =table

M

N

O

P

X

Y

Z